P9-DOH-593

The
LOST
WHALE

The
LOST
WHALE

*The True Story
of an Orca Named Luna*

Michael Parfit *and*
Suzanne Chisholm

Narrated by Michael Parfit

ST. MARTIN'S PRESS ❧ NEW YORK

www.stmartins.com

All photographs, unless otherwise noted, are courtesy of the authors.

Frontispiece: photograph of Luna's dorsal fin with plume of spray.
For many of the people of Nootka Sound, Luna's towering blasts of breath became a natural part of the landscape, something they noticed but accepted as natural to their world, like the sound of kids getting out of school. Luna was part of what made their own lives special.

ISBN 978-0-312-35364-3 (hardcover)
ISBN 978-1-250-03198-3 (e-book)

First Edition: June 2013

10 9 8 7 6 5 4 3 2 1

For Christopher Chisholm Parfit

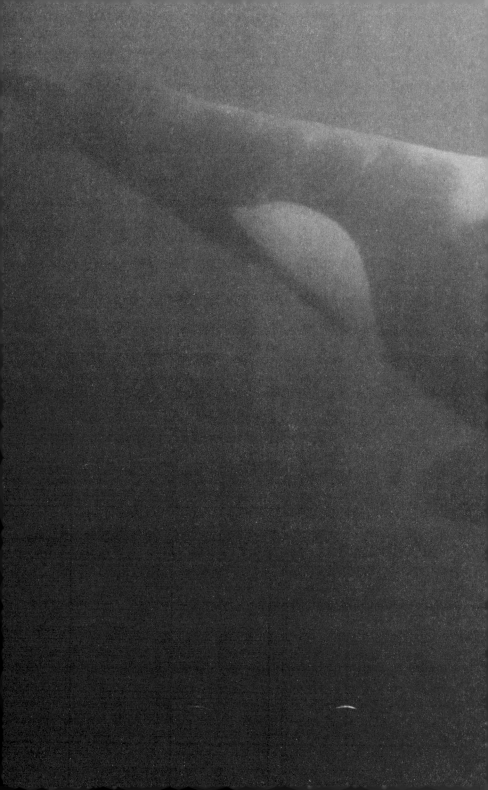

Part One

~~~~~

CONTACT

CHAPTER ONE

April 2004

I t was a clean but restless day, with hard light on the water and an edge in the north wind, the kind of day in which the sky doesn't tell you much except not to settle in.

It was the off-season in the islands along the border between the United States and Canada on the west coast of North America, in one of the few places where the border doesn't go in a straight line. The marina at the Rosario Resort and Spa on Orcas Island, about a hundred air miles north of Seattle, was mostly quiet, except for a few uneasy sailboats with masts and lines clattering like empty flagpoles.

The boat ride from the customs dock had taken about half an hour in lumpy water with a cold wind. All we had was an open twenty-foot boat with an outboard motor and a leaky canvas top, and there had been forty-five minutes of splash and spray even before we got to the customs dock, crossing from our island home in Canada. So Suzanne and I tied up with relief and walked up the dock toward the hotel and into the life of a whale.

We were joining a group of people whose interest or profession was the management of marine mammals. They gathered in a big conference room on rows of good padded chairs, not the folding metal kind. The long table at the front had two tablecloths and a short skirt on top of a long one that reached the ground so you couldn't see people in the panel of speakers wiggle their feet when they were exasperated at what their neighbors were saying. It was quiet, except for what you were supposed to hear.

I sat in one of the front rows. Suzanne was somewhere farther back. We sat with our small video cameras on tripods next to us. We were writing an article for *Smithsonian* magazine, not making a movie, but we used cameras for backup for our imperfect notes and because our editors wanted evidence, and cameras are good at evidence.

The room was full of the things that humans do: voices murmuring, chairs moving, clothes rustling, people crossing their legs and leaning forward, leaning back. We were so many and so close that we shared the air as intimately as our voices. We became a massed breathing thing packed into a room, like a school of herring leaning into the tide.

And the voices all turned one way, too. All spoke of one living being who was not there, as if all of us were whispering together about a movie star who should have treatment, or a candidate who needed advice, or a romantic thief who should be caught, or a soul to be saved with our wisdom. The missing subject of all this talk was a killer whale, an orca—a very young one.

Suzanne and I had seen photos in newspapers of a small orca's head poking up beside a dock, with kids leaning over the side to touch his nose, or of him raising his head to look into boats full of delighted people. These shots illustrated bits of text about how the young orca, whom people called "Luna," had become separated from his pod and turned up all alone in a distant fjord, where he had started to befriend humans. The most recent stories reported that the Canadian government was planning to solve this problem by catching the little whale and moving him.

There was a shot from one newspaper in which Luna was practically touching noses with a black dog on a boat. There were photos of hands reaching out, and the whale lifting himself partly out of the water to touch them. There were photos of people rubbing the whale's tongue. The images had been printed all over the world. We had those pictures clipped and in our files, but we didn't need to bring them with us, because everyone else here had the same shots, stuffed in their briefcases or seared into their minds.

A man named Marc Pakenham sat at the table and spoke. He had a large and flexible face sculptured with broad strokes. His expression seemed to be burdened by a thoughtful melancholy.

"This whale's character has been maligned a little bit over the last few years," he said.

Not knowing the story, we didn't know what he was talking about. But everybody else seemed to understand.

"In my experience," he went on, "and that of the other people who have worked with him—and I know Kari and Erin and a few other people have had occasions where we've been closer to Luna than we wanted to be—I don't think anyone can fail to be moved by the fact that this is a good whale."

If we'd been doing an interview with Marc, we could have asked him why, exactly, he felt the need to defend the moral character of this whale. Who was attacking it? But we said nothing. Marc continued his defense.

"If there is such a thing as a bad whale," he said, "this is not a bad whale."

Next to Marc at the long table sat Kari Koski, one of the women he had been talking about, who had spent a few weeks working with Marc's organization in Luna's neighborhood. She was almost the opposite of Marc. He seemed weighed down with some kind of wry sorrow, but she was not. She was radiant without seeming naïve, like a person who knows the darkness but shines anyway because shining feels better. She spoke of Luna as if he were a child in her family, as if she could pour her love for him into the room, knowing she had enough to flood us all with it.

"We've got a little whale that's coming up to the boat or the dock," she said, "and he's looking you in the eye, and he's squeaking at you, and it's what everybody comes out on a whale-watching trip hoping and wishing to get, it's a personal communication and interaction with a whale."

She glanced around the room with an affectionate, encompassing look.

"And I think we're up against a lot," she said, "when we're asking people to put their human emotions aside."

The meeting was full of detailed information that made only partial sense to us. The whale was a member of a group of whales called L Pod, part of a community of just over eighty, known as the Southern Residents, that spent about six months of the year in the waters near the southern end of Vancouver Island. The whales were officially endangered and were much beloved by the millions of people who lived near them.

The Canadian Department of Fisheries and Oceans (DFO) had announced that it was going to catch the little whale in the remote fjord where he had been for two and a half years and move him closer to the pod to which he belonged. There were several options, but the most probable involved catching him by subterfuge or force, putting him in a net pen, testing him for several days, bolting a satellite tagging device to his dorsal fin, lifting him into a truck, driving him about two hundred miles, and putting him back in the water near the Vancouver Island city of Victoria.

There was no disagreement in the room, but it was clear that there had been. Everyone went to great lengths to praise everyone else for at last working together to solve the problem. Everyone smiled at one another and shook hands. The smiles looked sincere.

The woman who was in charge of Luna was small and had dark hair. Her title was taller than she was. She was the marine mammal coordinator for the Department of Fisheries and Oceans. Luna was in her territory and portfolio.

Her name was Marilyn Joyce. She did not seem nervous in front of the assembly, but she did not seem fully at ease, either. She read from a statement, looking down and up with that hint of wariness and self-conscious precision that tells you that this person thinks she had better be careful what she says.

"We really did hope that Luna could just go on his way without us interfering with him," Marilyn said, with a kind of half-apologetic glance up at the audience, in which I read both embarrassment and something that seemed a little harder.

"Who knows what he has on his mind," Marilyn continued. "But anyway, we're making decisions for him now."

We were on Orcas Island for two days. The next day, the wind had changed direction and picked up, and it seemed colder now. Late in the day, we headed back to our chilly boat and the rough journey home across the shipping lanes, a windblown strait, and the border. So we thought mostly about rough water and the approaching darkness. But we could not help thinking about the whale known as Luna.

It was like starting to read a five-book series of novels on the third book. Who were these people and what was going on? What was this unexpected life from the alien world of the sea that for some reason sought the company of humans? Why was that wrong? And what were those human emotions that people had to put aside?

We moved out of sheltered water near a wooded lump of rock called Battleship Island. We went through a tidal rip where the wind fought the current. The rip tossed us around, and we bounced out of the chop into the longer waves of the strait, dusk rising like fog. We knew that sometimes there were lost logs out there, and our boat was small and fragile. We both stared hard at the thrashing water just ahead. We couldn't afford to look up into the distance. But if we looked backward into the past, the early history of the little whale was right there, in the waters near Battleship Island.

CHAPTER TWO

September 1999

It was a warm September day on San Juan Island, near the U.S.-Canadian border, with the water just starting to get restless under winds that weren't yet marshaled into force by the roaring lows of autumn. Astrid van Ginneken answered the telephone and immediately took off to go out in a boat.

She was from Holland, and was working, as she had done every summer since 1987, in the seafront office of the Center for Whale Research, on San Juan Island. This is the headquarters for Ken Balcomb, one of the legendary orca researchers of this coast, who is senior scientist of the center. On this morning, Astrid had gotten a call from someone who said he'd seen a solitary orca breaching again and again down the island's coast to the south. It seemed odd to her, because you almost never saw these whales alone. So Astrid went out in a boat with a colleague to find out what was happening. It took them about twenty minutes.

A killer whale is impressive to see, but the sound of its breath is the thing that turns your mind. That exhale and inhale, great volumes of air forced out hard and then taken back swiftly, but softer and ending with a little sibilant click as the blowhole closes, gathers your attention. It seems so urgent. Everything is focused on this: to breathe, to breathe, to breathe, to breathe. When you hear it, it seems more hurried than the way humans breathe, but it also feels like a need—a desperate need—that we can understand. Whales start off as strangers to us, but when we hear them breathe, that begins to change.

The whale that Astrid found from the Boston Whaler outboard was not far from Battleship Island, near a place called Kellet Bluff. Astrid saw her in the distance, visible as a tower of breath and a dorsal.

These whales were all numbered as part of a research program that Ken had conducted for over thirty years. Astrid knew the number of the whale from the shape of a gray patch behind the dorsal. She was L-67. People also called her "Splash." She was alone. But no, she wasn't. There was a tiny new orca right beside her. This was strange.

Orcas are never alone. They are considered among the most social of all animals. And when they give birth, they are even less likely to be alone. For births, other orcas gather around.

"Adolescent females," Astrid told us once, "are usually very, very interested in baby-sitting calves or being near mothers with their calves, as if they feel soon the task will be upon them."

The calf, like most newborn orcas, looked plucky to the humans on the boat. He came up beside his mother very quickly compared to the big heave of her body, almost like a kid taking a hop just because he's alive. He also looked pink. Baby orcas have a tinge of orange or pink under the white patches; it looks like a stain, but it doesn't come from the outside. They have thin blubber, so their flesh and blood glow through, like the raw materials of life asserting themselves against the blue-green chill of the sea.

But mother and child were alone. There were no other whales around. The adolescent females were not there. The older females who usually seem to be there to help were not there. But it was not possible, even with all the records of orcas seen here year after year, for any of the human observers to know what this unexpected solitude meant.

As the Boston Whaler attended this odd new family, Astrid, as close and hovering as a maternity room nurse but unable to offer kindness or advice, picked up something emotional from the young mother. Astrid's sense of awareness of the orca's feelings was not something mystical; it was that curious but familiar sense of another's need that we sometimes call *compassion* or *empathy*, which Astrid felt so strongly when she met orcas that she later wrote a long book about life from an orca's perspective. Now she sensed the young mother's discomfort with the alien buzzing presence of humans and their boat.

"We followed them as they were crossing over to the other side of the strait," she told us. "Then we decided we didn't want to bother them anymore, as the female was obviously a bit stressed."

That same day, a small group stood with Ken Balcomb on the deck of the San Juan Island headquarters of the Center for Whale Research.

Most of the people on the deck had been around here in the seventies and early eighties, back when people who studied orcas were "just a little band of slightly off-the-edge people who would go out and spend hours and hours taking pictures of whales."

The guy who said that was Howard Garrett, Ken's half brother. He was talking about people like Ken who were working on orcas before theme park orca shows, the *Free Willy* movies, the *Flipper* TV shows, and the stunning research about the size and complexity of whale brains, which changed the image of orcas from bloodthirsty killers to the smart, social creatures we recognize today. Howie Garrett was one of those on the deck that day, along with his partner, Susan Berta.

They were looking out across Haro Strait, west toward Vancouver Island. There were no whales in sight.

The archipelago here, called the San Juan Islands in the United States and the Gulf Islands in Canada, is surrounded by about seven million people, between Seattle and Tacoma to the south, Vancouver to the north, and Victoria to the west. The whales that come every year into this civilized playground are called the Southern Resident orcas. They're a small band livingly bravely off remnant runs of salmon in waters laden with poisons. They are made up of three pods: J, K, and L. Often during the winter, you can see J Pod in these waters, but K Pod and L Pod vanish altogether.

Every June, the Southern Residents return from winter's unknown quests to the north or south, following the Chinook salmon and drawing swift whale-watching boats out of harbors everywhere like hummingbirds chasing moving flowers.

Ken Balcomb is bearded and looks habitually bemused, Howie is earnest and sincere, and Susan is a sweetheart who loves whales and believes that they have a spiritual as well as physical relationship with humans.

Howie was here on a kind of vacation. He was working on a campaign to get a Southern Resident female called "Lolita," who had been captured in 1970 for aquarium use, released back to the northwest sea from a tank in Florida. He was about to head back to Florida and a terrible little apartment, which was all he could afford. But Ken had heard the same report of a lone orca that had already sent Astrid on her run to Kellet Bluff, and he thought that was odd, so he and the others were standing out on the deck to take a look.

When you have been around whales as much as this group, a plume in the distance is not exotic, but it's still wonderful. To this group, these whales were part of their community, and a plume was like the familiar gait of an old friend. So when they saw a single plume in the distance, its blast of breath cheered them.

When the whale's fin rose again in the calm water, there was an immediate recognition. It was L-67. Her pod, L Pod, was the original family of the Florida captive, Lolita, so Howie was delighted. He and Susan believe that these whales swim in a different tide of experience than the one humans perceive on the surface of life, so there was meaning in seeing this emissary from the exiled one's family.

In photos, whales seem very easy to spot: big fins, backlit spouts, a foam of water. It's not like that in the day-to-day world. What's that? A log bouncing in the swell? A bit of sea running into a wake with a vertical splash? A whale? Oops, now it's gone! Which way was it going? So the observers were doing that as they watched Splash, and then—

"And then," Susan recalled, "Ken goes, 'Wait. What's that behind her?' And there's this little fin and we were like, 'Wow! It's L-67 with a baby!' "

Now this group, too, had seen the new baby.

"I think we were all just like, 'Gasp!' " Susan said. "I remember Ken getting that smile he gets when something really stupendous or surprising happens. He just kind of chuckles and smiles in this very low-key way, but you know he is very excited."

For Howie and Susan, this day shone with meaning.

"I totally believe that whales have this connection with us," Susan said. "These coincidences keep happening. And it just felt like that, especially L Pod being Lolita's family, and Howie had been in Miami, living in an awful place to try to bring her back, and I thought, What a neat gift to have L-67 come by with her new calf and show us."

Howie flew back to the Lolita campaign and the awful place in Miami the next day, but now that he knew there was a new baby among the Southern Residents, he was happy.

Astrid van Ginneken seems to be at home in the wind. She does not look disheveled. It's the opposite: She's smooth and angular and forthright, as if she had been born on the prow of a sailing ship on northern seas. You can see how she might feel akin to these swift, smooth lives in the water, shaped for movement in a world that is always going somewhere itself.

When Astrid went out there the next day, she expected to see L-67, Splash, with the new little orca, now designated as L-98, beside her, and she wondered if any other orcas would be around this time. But what she actually saw was confusing. The calf had switched mothers.

Now the little orca was swimming next to an older female from K Pod nicknamed "Kiska." Seeing this, Astrid and others thought that perhaps the glowing new baby was Kiska's and had just momentarily been swimming with Splash the day before. But Splash was hanging close to Kiska, and it appeared that she was trying to be near the baby, too. Astrid and the other people who were studying these whales recorded these events in their logs that day, just like all their other observations, but they had never seen anything like it.

Like a stir of gossip, the itch of this little mystery passed among the woods and waterways of these islands, from one boat to another, at the dock, at the store, and worked its way through the small and scattered community of people who followed the whales. And someone came along with another clue: A little while before, a female orca who may have been Kiska had been seen carrying a dead baby orca around across her back.

"So," Astrid said, her empathy alive to the grief this image brought to mind, "it could be that she actually lost her calf and was so devastated about that loss that she kidnapped L-98."

Something else was happening that late summer. Another young mother orca, whose nickname was "Nootka," washed up dead on an island a few miles to the north. She had a prolapsed uterus. Childbirth had killed her. But her new baby still lived. This baby had been born just before Luna, so it had been recorded as L-97.

The baby was nicknamed "Tweak." It was tiny. On Astrid's last day on the water that year, she saw Tweak with members of its extended family, including its grandmother, uncles, aunts, and its older brother.

"Little L-97 only lifted its head to breathe," she wrote a few days later, "and did not make the bowlike surfacings, typical for calves. The contours of the skull were visible and it was clearly emaciated."

But as the baby struggled to swim, on one side appeared the big dark back of its grandmother, and on the other rose the moving wall of an uncle. The two big whales moved in careful formation through the water so that the struggling baby could keep swimming in the embrace of their wake.

Two days later, Tweak was, unexpectedly, still alive, still with its extended family, and the humans just watched, so completely unable to help and so wishful.

"Then, the greatest thing happened," Astrid wrote. As people watched, out there on the edge of the whales' endless marathon, little Tweak's older brother caught a salmon, tore it to pieces, and scattered the pieces in the water in front of the baby.

"It was not possible to see if the calf actually took it," Astrid wrote. "But there was no doubt that something had kept him going through the past days and that his family was fighting for his life."

In late September, the dance between Kiska and Splash around Luna went on, the glowing child swimming first with one, then with the other. Then one day, someone saw Splash sweep past a boat with Luna nursing, and that was it. From then on, Luna and Splash were together, and Kiska went back to being bereft.

"It was the most unusual beginning of a whale life that we had documented," Ken Balcomb said. "And, you know, it just kept evolving into more unusual."

In mid-November of that year, the whole community of the Southern Residents went traveling in the wide, wild, winter seas. When L Pod came back in the late spring of 2000, Luna was there with Splash. He had made it through the winter. But little Tweak was gone.

The researchers saw Luna several times that first full summer of his life. He had already developed something of a personality. To them, he seemed much more independent than almost all the other babies. He was just as social as all orca babies—he was always seen with an older orca. But he was in some ways more social than most of the other young ones, who stay almost exclusively with their mothers. Luna was out and about. He was seen swimming with many different L Pod orcas.

"Some of them are momma's boys," Ken Balcomb said. "Others are like Luna. But he's probably the extreme: He was wandering around, just happy with anybody."

The researchers' logs also show energy. They mention him cartwheeling, tail lobbing (putting his head down and waving his tail in the air), swimming upside down, lunging, rolling, and slapping his little pectoral fins on the water.

That summer, there was a Name the Babies contest, an annual event organized by the Whale Museum on San Juan Island. A young girl from Bellingham submitted the winning entry. The little orca should be called "Luna," she wrote, because "the whale explores the ocean like the moon explores the Earth."

In the fall of 2000, the Southern Residents vanished again for the winter. But when L Pod came back with the other whales in the spring of 2001, several orcas did not return.

One by one, as people from the Center for Whale Research did the annual census, they noticed gaps: Orcan, Squirty, Oskar, Cetus, and two calves who were so young, they had not been given names. All were missing. The population was now down to seventy-eight. It was a decline of 20 percent since 1995.

One of the missing was the little whale L-98, Luna. There wasn't much chance that he could have survived. He would have barely been weaned. It seemed to be the end of his story.

By now, Howie Garrett had moved home to the Puget Sound area. Lolita, the L Pod whale he'd been trying to get released, remained in captivity in Florida. Ken, Astrid, Howie, Susan Berta, and all the people who followed the whales felt as if they had lost family members.

CHAPTER THREE

April 2004

On a cold and windy afternoon in April 2004, Suzanne and I sat on the concrete edge of the government dock down the hill from the town of Gold River, on the west coast of Vancouver Island. The dock was at the east end of a piece of the fjord named Nootka Sound, an inlet called Muchalat.

Seagulls strolled around on rafts of logs just to the west of the dock, their feathers ruffled by the wind. A flag flew out flat and crisp, its edges crackling, at the stern of an old freighter called *Uchuck III*, which was tied to the dock. The flag's edges were torn from frequent wind. Sea lions barked in the distance. But there was no whale.

Suzanne and I had rented an old Ford Taurus station wagon in Victoria and driven north. Suzanne, for elaborate reasons, mostly because she could not help nicknaming almost every animate and inanimate object, called the old wagon "Pops."

We had put our two uncomplaining dogs and our rolled-up inflatable boat in the back of Pops and had driven half the day up-island until we got to the town of Gold River, a remote village that looked curiously suburban, built around a shopping center and two gas stations an hour and a half's drive on winding roads from anywhere else. Then we drove seven more miles down a winding road, beside cliffs and waterfalls that sprayed the road and passing cars, to a place where the hulk of a huge pulp mill stood silent by the water and the government dock stuck a high concrete wall and a small group of wooden floats out into the water next to the mouth of the river that gave the place its name.

We parked the car in front of the office of a small seaplane charter operation called Air Nootka, just back of the dock. Inside the office, there was a sign. It said NO, I DO NOT KNOW WHERE LUNA IS. NO, WE DON'T DO INTERVIEWS.

We sat on the dock. Gusts of wind made ruffled patches on the dark gray water. Heavily forested hills rose straight out of the water all around. In the distance, snow and rock showed high above the hills, some peaks almost seven thousand feet above the sea. Occasionally, a boxy aluminum crew boat (which everyone here called a "tin" boat) came roaring around the point to the dock to load or unload loggers from distant camps. Every once in a while, a car came down to the dock and someone would come over and would notice that we were watching the water.

"Is he here?"

"Sorry. Haven't seen him."

The car would drive away.

A couple who had driven up from a town over a hundred miles south said, "Is he here yet?"

"Haven't seen him."

"We were down here before lunch, and we shouted and sang and slapped the water, but he didn't show up."

In our lives, other things were going on. My father, who lived in California, was on a long journey out of the world. He had Alzheimer's, and although he was not in danger of dying soon, he had already left us. I had said good-bye to him on a visit, talking to him as he slept and then leaving the hospital in tears. Now I tried to talk to him on the telephone, but all he said to me was, "What?" He didn't seem to know what the telephone was.

He was British. He had been a filmmaker, an artist, and an Anglican priest. Now he was in a long-term-care hospital, and we had no idea how much longer he had. I talked to my mother every day, and she went to see him twice a day and read to him from books he did not understand.

He had been a watercolor artist, and I remembered from my earliest days the magic of watching a scene in front of us come to life on the paper. When I saw places like Nootka Sound, I could not help thinking what he would have done with the scenes we encountered everywhere, with their muscular contrasts of bright water, dark mountains, and stormy skies.

I often remembered his hands. He had a benign tremor in his hands for much of his adult life. It was so pronounced that it was almost impossible for him to carry a cup of tea without spilling. But when he sat down at an easel to paint, what appeared under his brush was not tremulous. His hands still shook as he painted, but he had figured out how to rest the brush on the paper so almost no involuntary movement got through to the page, and the trees he painted had delicate lacy branches in their upper reaches that you would never imagine he could have produced. He never spoke of this; he just accomplished it. It was something to admire and not to forget.

We waited out the day until the sun went off the snow on the mountaintops, and Luna still didn't come. The dark ruffles on the water in the middle of the bay grew narrower and began to go away. The flag on *Uchuck III* folded up and fell asleep in shadows. We didn't hear the sea lions anymore. The seagulls settled down like hens. A river otter swam by in front of the concrete pier. In the rising tide and the river outflow, *Uchuck III* squeaked against a piling. Luna didn't appear.

CHAPTER FOUR

July 2001

On a still July morning in the year 2001, the crew of *Uchuck III* lifted the fixed ropes on the government dock at Gold River off the bollards on the port-side decks, and the ship moved slowly out of the dock. Donna Schneider, the ship's cook, went into the galley and took the fresh muffins for the passengers out of the oven.

Uchuck III was 120 feet long. It had once been a minesweeper. That year, it was a lot like Gold River, a town originally built to house mill workers, whose mill had just shut down. Gold River was the town where Donna lived, and now she was watching her friends move away. Like Gold River, *Uchuck III* was clean, tidy, and reliable, but now its original job was gone. The ship had been put back together out of a bunch of oddball bits and pieces salvaged from a brassier past. The town itself was still in pieces.

The fjord of Nootka Sound was like a living creature. It breathed. In the mornings, it exhaled. On summer mornings, the cool night breath of the high country drifted down the long, narrow passages of the sound and scuffed the reflections off the arms of sea that reached so many miles into Vancouver Island's mountainous heart.

On this morning as *Uchuck III* sailed west, Nootka Sound breathed out, and *Uchuck III* went along with the morning breeze. The ship cruised at twelve knots, and it took the world's rush and calmed it down to just a hiss of water, a rumble of engines, and a languid wake that rolled up the sound's steep shores and, reflected, rolled back out again. Under the mountains that crowded the water, the gray-blue cloud of the ship's diesel smoke, carried at the same speed as the ship by the soft breath of the canyon's exhale, hung above the ship like the ghosts of sails.

The ship mumbled its way up past Victor Island, past Jacklah River, past the log sort at McCurdy Creek, then past a small collection of huts and floating logs and the battered green boat *Jervis Bay,* all part of the home of Glen Hammond, whom people called "Radar." Radar was a log-salvage operator and a beachcomber, and he liked to say that *Jervis Bay* had been underwater for three weeks before he brought it up to serve his old-fashioned independent life. *Jervis Bay*'s bow rail looked as if it had been not only underwater but also under a logging truck. It was bent like a pretzel.

Uchuck III motored along past another log sort at Houston River, then made a bend to the north at Gore Island, past a big bay named Kleeptee, up to a promontory called Atrevida, from whence today's skipper, Sean Mather, the son of the regular skipper, Fred Mather, could see the wooded bluffs of Bligh Island dead ahead. The island was named for the British officer you think it was named for, who came here with the great explorer James Cook in 1778, before things went permanently rotten for Cook in Hawaii and pretty badly for Bligh a bit farther south.

As the ship passed the stony outcrop of Atrevida Point, Donna Schneider came out of the galley and looked aft, out where the long rolls of the wake slid away like something living moving underwater. And suddenly there *was* something living there.

For Donna, the work on *Uchuck III* was usefully normal in a world of uncertainty. The mill had closed down in 1999, and like most mill towns on the slide, Gold River was dying hard. People stayed, hoping for the mill to be purchased and revived. But the toll added up. If you were worried and awake at two in the morning, one man told us later, you could go out and walk around on the street and see lights on in a lot of windows. "You're thinking," he said. "You're trying to make decisions. There are a lot of people awake doing the same thing."

Gold River was a good town, clean and friendly, so people stayed and stayed; then suddenly they were gone. Friends seemed stalwart and enduring, then evaporated overnight. So for Donna, the trip down to the squat little array of pilings that made up the docks at the end of the road from Gold River was a reassuring trip to a past of reliable employment and a consistent group of colleagues. On the ship, time went along in its normal way, one cedar tree going past at a time.

But then things changed on Nootka Sound.

The ship emerged from the narrow waterway called Williamson Passage, hemmed in on the port side by Gore Island and to starboard by the craggy mainland, and moved out into a wider piece of water known as Mooyah Bay, where two arms of Nootka Sound came in from the sea and met before narrowing further to go in among the higher mountains.

After coming out of those narrows, the gathered waters near Mooyah Bay looked expansive. They spread out ahead like a pasture seen from a lane. Distance, constrained by mountains inside the passage, had meaning again. Cliffs receded, and the grander outlying ridges were revealed. A wall of mountains stood like a spine to the north.

On this day, as *Uchuck III* motored into this generosity of waters, Donna Schneider looked aft, along the widening wake. There was a splash. She watched and waited. There it was again. Something, maybe a porpoise, was following the ship.

She went up the stairs to the pilothouse. Sean Mather knew why she was there. She loved whales.

"I was looking at that," he said. "I think it's a pilot whale."

Donna was pleased.

"And that's what we thought," she said later, "that it was a little pilot whale. And we thought, Well, we get to see a lot of whales this time of year. And we were all happy. Well, a different kind of whale! Write it in the book." The little whale stayed with the ship for a few minutes, then disappeared.

On Nootka Sound, the gentle exhale of cool air coming down from the mountains ended, as it did every summer day. For a moment, there was calm. But just for a moment. All morning, the high country, with its dark stone cliffs and rugged canyons, had gathered the sunlight and turned it to heat, and soon the heat began to rise. As the warm air rose, it drew cool air in from the sea and up through the narrow canyons. In the canyons, this breath was narrowly focused by the close walls, and it began to roar. Long lines of spume lay across the water. Waves danced sharply and threw spray. It was a storm made by sunlight.

Some of the people who owned boats here wouldn't go west in summer between 11:00 A.M. and dark, because that's when the upslope wind blew a gale in their faces.

Uchuck III returned in the afternoon of the next day and rode that wind home. Late in the day, the ship once again passed Mooyah Bay. Donna was watching a little more carefully this time. She went back to the upper deck in the stern.

There it was. The little whale popped up again in the wake behind the ship, but this time she could see it well: dark skin, white patches. She went back up to the bridge and said to the skipper, "Sean, that's not a pilot whale. That's an *orca*!"

But it was so small.

Maybe that made all the difference. If the whale had been a thirty-footer, with a fin like a broadsword and breath as sonorous and aromatic as that of an Italian baritone, perhaps things wouldn't have mattered so much. But it was little. And that familiar thing hit Donna, that same thing Astrid felt and most people feel when they sense emotions from others: empathy. The little whale seemed lonely, and her heart was stirred.

Then, after a few days of passing through Mooyah Bay and seeing the same little whale in the wake, the crew saw something that looked wrong. There was a big loose log out there in the water, and they could see the little whale under it. It appeared to be stuck there.

"I was quite frightened," Donna told us later. "I thought, Oh, my God! He's tangled in something."

So Fred Mather, who was skipper that day, slowed the boat down. As it coasted and the noise of the engine dropped to a murmur, the little orca came out from under the log.

"He was just trying to rub his back on it," Donna said. "And then he actually brought the log over to the boat. Then he was spyhopping on the other side."

Spyhopping is a term that comes from whale scientists, who have used it to describe what many species of whales do. They come straight up, partway out of the water, nose-first, which brings their eyes a long way up out of the water, much higher above the surface than they can get by just rolling over on their sides. Apparently, this gives them a different look at surface things, like people in boats.

So the little whale started spyhopping, first on one side of *Uchuck III,* then on the other, which made the passengers rush from side to side.

"The passengers were just in awe," Donna said, "just like we were."

Over the next few weeks, the crew members watched the little whale. They enjoyed it, but they always thought that the next time they came back up the sound through Mooyah Bay, he wouldn't be there. Orcas and other whales often showed up for a few days, then disappeared. It was great, but it never lasted.

"But he kept showing up, and he kept showing up," Donna said. "And when we kept seeing him, we went, 'There's something kind of weird here.'"

CHAPTER FIVE

July 2001

Eugene Amos's mother was buried at a place called Yuquot, at the mouth of Nootka Sound, not far to the northwest of Mooyah Bay. But Eugene didn't know where. No one he knew remembered.

Eugene Amos was an elder among the small group set aside by law and custom as the Mowachaht/Muchalaht First Nations of Nootka Sound. He lived in a small community on a reserve called Tsaxana, which is up a hill a bit over a mile from Gold River. About 175 people lived there. Every once in a while, he would take *Uchuck III* or use Maxi's Water Taxi charter service to get out to Yuquot, which is also known as Friendly Cove because Captain Cook gave it that name when he met Eugene's ancestors there in 1778.

At Yuquot, Eugene sometimes went looking for his mother. Up beyond the open field where the children used to play, on the way to a lagoon that gets warm enough to swim in during the summer, there's an old graveyard. Around the graveyard are moss-covered trees and a depth of moss and fern and deadfall that make time seem slow. But the graves speak of its advance.

Somewhere in or near the old graveyard lay Eugene's mother. Eugene had never found a stone, but he kept looking. Ray and Terry Williams, the last First Nations residents of Yuquot, wanted to help him, but they couldn't find it, either. But Eugene still thought of Yuquot as home.

Yuquot means "where the wind blows from all directions." It was an ancient village site on a bay made by a hook of land at the mouth of the sound. The cove is tucked behind a gravel beach that faces the wind and the swells the wind drives before it, and breaks those big shoulders of the sea into foam. On the beach where the waves break, on the other side of the hook from the bay where ships anchor, there are millions of dark pebbles.

People come to Yuquot, and such is the force of their feeling for this place—some in awe of the history, some in awe of something they perceive as spiritual—that they want to take some of the pebbles home. Sometimes they have to be asked not to take so many. Even gravel runs out.

By the summer of 2001, there wasn't much left at Yuquot. There was a lighthouse on the point, a white-and-red complex of walkways and metal roofs, one of the few manned lighthouses left on this lonely coast. Three buildings stood down near the log-strewn beach on the calm side of the arm of land, where Ray and Terry Williams lived. And there was a church up the hill, a weather-beaten church that looked Christian on the outside but not when you went in.

Inside, as your eyes adjusted to the dim light, what you saw up in the front beyond the rows of pews, where the cross and the altar would have been, were tall shapes with wings and faces. They were sentinels of the mystical from further back, even, than Jesus: totem poles. Instead of the face of Christ, what you saw in this place of worship were the faces of eagles and wolves and killer whales.

Yuquot was just these remnants and a low basin a couple of hundred yards wide, a patch of grass surrounded by rising ground. In Europe, you would think of this shape as an ancient fort melted down to a perimeter mound, but here it meant something else. It was more like the cupped container made by two hands pressed together, holding voices. If you knew about Yuquot because you'd read about it or if, like Eugene Amos, you had so many memories of it that you couldn't tell whether they were your own memories or memories your father told you about that his grandparents had, then the cupped hands of the little basin of land, which looked so empty in the wind that blew the long grass around, was, in fact, full to the brim with the resonance of past lives.

For more than four thousand years, people have lived at Yuquot. Writing had not yet been invented four thousand years ago, but people were already living at Yuquot. In Europe and Asia and South America, civilizations rose and fell, and people lived at Yuquot. In the culture that the Europeans brought to North America, there was no equivalent to the depth of time through which Eugene Amos could reach to know who he was and where he came from.

Sometimes Eugene's younger sister Louise also looked for the grave. Louise and Eugene were close; they shared an ebullience and zest for life, and an ability to talk, at length and with clarity. There was something restless in her, too, that made her want to find the place where her mother was buried. She went to Yuquot once in the early 1990s, Eugene remembered, to look again.

Louise liked dragonflies and hummingbirds, Eugene told us, because in the old legends they were connected to healing. Like so many pieces of the natural world with which the people of Nootka Sound were so deeply tied by time and legend, these other lives were woven together with the lives of humans. "Knowing those legends and stories," Eugene said, "my sister had a great love for dragonflies."

The day that Louise visited Yuquot, though, was in the fall, when the summer birds and insects had mostly left the land. She looked among the ancient trees and mosses and read many old stone words about other people's moms, but she could not find hers.

"She had been out there," Eugene said, "and she had made her search and she could not find anything, and she was feeling very depressed." But the people in Yuquot have long looked to all the lives that surround them, the mammals and birds and insects, to find omens for their own lives, and that happened to Louise.

That evening, in the permanent twilight of the old forest, the air whirred with the sound of dragonflies. They came up out of the woods and paused around her, a little cloud of winged life passing by, and from them she took a message.

"These dragonflies came out for her," Eugene said. "And they accompanied her, they flew beside her, and they flew around her, and she cried. She just felt so at peace. She said it seems like the message she was getting was, 'Quit worrying. I am all right. I'm okay. You worry about you.'

"The dragonflies," Eugene went on, "were her messengers of peace and serenity."

On July 14, 2001, it was Eugene who would need the dragonflies. But he was in the city of Vancouver, and the dragonflies did not come.

The fourteenth was the birthday of one of his nephews, Joshua, who was turning twenty-five. Joshua was Louise's eldest child. It was also the day of the wedding of another sister, Irene, who was much younger. She was getting married in the little town of Zeballos, deep in the heart of Vancouver Island, farther north and even more remote than Gold River.

But Eugene was in Vancouver. He was fifty-five, and things were not easy for him. He was not as fit as he once had been, and he was coming to terms with the idea that neither of his two favorite jobs, fishing and logging, was available to a man of his age. So he had just gone through a program called Transitions, which sought to counsel people in crisis about how to shape the next phases of their lives.

"You look at how you perceive yourself," he said, "your strong points, your fields of expertise. You just go through yourself, and kind of take a look at your characteristics and your work ethic and what kind of work you enjoy, indoors, outdoors, manual, or the brainiac sort of thing. I think as a result of the program, I realized a whole bunch of truths about myself. It was like finding myself at a deeper level, you know? At a deep philosophical level, so to speak.

And it dawned on me that the gift of gab might serve me well. I knew it was going to be hard. I thought maybe I could make it, being self-employed. And why don't I do what I do best? Why don't I just carve?"

As these ideas were coming to him, he worked doing food prep and dishwashing at a community center called the Gathering Place, which served the homeless in Vancouver.

At about 3:30 on the afternoon of July 14, he had finished work for the afternoon and was walking back to the hotel where he was living. A car came up beside him and honked to get his attention. In it were friends: George David and his wife, Gwen. George was from Clayoquot Sound and Gwen was from Ahousaht, farther up the west coast of the island. Eugene had gone to high school with George and had known him ever since. Another friend, Clarence, was also in the car.

The car stopped, the door opened, and George and Gwen invited him to go for a ride. He got in. But he could tell they were troubled. "They were very quiet," he said. "And nothing really dawned on me. I just figured, Oh, they have had some bad news of some sort."

They drove to an area of green, a park near the Vancouver Planetarium. They stopped and walked out into the park, where trees cast shade and there was some peace. They sat on a bench. George sat on one side of Eugene, and Clarence sat on the other. And now George wept. Tears ran down his cheeks.

"Eugene," he said, "your sister Louise was killed in a car accident."

She had been killed in a head-on crash on the way to the wedding. She had only a few miles to go.

Eugene got through the night, but he does not know how, only that he did not drink. The next day, another friend gave him a hundred dollars for a bus, and he got to the town of Campbell River, about an hour and a half's drive from Gold River. There he hitchhiked back to Gold River and Tsaxana with people who had been playing bingo at the parlor in Campbell River.

When he got to Tsaxana, Eugene found the place already suffused with grief. Ambrose Maquinna, the beloved former chief of the band, had died the day before Eugene's sister was killed. Mike Maquinna, the chief's son, had been in charge of the First Nations band for three years, but Ambrose was still the big white-haired figurehead everyone turned to. Now he was gone.

Now everyone in Eugene's little band needed the dragonflies. But it wasn't dragonflies that came. It was a whale.

Not long after Luna was seen by the crew of *Uchuck III,* a story about the little whale started going around Tsaxana. The story was told by a man named Jerry Jack, who was one of several hereditary chiefs in the complicated hierarchy of the Mowachaht/Muchalaht people. Jerry was the next one down the chain of esteem from Mike Maquinna, the son of Ambrose Maquinna. He was telling a story he later told Suzanne and me.

The lives of First Nations members in Canada are filled with gatherings; they are a social people. But their tendency and need to gather is also driven by the endless negotiations that most Canadian tribes have conducted for generations with the government of Canada over land claims. The culture of modern First Nations people includes regular treks to meetings at conference centers, offices, and hotels to talk about history and money. So one day in the year 2000, Jerry Jack and Ambrose Maquinna were at yet another one of those meetings, together in a conference room at a hotel in another town to the south.

Ambrose Maquinna was sitting at one table and Jerry Jack at another. Ambrose was older than Jerry by around ten years. They shared an easy friendship. Jerry leaned back in his chair to get close to the nearby table.

"Hey, Chief," he said, "how old are you?"

"I'm seventy-four," Ambrose said. "I'm getting closer to heaven."

"And he was laughing away," Jerry told us, laughing himself. Then, he said, Ambrose made a prediction.

"'When I go home, when I die,' he said, 'when I go home, I am going to come back as a *kakawin*.'"

Jerry Jack laughed again as he told us this. "A *kakawin*," he said. "A killer whale."

Not long after Louise's death, Eugene Amos moved back to Tsaxana permanently. He worked part-time at the Gold River School and the rest of the time carved ravens and orcas out of slabs of yellow cedar. Eugene is a wiry guy who sometimes lets his hair grow into long gray waves and sometimes wears a goatee, then cuts everything when he thinks it is time. He no longer looks durable enough to be a logger, but he likes to tell you that it was his light, wiry body that made him so sure-footed on the boom sticks and the logs.

In late August of that year, Eugene went back to Yuquot. Yuquot is a good place for wounded people to go. It was the time of Summerfest, the annual two weeks when the people who once lived there return home to Yuquot and bring their families.

Eugene put his camping gear on *Uchuck III*, but he rode out to the little bay on the Pacific in Max Savey's tin boat, *First Citizen*. Max is a member of the Mowachaht/Muchalaht First Nations and is another one of several secondary hereditary chiefs, like Jerry Jack. Max and *First Citizen* form the entity called Maxie's Water Taxi.

The morning that Eugene went out to Yuquot was calm. It was one of those days when Nootka Sound seems to hold its breath between early morning and the afternoon storm just to stare in amazement at its own brave mountains.

First Citizen raced through the reflections as if drawing a line to cut glass, leaving a long scratch of foam on the stillness. Eugene, who knew this landscape as well as any other in his life, was still captivated by the beauty.

"It was a perfectly calm day," he said, "where everything is just kind of mirrored. Double images. It was in the morning. It was just a beautiful day, and it was warming up really quick."

When Max came out of the narrows of Williamson Passage and into the broad space by Mooyah Bay, the stillness was creased by a small black fin. Eugene remembers that *First Citizen* slowed so the people on board could take a look. To some, the little whale was the spirit of Ambrose, but to Eugene, the whale represented not just the departed chief but also his sister.

"The whale's presence does that for me," he told us later. "It brings back everybody who was important to me, and who still is important to me."

For the First Nations, life, wild animals, and a sense of the supernatural are blended generally into experience, and whether the whale represented one spirit or many mattered less than the general sense of who orcas are.

"There are supernatural creatures in our belief system," Eugene told us later. "*Qwayac'iik* is the wolf. He is one of our most respected creatures on the land. His counterpart in the ocean is the orca. He is connected with truth and justice."

Eugene stood in the boat and watched the small black fin slice the water. For him, as it was for many of the First Nations people, there was not just a sense of empathy that they felt in their own hearts for a little whale on his own in Nootka Sound. They also felt that the spirit of the whale had empathy for them, for their own need for truth and justice, for their own loneliness, for their own sorrows.

"He was just a little guy then," Eugene told us. "He was only nine or ten feet or something. He was just a little guy. I thought of it as being a small miracle. And it brought me a sense of peace, in that life goes on."

CHAPTER SIX

November 2001

O n a gray day in the fall of 2001, Sheila and Rick Millard were
out on Nootka Sound in a seventeen-foot fiberglass outboard,
heading back to Gold River from their cabin. Rick and Sheila both
lost their jobs when the mill shut down, but they stayed and finally
found work in the logging industry. Now they could still go to their
cabin on the sound about every other weekend.

Nootka Sound is overtly magnificent in the summer, but for the rest
of the year it is mysterious. Much of the time, the highest peaks are hidden in cloud, rain, and snow. Mist curls up in canyons as if to hibernate,
or infiltrates the woods like the thought of rain seeping into your mind.
And when the rain comes, it falls in curtains as gray and heavy as
chain mail, and it falls hard across the water, as if to bar your passage.

On this day, it wasn't raining, but the summer shine was long
gone, and in the general coolness, the afternoon winds were now
quiet. In the broad sheltered avenue of Hanna Channel, the water was
still and dark, with long ripples as languid as if they flowed through
syrup. The little outboard slipped across this untroubled sea with
hardly a bump and emerged easily into the expanse of water near
Mooyah Bay. And there was an odd splash in the distance.

"Did you see that?" Rick said.

"Yeah," Sheila said. "It looks like something jumping out of the
water."

The splash was quite a distance away, Sheila remembers. "So we sort of slowed down and putted over there. And we thought, Oh, it looks like a whale. And we realized how tiny it was."

Like most boaters on the coast of British Columbia, the Millards had seen a brochure called "Be Whale Wise," which sets out the rules for watching whales. So they didn't try to get right on top of this little whale. The brochure instructs you to stay a hundred yards or more away and slow down or stop if you see whales within four hundred yards. So they stopped. But the little orca hadn't read the brochure.

"He just zoomed right on over to our boat," Sheila recalls. "He was rubbing on it."

"Oh, it's a baby whale!" she said to Rick. They looked around. They knew this sea and its abundant life well, so they knew that a little whale like this would not be alone. Where was his family? But there were no other fins, no other plumes of breath.

One of Sheila's first thoughts was that maybe the little orca had the wrong impression about what they were. Maybe, she thought, he was trying to nurse. Unlike many boats, theirs had a white bottom. She wondered if the whale was mistaking the bottom for his mother's white belly and was poking around down there in search of a milk spigot.

In a way, it was as if Sheila was giving the little orca an excuse for being there. No unusual barriers broken; it was just a mistake. But as the little whale kept playing with their boat, it became apparent that he wasn't trying to nurse. He was there for the company. He wouldn't just rub; he'd also look. He'd roll on his side and look up at them with one dark little eye, as if asking some question they couldn't understand, much less answer.

What do you do?

A somewhat impractical thought instinctively crossed Sheila's mind: Maybe they should take it home and put it in the tub.

Well, no. But even as they tried to gently motor away, the little whale followed, as if determined to hang on to a hand.

"But it was getting late," Sheila says. "So we had to leave."

They gradually accelerated. The little whale followed. But as they reached the edge of Williamson Passage, just past Atrevida Point, the orca let them get away.

"Oh," Sheila says, "it was just heartbreaking."

She looked back. In the distance, a white plume of mist lifted and blew away, and a tiny black fin appeared and disappeared.

Cameron Forbes and his wife, Catherine, were sure they were too late to see the little whale. Usually, by the time you hear about a solitary wolf prowling a campground or an albino sea lion barking on a log, it's too late and the phenomenon has vanished.

So when Rick and Sheila Millard told Cameron and Catherine about what they'd seen, they thought they'd missed the whale.

Cameron and Catherine own and operate a fishing resort about twenty nautical miles from Gold River. It is up the sound, toward the open ocean. The resort is called Critter Cove. It's a tidy bunch of floating docks with charming cedar cabins and a restaurant. In summer, hundreds of sportfishers drive up from Vancouver and Washington State to fish these extraordinarily productive waters, often so close to one another on the best holes that they might as well be trolling for Porsches on Interstate 5. But in the winter, there's just a caretaker living out a superior form of loneliness on the place, and Cameron and Catherine go out often to do maintenance and check on the cabins. They go back and forth in their own small tin boat, which has a cabin and two outboard motors.

One November day, they headed out on a routine trip. Everything was gray but placid. On days like this, Nootka Sound did not seem hostile, just remote, a face turned away from the intensity of life.

They proceeded into the gray world. Their kids, Tucker, who was almost one, and Bryce, who was two, were bundled up in tiny red life jackets. The family had plenty of color and energy to brighten even a land drained of color by November. In small chop, the boat roared along, steady as a train, but there was a hammering beat of small waves on the metal and a rattle of drops smacking the window.

Looking for the little whale, they finally saw him. He was just a small black fin out in the big patch of water, the fin not much different from a branch stump on a log, except that it moved and disappeared. Cameron stopped nearby. Then they, too, had their moment. The little whale noticed them and swam over. He didn't come right up to the boat, but he got very close and looked at them.

"When you see wild whales," Catherine told us later, "they look at you, but they carry on. This is a whole different thing. Because he doesn't just sort of go on by and do his business; he comes up and looks at you and shows you stuff. He's flashing his tail, and doing all this within fifteen feet of your boat. He is trying to communicate with you."

In the summer, there's usually abundant traffic through this part of the sound, mostly fishermen pursuing salmon or loggers heading for their camps. In the winter, Nootka Sound can be an empty place. This day, there were no other boats in this stretch of water. It was just one little family and one little whale, looking at each other across the chill beginning of the long winter's rain, as if each was trying out an odd sort of personal connection that neither could quite understand.

The remarkable presence in Mooyah Bay stayed there throughout that gray season. Cameron and Catherine, Sheila and Rick, Donna Schneider and *Uchuck III*'s crew, and five or ten other people of Nootka Sound kept in touch with the whale. Cameron called him "Patch," because that was a friend's nickname and it fit. So Patch became a piece of a little Nootka Sound community of people who chose not to tell a lot of other people of the marvels they saw.

"It was kind of like he was our whale," Cameron said. "We were protective of him. Because you know people, and people are jerks."

Patch was both entertaining and endearing. He seemed determined to make a connection between himself and the people he met, but he was tentative, as if he was hungry for it but was also scared. As Cameron and Catherine approached across the water, Patch would leap in apparent greeting, then would race over to wherever they stopped. But then he wouldn't come right up to the boat. He'd stick his head out of the water, open his mouth, and make little squeaking sounds, just keeping a bit of safe distance between himself and the people.

His antics were complicated and funny to those who watched. He would slap his pectoral fin or his tail on the water. He would put his head straight down and stick the aft end of his body up out of the water, letting his tail flop and fly in the air like a flag. Sometimes he'd go down, catch a fish, and bring it up, holding it up in his mouth so they could see it.

"It was as if he was saying, Look what I've got," Catherine said. "He was certainly showing us what he had caught down there."

But what made it so striking was why the little guy was doing all this. He hadn't come for food. He was there for the company. When Donna Schneider, Cameron and Catherine, or Rick and Sheila looked across that gap between them and Patch, what they saw was not just a bulbous little animal in tuxedo colors with an array of spectacular teeth. They saw an awareness, a presence, and a longing. And they responded.

"You realize, Oh, man, this is not a reptile," Cameron said. "He has got emotions. And that is why you know that he is not a predator toward you. This is somebody just wanting to bond. You look in his eye, and there is more there than with most of my guests. There really is."

The way Cameron and all the others reacted to the little whale felt like instinct: When Patch looked at you, the look had need in it, and your empathy lit up right away.

"How do you know that a puppy needs attention?" Cameron said. "You just know."

CHAPTER SEVEN

November 2001

One day in the late fall, a helicopter growled and clattered its way slowly up over the pass between Campbell River, on the east side of Vancouver Island, and Gold River, to the west, then descended toward the narrow stretch of Nootka Sound that leads in from the sea to the Gold River docks. It was a great, sunny day, not at all normal at this time of year.

From the air, Nootka Sound looks very different than it does from the water. From a boat, the seaways of the fjord are shining avenues attended by the somber forms of hills that seem to kneel at the water's edge, but from the air, the waterways are slender intrusions into a landscape dominated by rock and tree. From sea level, there are only glimpses of the highest arrays of peaks, but from the air, the ridges and peaks crowd around like gray stone armies, with blades edged with ice, marching through the weeds of the forests.

The helicopter passed among these multitudes and descended. Closer, the waterways widened, and the area around Mooyah Bay opened like a pool in a braided river, a broadening where passages met and then diverged. The helicopter dropped lower. The people inside were looking, skeptically, for a little whale.

The two scientists in the helicopter were among the world's most seasoned orca experts. They were John Ford and Graeme Ellis, who many years before had joined Ken Balcomb to write the book *Killer Whales,* which is required reading for anyone who cares about the orcas of North America's west coast.

John Ford is lead orca researcher for the Canadian Department of Fisheries and Oceans. He is a former orca trainer who is now a Ph.D. biologist. He had left the Vancouver Aquarium staff to join the Department a few weeks before the helicopter trip. Graeme Ellis is a scientific technician for the Department. Graeme went even further back than John in the captive business. Years before, in the 1970s, he was involved in the captures of transient orcas and Southern Resident whales that were swept up out of the sea for the aquarium industry.

The mystery of killer whales is vast, and despite the knowledge about them that has been gained over the past three decades by people like Ken, John, and Graeme, the mystery has only deepened.

At first, it seems that they know a lot about them. They know that there are three groups of orcas that live around the island—offshores, who spend their time out in the grand ocean, and about whom nobody knows much at all; transients, who pass through occasionally to eat red meat like harbor seals and sea lions; and residents, who come back from unknown winter journeys to spend summer and fall near Vancouver Island and eat only fish.

Each individual resident orca is known by the unique shape of its dorsal fin and the patch of light gray on its back, and each has been given a name and number. Once individuals began to be identified, research revealed that the resident orcas are intensely social, probably a lot more social than the individualistic people who study them. There are two types of residents: Northerns, about 250 whales who spend their summers at the north end of Vancouver Island, and Southerns, the remnant group that spends summer and fall seasons going back and forth across the border between Canada and the United States, living in highly polluted waters in one of the most popular archipelagos in North America.

Orcas' brains have revealed enormous capacities in the same areas that give humans such a broad grasp of the world and also the power to subdue it. John Lilly, a maverick physician and writer whose books, particularly *Man and Dolphin* (1961) and *The Mind of the Dolphin: A Nonhuman Intelligence* (1967), changed the way many people saw those remarkable animals, wrote that the orca may be the most intelligent creature on the planet.

"They are incredibly perceptive animals," John Ford told us. "They have individual characters, personalities, if you like, that are strikingly different in different animals. They also respond differently to individual people."

The aquarium orca shows where he worked years before were attended by as many as five hundred people, a buzzing, colorful, chirping crowd, but if John walked along the path behind the crowd, the whales would follow him with their eyes, even when he was out of uniform.

"And the dynamics of working with them," Ford said, "in the context of trying to persuade them to do what you want them to do as part of the show's routine, was always a challenge, because they seemed to make a game of changing things. Often, in such a subtle way that you did not realize it, your behavior was being modified by them."

But as it has been for many species people have studied at length, all this new knowledge had opened huge new windows of mystery. The men in the helicopter knew that the orcas use a complex repertoire of calls, whistles, and clicks both to navigate underwater and to communicate among themselves, but they had no idea how that communication and navigation actually worked. They knew orcas could catch swift salmon in murky water using sound the way ships use sonar, but they had no idea how the orcas perceived that underwater world—could they be "seeing" with sound with perhaps as much detail as we perceive with vision? The scientists knew orcas could easily travel a hundred miles a day, but they didn't know where the

Southern Residents actually went when they left the Salish Sea for the winter.

They knew that the many details they had learned by watching from the surface was just the surface. What remained to be learned was huge.

One thing that had become clear, though, was basic and important: These animals are highly social. They have intricate patterns of relationships that they seem to maintain across generations. They live together in small groups dominated by females. The groups are called matrilines. Males leave these groups only to mate, then return, and never permanently leave their mothers' groups. So there was one generalization that the people in the helicopter could make with confidence: These orcas do not live alone. So they thought that the people of Nootka Sound had probably just been seeing a porpoise.

The helicopter trip was a scheduled run to the west coast of Vancouver Island to survey sea otter populations, but the scientists decided to divert from the course for ten minutes or so to take a look at this supposed orca.

"I mean, we could not go out on a dedicated trip in a helicopter to look for a whale," Graeme told us.

"What can I say?" he went on. "We get whale sightings all over the coast all the time. We don't run out and check it out. But it sounded kind of like an unusual report, so we thought, We're there. Let's have a look."

The helicopter descended. Graeme didn't think they'd spot anything. But he was wrong. As they flew over, Patch launched himself right out of the water and made an enormous splash. He left a bull's-eye of foam. Nothing shy about this little whale.

Graeme recalled that someone said, "Oh, look, there it is! There *is* a whale down there!"

The helicopter climbed up away from Mooyah Bay and on toward the coast, now only a few air miles away from the otters. But Graeme was intrigued. This was definitely not normal.

"I wanted primarily to photo-ID it, to see if I could find out who it was," he said later. "To me, that was most important: to try to figure out why a young animal like that would be on its own."

It was late November before Graeme could get to Gold River. His office was in the city of Nanaimo, about a three-hour drive from Gold River, and he had to bring a boat with him.

"My memory of going to Gold River is either snow or rain," he said. "Towing that boat in snow, that's what I remember. I mean, what am I doing?"

Graeme drove through Gold River down to the launching ramp, which is run by the Mowachaht/ Muchalaht First Nations. On the bank beside the ramp were three abandoned houses, left when the band, driven from its home on the water by the fumes of the pulp mill, built its new village of Tsaxana up the hill from Gold River. The ghostly houses watched implacably as Graeme launched the boat and headed west, over dark water, in rain and under heavy clouds.

Over the previous thirty years, the scientists who were drawn to these whales by their mystery unraveled the very first bits of it by identifying individual whales. The shapes of dorsal fins and saddle patches had been assembled into family trees. Now, whenever a new whale is born, the first task of scientists who work this beat is to photograph the little newcomer's saddle patch and get the animal recorded on his or her tree, like a hospital administrator logging in a patient or a society matron tracking aristocracy.

So Graeme needed to take a photograph and compare this whale to the whales recorded in the books.

The photograph was hard to get. But Graeme had been looking for whales in rain and chop for many years, and Mooyah Bay was at least a limited space. Soon enough, there was a plume, and there was the little fin.

Graeme comes across as a pessimistic, almost cynical man. He seems to cultivate that image. It goes well with science, particularly the science of creatures that have become, over the relatively short period of his professional career, the focus of a lot of human reverence. But he doesn't pretend to be disinterested. Like many scientists, he has been trained to be dispassionate, but empathy remains. Graeme's cynicism seems to be a cover, built to hide the emotions he is supposed to put aside.

So the first thing he worried about was how this very young whale could possibly survive here alone.

"The whale was young enough that we did not think it would have the skills necessary to feed on its own," Graeme said. "We wanted to be able to judge his health from his appearance. They mask problems really well, it seems. So you don't really know from the outward behavior that there's anything wrong until they drop dead."

There was one quick clue that he looked for right away. When an orca is sick or hungry, it tends to lose fat behind its head first, so there's a narrowing where you visualize a neck might be. That creates a shape that scientists, in an uncharacteristic burst of vivid imagery, call a "peanut head."

"That peanut-head appearance is a warning alarm that all is not well with these animals," Graeme said. "So we were quite concerned about that."

But when Graeme was close enough to see all of Patch as he came to the surface, the peanut-head shape wasn't there. Patch was doing well—so well, in fact, that someone else who saw him said he looked as fat as a watermelon. So Graeme took his photos and left that canyon full of rain.

Back at the office, he went through photos of young Northern Residents first. No luck. Then he looked at the Southern Residents. Jackpot! There was a familiar saddle patch in the photo of L-98.

He sent the pictures to Ken Balcomb. He told him not to tell anyone. Ken verified the identification and kept it quiet. But the news was stunning: In twenty-five years of recording the locations of the orcas of the Pacific Northwest, Southern Residents had never been reported in Nootka Sound.

Patch now had a new name. He was Luna, L-98. Luna wasn't dead after all. He had gone off exploring the ocean.

Graeme made his fateful discovery in November. He told John Ford. But they kept it quiet. They didn't want to cause trouble.

CHAPTER EIGHT

December 2001

W e need to have a little meeting," John Ford said quietly to
Marilyn Joyce, making sure other people at the marine mammal conference couldn't hear. Marilyn was the brand-new West Coast marine mammal coordinator for the Department of Fisheries and Oceans, which meant she was in charge of orcas.

The conference was going on in the city of Vancouver in December. It was organized by the Society for Marine Mammalogy, so Marilyn was there as part of learning her new job.

Marilyn had been the marine mammal coordinator for only a short time, and she was feeling pretty good about the job. She had been working for the Department since 1986 and had spent much of that time working in fisheries management, which often involves acrimonious battles among sportfishers, commercial fishers, and passionate conservationists. When she got the marine mammal job, Marilyn saw a field in which, at least on this coast of Canada, nobody was trying to kill the resource and everyone wanted to conserve it.

"So I was tremendously excited about this new job," Marilyn told us. "Because everyone wanted to do great things for whales, seals, and sea lions. And I thought this would be a really great position to be working in, and there would probably be less conflict than where I'd worked in the past."

Then John Ford came up to her and suggested the meeting. "And we should be pretty low-key here," he went on, "because we're not quite sure what this means."

Well, that was an enticing thing to say. So Marilyn convened the meeting. It was a small gathering indeed: It included only Graeme, John, Marilyn, Ken Balcomb, and a few other scientists from the United States and Canada.

The group assembled quietly around a table. There, John and Graeme produced a stack of photographs, like detectives bringing out shots of the bad guy.

"It was all kind of hush-hush, top secret," Ken Balcomb said later. "Get us into a side room, a small, select group of marine biologists. For some reason or another, they were trying to be political already. We don't want to leave the wrong people in or the right people out. We want to include people, but we don't want to have it too big, and it's got to be people who can keep their mouths shut."

The photos went on the table, and they were not shots of some guy with a three-day beard and an attitude. They were shots of a goofy baby whale.

Graeme and John delivered the secret: *We have this little whale by itself in Nootka Sound. It's L-98. It's from L Pod. Didn't come back this year. We thought he was dead.* They all looked concerned.

Marilyn Joyce had one last little burst of innocence, and perhaps some compassion of her own for the little whale's solitude.

"And I said, 'Oh, that's interesting.'"

No doubt, looks passed around the table, quick glances running between these old hands at the killer whale business, men who had seen the images of orcas evolve in the public eye from being murderers to being lords of the undersea, and who knew that there is nothing that is just "interesting" about an orca.

"And they shook their heads at me, and said, 'No,'" Marilyn told us later. "'You don't understand! This is highly unusual and is not going to be easy.'"

Ed Thorburn was an enforcement officer for the Department of Fisheries and Oceans. He had a crisp mustache and a severe look that said, Don't poach abalone on my watch.

In 2001, Ed's beat included Mooyah Bay, but he didn't go there very often because people didn't fish there. So in the fall, as he went about his business policing fishing seasons, he didn't see Luna.

When you're a law-enforcement person accustomed to dealing with abalone smugglers and salmon crooks, just how seriously do you take it when someone calls you up and murmurs in your ear, "Don't say a word, but you've got a whale in your water." Well, okay. And?

"It was John Ford and Graeme Ellis who called," Ed says. "They said, 'We are not telling anybody; we're just keeping it as quiet as we can, hoping that his mother will come back.'"

On a calm but drizzly day in December, not long after the call, Ed drove his boat through the labyrinth of Nootka Sound toward Mooyah Bay. Ed's boat was a big black-and-gray Zodiac named *Rugged Point*, with a console in the middle but no real shelter, so he was used to wind and rain. But it was a fast boat, with twin 150-horsepower outboards, and on a calm day it could fly. So he came roaring around the corner of Bligh Island and looked east across the junction of waters near Mooyah Bay, where layers of ridgelines stood one after another and disappeared in grayness before they reached the sky.

At first, he didn't see anything. He slowed the boat down to a crawl and motored slowly across the still water, past the automatic light and the outcrop of mossy rock at Anderson Point. It was so calm that once the boat slowed, he could watch his wake reach the shore and wash up on the dark stones.

The boat idled along and eventually came around the point near the log sort in Mooyah Bay. Still nothing.

Then, seen through binoculars, there it was: a tuft of white mist that faded quickly, and a tiny black fin that rose and fell in the expanse of gray.

There were no other boats there, and even the logging camp seemed empty. It was just *Rugged Point* and a very small whale breathing in the distance. Ed turned the boat to leave. This might not be such a hard secret to keep. But there was something about the solitude of that small plume in the expanse of Mooyah Bay that caught Ed's attention. Soon he would come this way again.

One month after the marine mammal conference, on January 3, 2002, Orca Network, the organization run by Howie Garrett and Susan Berta, received a report of a lone baby orca in Swinomish Channel, near La Conner, in Washington State, about two hundred nautical miles from Nootka Sound. A few days later, the baby orca was seen swimming near a tanker off Edmonds, Washington, and a few days after that, the whale was seen and photographed near Vashon Island, near Seattle.

When Ken Balcomb heard about this, he thought, Well, Luna came back!

John Ford thought so, too.

"I just thought, logically, it was most likely the same whale," John told us later. "Because the chance of having two independent situations was more remote than this whale simply moving down into Puget Sound. It was a Southern Resident, after all."

John Ford can be an assertive guy, in a deceptively mild-mannered way, and he wrote an assertive memo that turned what was likely into stated fact: "On January 14–15, the whale was observed in a photograph on Vashon Island, Puget Sound, and its identity was confirmed as L-98."

But John and Ken were wrong. The baby whale near Seattle was not Luna. She was soon identified as Springer, a young female member of the Northern Resident community of killer whales, who spend their summers near the northern tip of Vancouver Island. But Springer was smack in the middle of Luna's home range. It was as if, after all these years in which these whales had never separated, it was happening all over the place.

The general public knew about the little whale near Seattle, but not about Luna. And the scientists still said nothing. But it was a re- markably odd situation. There was a Canadian orca calf in the United States, and an American orca calf in Canada. It was like an interna- tional exchange. Except nobody knew how these two lost whale kids would get home.

CHAPTER NINE

January 2002

Graeme Ellis sure hit the bad days on the road to Nootka Sound. In January, he drove up there again, this time in snowfall, hauling that boat and trailer back over the two slippery little passes between Campbell River and Gold River and at last getting to the Mowachaht/Muchalaht Marina, where the Gold River itself empties into the sound.

This time he brought a friend and colleague, Lance Barrett-Lennard, a marine mammal scientist who worked for the Vancouver Aquarium and who had also attended the clandestine meeting in Vancouver. Lance specializes in genetics, but the science of whales is not a large enough field to allow him to focus on only that one angle, so he covers a lot of other ground, too. He wanted to assess this curious event and see the whale for himself.

By the time the two men got to Nootka Sound, Lance may have wondered whether his curiosity over this whale was truly worth all this unpleasant travel.

"It was a foul day," he said. "It was snowing and raining. It was a nasty day."

Not only that but out on the water it was also windy. The two men drove the boat through the clatter of chop the fifteen nautical miles out to Mooyah Bay and started looking for Luna through wet snowfall and wind. After a bit of squinting and binocular cleaning, they saw the little whale and motored in his direction.

It can be bleak and lonely indeed on that patch of water. Winter rains wash the color out of the day, and wind turns the cold air raw. As you bob around on this unsettled surface, your face rain-blasted, your fine and expensive rain gear leaking, and a realization dawning that your boots are not waterproof, either, your mind can become somewhat jaundiced about the value of your endeavor. Particularly when the whale you have come all this way to see proves to be elusive.

"His behavior," Lance said, "was typical of a killer whale feeding. You know, it was just like, I'm busy right now."

The two men followed Luna around as he foraged. They spent their time scooping at the water, with a swimming pool net, cleaning it. Killer whales are messy eaters. They leave scales and bits of fish in the water. The fine-mesh pool cleaner gets the stuff.

By analyzing the debris later, the two men realized that Luna was being creative in his feeding habits, which might be the reason he was able to get enough to eat to survive at such a young age.

"The thing that struck me upon first seeing him," Lance said, "was that he seemed to be in good shape. And for such a young killer whale to still be in good shape, after at least six months, ran counter to everything we thought we knew about killer whales. Everything about young killer whales, both in captivity and in the wild, makes them seem totally dependent on their parents. We thought that it would be like laying a baby in the forest, and coming back and finding it alive."

The debris Luna left was not from salmon. It was the scales of pilchards, a type of sardine that resident orcas don't normally eat. But that year, the pilchards were thick.

"So," Lance told us, "Luna ended up in a situation where he could almost swim through the water with his mouth open. And that was the first time that we had any record of any killer whales anywhere eating pilchards." This kid was, at least, adaptable. Was that the species, or the individual?

Finally, Luna came over to the boat and rode its bow wave for a short time. This had one unintended consequence.

Graeme was using a small, expensive video camera to record Luna's behaviors. He had borrowed the camera from John Ford. He and Lance were going to great lengths to try to protect it from the rain. But as they were filming Luna's bow riding, the little whale did something almost as creative as his pilchard diet. He rolled on his back and flipped his tail, sending a cascade of water right at the two men.

"He just doused us," Lance said.

What a day! Wind, rain, snow, everything cold and grim, and now this little whale throws a couple of buckets of water on you. What's next?

Right. The camera. Graeme wiped it off in a hurry, then looked in the viewfinder to see if it was okay. The good news was that it was running and there was an image on the screen. But this was a fancy camera, with all kinds of things you could do to spice up your film, and now it was doing that stuff all by itself. On the screen, over the footage of a little whale playing, it was editing in balloons, hearts, and smiley faces.

"Uh-oh," Graeme said to Lance. "John's not going to like this. It's saying 'Happy Birthday.'"

In the connection of waters at Mooyah Bay, in those gray days of winter, the little whale's life was like a single sparkle on the water. Luna was there, and when people in boats stopped to look at him, he approached—but not too close. The connection between Luna and people was like a dance of what seemed to be shyness, with glances, turns, and looks between strangers. There was no touching, but the dance was slowly getting closer.

On one of the rare peaceful days of that winter, when the wind rested, Ed Thorburn, along with another enforcement officer, came to Mooyah Bay again to see how the little whale was doing. They found Luna busy pushing a big log.

"I had no idea how to deal with this animal," Ed told us later. "Nobody told me what should or shouldn't be done. So we parked our boat. And I stopped it probably a couple hundred meters from where Luna was. And he would push things closer to the boat."

Ed stood still in the boat. The big twin outboards were shut down and the ripples of the quiet bay made small clanking noises on the aluminum hull of the big inflatable. He and the other enforcement officer stood in the boat, silent, as if they were worried that they might disturb Luna. But Luna was working hard.

The log was about twenty feet long and at least two feet in diameter. It was a massive piece of wood, far bigger than Luna, who was only about twelve feet long.

To push it, the little whale would circle it once, as if stalking it, then come at the flat end, where it had been sawed off. Then he'd put his head down underneath it, turn on his side, put the edge of one pectoral fin up against it, and thrash his tail. The log would move slowly forward.

Because Luna was lying on his side in the water while he did this, his tail flukes, which normally moved up and down when he was swimming forward, swept from side to side. One side of the flukes stuck up out of the water as he swept his tail back and forth, so there was a lot of splashing. It did not look efficient. But he was, after all, only two years old, and nobody said he couldn't be clumsy.

Luna would work like that for a minute or so, then stop pushing. Then he'd twist until his little dorsal fin and blowhole were out of the water, give a sharp exhale and inhale, then stalk around the log once more and go back to pushing. While Ed watched, Luna pushed the big log in a full circle. He let it drift for a minute or so, then started pushing it again.

Luna pushed, and Ed watched. And Ed decided to change Luna's name, because it just didn't seem right to him.

"I thought, Boy, Luna is a girl's name. And I thought, Here he is, playing with these logs; I mean, he is pushing forty-footers around." So Ed came up with another name, after the star of the famous Canadian television series *The Beachcombers,* which ran from 1972 to 1990. It was about men who searched for logs washed up on the rugged BC coast, which they could then tow away and sell, making a ragged but fiercely independent living. The star of the series was an actor named Bruno Gerussi, who had died a few years earlier.

"So I started referring to him as Bruno because it was more appropriate to what he was doing, and he was a boy, and I thought, you know, *The Beachcombers.*"

Whatever his human nickname or designation was, Patch or Luna or Bruno or L-98, the little whale kept pushing the log. And time paused as the rain fell on the flat water and all you could hear on Mooyah Bay was the splashing sound of a young whale by himself, but not quite alone, because there on the boat nearby was a man in a uniform with a mustache and a severe, windblown face, watching.

"There are times in your life," Ed Thorburn told us later, speaking very deliberately so as to get it just right, "when you reach a point, and you say, This will be with me until the day I die."

One day in January, Graeme Ellis drove north again from Nanaimo, towing a trailer, with three other people who were in on the secret of Luna: John Ford, Marilyn Joyce, and Dave Huff, the veterinarian for the Vancouver Aquarium.

They drove up the winding road into the town of Gold River and slid the boat into the chilly mouth of the Gold River itself, where it flows past the launching ramp and mingles with the tide. It was less than an hour's run down the arm of Nootka Sound to Mooyah Bay, and in January there wasn't much company on the water.

But there was company in Mooyah Bay. Luna came over—not right up to the boat, but close.

This was the first time Marilyn had seen him. She was captivated. But she didn't call him Luna. She was careful to call him L-98.

For decades, many young people chose to go into biology because of the deep empathy they felt for the plight of other lives in a world increasingly dominated by humans and our often-harmful machines, structures, and chemicals. But these passionate and empathetic human beings then studied with professors known as behaviorists, who believed animals were, essentially, instinctive automatons whose appearance of having emotions could be more accurately described as being caused by simpler biological mechanisms. Most behaviorists also believed that affection for individuals among subject species can consciously or unconsciously skew the process and the results of research. Thus the students were taught that their emotional responses to animals—compassion and empathy—could be seen as weakness, as a lack of scientific discipline. Many of the students were also taught that the instinctive response they felt to animals, which told them that animals were suffering or experiencing loneliness, frustration, or pain, was misguided and wrong. Many were taught that it was wrong to assume that animals have anything like the same emotions humans have, so for humans to acknowledge or accept their own emotional response to the apparent emotions of animals was a sign of ignorance. Those human emotional responses, that empathy, had to be put aside.

That attitude has been changing over the past twenty years, with the development of the discipline of cognitive ethology and studies of brains and behavior that show evidence for emotions in animals that may be similar to those of humans. But many biologists still believe they have to be unsentimental to the point of coldness toward the animals they instinctively revere. So to many of the people who work more closely with animals than most of us, empathy remains a weakness.

Research animals are usually given numbers instead of names. This is mostly done to help with the spreadsheets. But numbering is also described as a way to remove sentiment from the process, because some people think that giving animals nicknames changes our attitude toward them. So scientists who are worried about looking unscientific, or about revealing too much sentiment about an animal, often insist on using the number, even when everyone else is using a nickname.

But even though Marilyn always called whales by their respective numbers, she found personality in Luna right away. Luna came near the boat, pushing a log about twelve feet long, then rolled it up across his head, slid it down over his dorsal, rolled it back toward his tail, pushed it in the air, and then turned around and started again.

"To me, it was just fascinating," she told us later. "Because he had such skilled dexterity with a log. You know, he was very young, and obviously this was entertainment."

But what she thought should be done for Luna was very different from what many others in Nootka Sound felt. To her, the best possible thing people can do for wild animals is to stay away from them.

"I think that's my underlying philosophy," she said, "whether that's whale watching or whether that's dealing with sea lions in a marina. I really want nature to go about its business with the least interference from us. Really."

On February 1, 2002, Susan Berta, who ran Orca Network with her partner, Howie Garrett, was stuck at home. She had the flu, which gave her an excuse for crying when she got the e-mail.

Susan and Howie live in a rural community on an island north of Seattle, and that night was the organization's monthly meeting, held in a fire hall down the road. But because Susan was at home, she got the e-mail while the meeting was still going on. When she read it, the tears began.

"I was so sick, I couldn't even drive the few miles to the fire hall," Susan told us, "but I thought, I have got to get this to Howie now!"

Susan tried to figure out how to get this e-mail to the fire hall. All the nearby members of her organization were also there, so they weren't available. Howie didn't have a cell phone. Finally, Susan remembered a friend who lived near the fire hall. She called her.

"Sandy," she said, "will you do me a favor? If I e-mail you something, will you print it out and take it to Howie? And then you've got to tell me what the look on his face is when he sees it. This is how you get paid: You get to see the look on his face."

A few minutes later, Sandy edged into the back of the fire hall. The talk was winding down. She slipped the piece of paper into Howie's hand.

What was the look on his face? Well, to start with, he didn't cry. His eyes got big. He didn't say anything.

"I was just totally dumbstruck," Howie told us later. "Wait a minute; this can't be!"

He went to the front of the room. The speaker finished. Howie took her place. He read part of the e-mail:

> Fisheries and Oceans Canada marine mammal scientists have confirmed sightings of a lone, juvenile killer whale in a remote inlet off the west coast of Vancouver Island. Department staff, with the assistance of the Center for Whale Research in Friday Harbor, Washington, U.S.A., have identified the whale as L-98, a two-and-a-half-year-old juvenile male from L Pod, one of three Southern Resident killer whale pods.

The secret was out.

It was a stunning revelation. When Luna had not turned up in the annual census, everyone who knew anything about orcas had assumed that he was dead. But he wasn't. For the first time since research had begun on these orcas over thirty years before, an orca given up for dead had actually turned up alive. And it wasn't just any young orca. This was L-98, Luna, who had been born in such strange circumstances, who been so spirited and independent as a new baby, and who had won so many hearts before he had been lost and mourned. Luna was back.

There was a moment of silence. Then a whoop in the audience. Howie grinned.

"Everybody just kind of said 'What?' They couldn't believe it. It was an amazing bombshell. I mean, it rattled the meeting considerably."

CHAPTER TEN

March 2002

On the west coast of Vancouver Island in the winter, a day with sun is lovely and transient, a cup of nostalgia that warms your hand before you even sip.

On the fifth of March, it was a day like that. The snow was still deep in the high country, and the sun made the ridges dazzling white. Along the shoreline, the snow had melted, so everything smelled of fresh air, sea salt, and cedar.

Ed Thorburn was back. His big inflatable boat, *Rugged Point,* drifted along in the slow current, with the outboard motors shut down. The water was so calm that the surface tension looked as thick as syrup.

The only thing that broke this skin was Luna. He came toward the boat, bringing a short log with him. The log was four or five feet long, each end cut off flat by someone with a chain saw. When Luna approached the boat, paddling on his back, glimpses of his white belly showing, he half-carried the log along on what you would call his chest if he were a human.

When he got fifteen or twenty yards from the boat, he rolled up-right and let rip with a long, noisy blast through his blowhole, spraying water all around and giving the very audible impression that he had a monumental case of gas.

"Don't be rude, Bruno," Ed said aloud.

There was something special about this day. On earlier days, Luna had been more coy, more distant, keeping farther away from the boat. But now, Ed and the other officer on the boat, whose name was Jake Joslin, seemed to be the direct focus of Luna's interest. What Luna did seemed deliberate, conscious, and somehow urgent.

He went underwater, then came straight up out of the water for almost a third of his length, so his eyes were well clear of the water and he could look straight at the boat. It was the same move that he'd done around *Uchuck III,* which scientists call spyhopping. Ed had his own term for it, which made just as much sense, maybe more: *eye popping.*

Luna popped his eye up, took a look, then went under, put his head straight down, then lifted his body in the water so that his tail rose straight up in the air. His flukes flopped at the top, as if his tail were waving—a tail lob.

He let his tail slide back into the water, went over to the log, then dived, came up away from the log, and swam straight toward the boat. When he got close, he raised his tail deliberately and brought it down hard on the surface, with a wide-open smack that sounded like a gunshot and made a shower of spray.

"Sees us," Ed said to Jake, an understatement. Luna disappeared, then did a towering eye pop near the boat and vanished underwater again. He came out, dashed over to the log, rolled over and put it up on his chest, holding it there with his pectoral fin, then rolled back over, took a breath, and slapped the water again: *pow!*

"Gotcha," Ed said to Luna from about four feet away. Luna slapped the water again, and Ed backed up a little.

"Trying to get us wet, are ya?"

Luna slid up the starboard side of the boat, and right below where Ed was standing, he lifted his tail again and gave a mighty slap and splash, right in Ed's face and in the lens of the video camera with which Jake was filming all this.

Luna then rolled over by his log, swam back toward the boat, then rolled upright, took a deep breath, and immediately gave a massive long, wet blast on the surface through his blowhole while he slammed the water with his tail yet again. The blast went on and on. It sounded like a jet aircraft running on beans, but it made rain so fine that it captured sunlight in a rainbow.

Ed chuckled fondly. "What an animal!" he said quietly. After a while, he said to Jake, "Certainly does seem that he likes to have people around, eh?"

"I was thinking he was entertaining himself," Ed told us later. "It gave him something to do. I didn't realize it was probably something to do with socializing."

"All in all," Ed wrote in a letter to John Ford after this day in the sun with Luna, "he seems healthy and active but very lonely."

Part of the legacy of the behaviorist approach to animals is the term *anthropomorphism,* the use of human terms to describe animal emotions. Many people would say that Ed's use of the word *lonely* to describe what Luna appeared to be experiencing was anthropomorphic. But what Ed said wasn't much different from what a fully credentialed scientist, Lance Barrett-Lennard, said to a newspaper reporter soon after he visited Luna on the "Happy Birthday" camera day: "This is a child whale. I think he has proven he is not a toddler by the fact he's been able to feed himself. But he's a little guy, all by himself, who is desperate for company."

On March fifth, that calm and sunny day, Ed and Jake just kept watching. Luna pushed and pulled his log right under the boat and up on the other side, where Ed was leaning on the tubes, looking down at him. The log came back up to the surface, and Luna was there right next to Ed, on his side, looking up at him through a foot of water.

"Well, well," Ed said to Jake, or maybe to Luna. "What a sight!" Ed, perhaps instinctively, put out his hand and waved as Luna passed by.

"Killer whales really are much more social than humans in a way," Lance Barrett-Lennard told us later. He, too, had been trying to figure out what was going on with Luna, and he had his own ideas. "They're just never by themselves. So, for obligately social animals, and a species in which there is an extended period of parental care, the predictability of life, particularly for a young killer whale, lies in the social bond. So you have this whale, this young animal who is in a very unusual situation. And I think he was just really trying to build some kind of predictability into his existence."

Luna dived and disappeared. The two men looked around. He wasn't out by the log.

"Look at that!" Ed said.

From about twenty feet away, moving horizontally toward Ed at the surface, Luna slowly lifted his tail right out of the water. Wrapped around both flukes were a couple of strands of bull kelp, wiry, long pieces of vegetation that look like rope with leaves. Luna must have plucked them from near the bottom by twisting his body in the vegetation until his flukes collected it.

Luna dived deep, came up in front of the boat, and did two eye pops, looking at Ed, then went about fifty feet from the boat, put his head straight down and his flukes in the air and waved them back and forth, splashing.

"Beauty!" Ed said.

CHAPTER ELEVEN

March 2002

Jamie James and Roger Dunlop believed that strange things happened to them when they traveled together. One of those things had happened back in the summer of 2001.

Jamie was a Mowachaht/Muchalaht member who worked as the fisheries manager for the band. Roger Dunlop was the tribe's official biologist and Jamie's boss, but he was not a First Nations member.

One day that summer, Jamie and Roger had been counting sea otters in Roger's old gray Zodiac Hurricane. Sea otters are those absurdly cute furry creatures that float on the surface, eating shellfish by holding them against their chests and hammering them open with stones. The species was wiped out on the Vancouver Island coast after James Cook took fur samples to China and the otter-fur trade exploded. Now otters transplanted from Alaska were bringing the species back, and the band kept track of them.

That day, the big ocean swell was lazy and long. It lifted the smooth water gently and let it back down like something underwater breathing in its sleep. The otters were easy to spot near the lines of bull kelp that hung in the water near rocky shorelines.

Counting through binoculars, Roger saw a head on the surface. Another otter. No, it wasn't. It had pointy ears.

The head moved slowly through the smooth water, toward a beach. In the gently heaving water it reached the shore.

The animal came out of the water on a rock and gravel shoreline, with kelp draped on its shoulders like a cloak. It stood on the rocks of the shore and shook. The kelp slipped off.

It was a wolf. It trotted along the stony shore for about two hundred yards. Then it disappeared into the forest.

"I didn't really think anything of it," Roger told us, "other than here is a timber wolf coming out of the water with kelp falling off of it."

Jamie leaned over the side of the Zodiac and threw up into the sea. Later, both of them saw this as significant.

"That's a sign among Nuu-chah-nulth people," Roger said to us later, "of having encounters with supernatural beings."

"It's been told," Jamie said, "that maybe hundreds of years ago a young chief witnessed a killer whale come to shore, and it transformed into a wolf with kelp coming off its back like a cape. And it was so much power that the young chief fainted. We have a cultural experience with everything, going right from the ocean to the land to the sky. Everything."

In March 2002, Jamie and Roger went out to count otters again. They got up at 5:30 and went out in the same old Zodiac in the still, dark morning. They had to pick a day calm enough so they could see the otters in the larger body of water outside the mouth of Nootka Sound. As they motored west, mist hung in shreds from the wet trees, barely moving. The Zodiac was the only swift thing in the day.

Jamie and Roger counted otters as the day grew from dark gray to bright gray, until the chop made it too difficult to see those little heads on the water. Then they started back.

Now that the counting was done, they had a little time before the early March darkness came down. So when they saw a distant spout as they were passing Mooyah Bay, Roger stopped the boat to see what these whale stories they'd been hearing were all about.

Soon enough, Luna came over. He swam right up, rubbed against the boat, went underneath, circled the boat, then rubbed against it again. For people like Cameron and Catherine Forbes, this was becoming normal. But for Jamie and Roger it was astonishing.

"I've never seen a killer whale so close in my life," Jamie told us. "It was the most friendly animal."

The old gray Zodiac wasn't a lot bigger than Luna. The little whale rubbed against it and blew fishy breath in the faces of the two men, who were grinning at Luna and at each other. It wasn't a solemn moment of power like the time the wolf walked out of the water, but it was still something special.

"We were like little giddy boys," Jamie said. "Look at this whale! We were kind of bouncing all over the place." They had often seen killer whales before, but this was different.

"Killer whales come in all the time," Jamie told us, "but for a killer whale to be interested in you? It was pretty wild. This killer whale is looking at you. He has actually got an interest in you. And that is really a strong bond. It was awesome. But we never thought he would actually stay."

CHAPTER TWELVE

April 2002

Paul Laviolette, who lived in Gold River and used to work at the mill, also owned a fishing lodge where he ran charters. But then he found out that he was allergic to fish. Not good. He sold the lodge, but what was he going to do with his boat?

Then Luna came along. And Paul did nothing legally wrong, but he got in trouble anyway.

At the time, no one on Nootka Sound seemed to think that there was anything wrong with Luna's efforts to swim up to boats and look at people. All the whale rules that were already in place were designed to keep people from chasing whale pods around. People weren't chasing Luna. Luna was chasing them.

Everybody knew those rules: Stay one hundred meters or more away from whales. If you're speeding and you see whales within four hundred meters, slow down or stop.

So that's what people did. The trouble was, if you saw a spout anywhere around Mooyah Bay, four hundred meters, five hundred meters, maybe one thousand meters away, and you slowed down or stopped, poof! Here would come a little whale to play beside your boat and look you in the eye.

That spring, people didn't get in trouble for stopping. Everyone seemed well aware that orcas were so social that what Luna was doing was trying to make up for having no related orcas around. That was just what he did, no big deal.

Even the Department of Fisheries did not seem particularly concerned about stopping the social stuff. Its worry seemed to be about avoiding food dependency. Marilyn Joyce wrote Ed, "We do not want people feeding it."

They weren't. At first, when Ed reported back to Marilyn, he wrote that people were being careful. He seemed to delight in the way Luna courted his human contacts:

All were very aware of the sensitivity and were very careful not to approach the whale, but allow it to approach them. The interesting thing was as each boat came into the area Bruno went to the boat and did a little show. When another boat came into the area and stopped, Bruno broke off and went to the new boat. Seems he is auditioning for a show.

Paul Laviolette was among those people. He would go out to see Luna in his twenty-foot-long fiberglass sportfishing boat, *Yabba-Dabba-Doo*. "We would just wait and he would show up," he told us later. Paul was impressed.

"My dog, he has one word," Paul said. "*Woof.* What's wrong? Are you hungry? You want to play? I have to figure it out. But then I get out there and here comes Luna." Luna didn't come as close as Paul wanted, so he put his hand under the water and waved it.

"So he puts his fin above the water and he is waving back at me," Paul said. "I'm thinking, He cannot be doing this on purpose. So I do it again, and he does it again. And then he takes off, chasing a fish or whatever. So he comes back and I put my hand under the water and I am waving. And sure enough, he waves back with his fin. And I think, Holy! Here is something that has got way more intelligence than the domestic animals that we are used to."

Since Paul couldn't imagine that he'd be allergic to a marine mammal, now he had a way to use his boat. So he put up a sign in the Ridge, a Gold River pub and restaurant. WHALE WATCHING, it said.

"Next thing you know, I'm getting phone calls," Paul said. " 'Can you take us out to see Luna?' Sure, no problem. We'd get out there in the morning and he'd hear the boat coming and just leap out of the water about a mile away. Here I am! Here I am!"

But then Paul got a different kind of phone call. It was from Fisheries officer Ed Thorburn.

In the days leading up to Ed's call to Paul Laviolette, Luna had been hurt. A prop from a passing boat had carved a cut into the side of his head, just behind one of his eyes. When Cameron Forbes and his family saw it on the way out to Critter Cove for Easter, it looked bad.

"It was a big cut," Cameron told us later. "A big gash. You could have put your hand in the cut. He came up, and he was like a big dog wanting to climb on your lap. If he wasn't so big, you would pick him up and cuddle him. And it was just like he was hanging his shoulders, and not feeling too good."

Ed did not hide how he felt about this. The empathy Luna had brought to life in Ed seemed to have grown each time he saw the little whale. Now, like Cameron and Catherine and many others on Nootka Sound, Ed apparently felt like Luna's protector, emotionally committed to helping him have a better life.

But for Ed, the direction of that commitment had changed. A few weeks before, he had been talking with admiration about how Luna approached each new boat. But now he had a different attitude.

His conversations with Marilyn Joyce and John Ford about Luna may have sounded a bit like a group of men and women talking about relationships, that endless human conversation.

Many scientists believe the need for managing relationships is one of the reasons social animals developed large brains. It's easy to see why; it's not simple. And this was indeed all about a relationship— not just between genders but across the lines of species, as well. It

was complicated and emotional and there was a huge lack of knowledge, but there was certainty in some voices. Those were the voices
Ed was tasked with hearing.

What John Ford said or wrote to Ed was probably much like what
he said later to us.

"In the short term," John said, "yes, you can see, this is a social
animal who needs some sort of social life. And is it our obligation
to fulfill that? There's a huge downside to that."

The downside, to John, Marilyn, and Graeme, was the possibility
that Luna would get so attached to humans that he might not seek out
his pod if it appeared nearby. All three of them had also been at least
exposed to, if not convinced by, the idea that emotional relationships
with animals were not something good scientists had. So to them, the
best thing a person could do when faced with Luna's hunger for contact was to put compassion aside and turn away.

"You can't help but have a lot of empathy for this whale," John told
us. "It is clearly almost begging for attention. It is very, very hard to
not gratify that, just to take your boat and speed away from him. It's
tough. But I think it was the right approach. This whale is best off if
he remains a whale."

This was hard for Ed. He was torn between this rational analysis,
conducted far from Nootka Sound, and the look he saw in Luna's
eyes.

"You would've had to be a pretty coldhearted person," Ed told us,
"not to see the desperation in this whale, trying to socialize. When
he pops up, and he looks at you, you can see—I mean, the eyes are
the window to the soul."

But the mandate was clear. Ed didn't really have a choice. "I felt that
he was desperately lonely and needed the socializing," he said later.
"But everything I was told was that it was a bad thing. So that was
where I stood."

And once Ed stood, he stood firm. After the cut on Luna's head, Ed's memos show a man intent on stopping the contact: "Talk around the community of Gold River is that people are getting so close they can touch Bruno," Ed wrote. "In fact I am aware of two or three people who have rubbed his nose. I am prepared to charge people [with] touching and/or with disturbing whales or some such thing. Is there expert witness testimony to support such a charge?"

There was no immediate answer, at least in writing. But the change had happened. People who connected with Luna in Mooyah Bay were about to feel the lash of the law, delivered through the severe face of Ed Thorburn.

But was Ed really convinced that solitude was the right thing for Luna? The next time he recorded a visit to Luna was on the nineteenth of April. On that day, when Luna begged for attention, Ed did not take his boat and speed away. The following Monday, he reported in another of his memos that he had spent an hour and a half with Luna that day.

What did Ed and Luna do in all that time? There is no record if Ed spent any of that hour and a half thinking through how to reconcile Luna's apparent loneliness with the door Ed was now going to try to close against him. If Ed did contemplate that, he did not come up with any solutions, at least none that he had made public.

When Ed wrote his memo, he expressed no ache or confusion. All he put down about that ninety minutes on the water with Luna was, "He is still too friendly."

CHAPTER THIRTEEN

June 2002

The rains were gone. Summer was almost here. It was a bright day at the beginning of June on Nootka Sound. The sun baked the mountains and the heat rose, building wind.

Sometimes the wind sweeps up Nootka Sound all at once, like an army on running horses. You can be zipping along in your boat on water that's almost still, riding across the dark green reflections of the trees and mountains that climb almost vertically out of the water, and then off to the west there's a darkening line, a front of much deeper blue, where the wind breaks the water into chop.

Then, as you advance, the wind cascades over you like a line of surf. The waves jump up under the boat with a thump and clatter. Suddenly, there's spray all over the place and the whole climate seems to have changed.

That afternoon, *Yabba-Dabba-Doo* bashed through the wind and waves westward from the Gold River docks into Mooyah Bay. It stopped, swung sideways to the wind, and drifted. Paul and Judy Laviolette were waiting for their friend Luna to show up. Four hundred meters? They hadn't even seen him. He might have been a mile away. They just stopped.

Poof! With a blast of mist, Luna was there, a round blue-black back, a splash of water, a smell of fresh fish on his breath. He swung his tail down in the water and poked up his head, resting his chin on the side of the boat, apparently in expectation.

Judy Laviolette leaned over, her curly blond hair only half-tamed by a baseball cap on backward. Without apprehension or hesitation, she put both hands on the sides of Luna's face and gently rubbed his skin. Luna bobbed in the moving water, then blew his breath slowly out—not the way he normally did, in a sudden poof, but very gradually, with the flap of his blowhole pressed almost tightly closed, just letting out enough air to make a loud, long raspberry.

"Excuse yourself!" Judy said, laughing. Luna sank down into the water, came back up, and blew a cloud of thick, fishy mist in Judy's face. *Poof!*

"How do you like that breath of fresh air?" asked Paul Laviolette from behind the little video camera that was recording all this.

Luna dived, then came up alongside the boat, and Judy rubbed his back from his blowhole to his dorsal. Luna swung down into the water again and brought his face right up to hers and let her rub one hand all around his nose.

"What are we going to do with you?" Judy said very quietly, just to the whale. "We've got to find your family."

This sort of thing was happening on Mooyah Bay a lot now. But it had taken a long time for Luna to get this comfortable around people.

"The first time he really came up and asked to be petted was in June," Catherine Forbes told us. "It was just before the summer got started. It seems to have happened almost overnight. From not being touched, and all of a sudden, somebody obviously touched him and was gentle, and all of a sudden, he was coming up to the boat and rolling over, and Oh, pet me!"

Ed Thorburn did not live in Gold River, and his office and the dock where he kept his boat, *Rugged Point*, at that time were in another town, Tahsis. But he had heard about the whale-watching posters that Paul had put up in the Ridge, so he got on the phone.

He told Paul that he shouldn't be taking people out to see the little whale. Paul wasn't convinced.

"I thought, Oh, yeah, right," Paul told us later.

Paul left his signs up at the Ridge. Ed called him again.

"I said, 'If you choose to do this,'" Ed told us, "'then we will make it very difficult for you to get anybody into Mooyah Bay.' I said, 'It is just not the right thing to do, because we're acclimatizing the whale.'"

Paul had given a TV crew some shots he had taken of Judy playing with Luna. When the clip was shown on a local broadcast, Ed recognized who it was. But he didn't tell Paul that he knew.

"I told him, 'We are investigating anything dealing with disturbing that whale,'" Ed told us. "'And if I find out who that person is, I'm going to charge her.'"

"And I thought, Screw you!" Paul told us. "This is new to everybody! Who's gonna make the rules here? You're not!"

Paul didn't take down the signs at the Ridge. People kept calling him up for charters to see Luna, and Paul would still take them out.

So Ed went out to catch him.

It was another one of those great summer days—cool mornings, hot days, wind in the canyons. A young couple from Seattle had seen the signs at the Ridge and called Paul Laviolette because they wanted to see Luna. "Sure. When do you want to go?" he said.

They got out to Mooyah Bay before the wind was fully blowing, and Luna came right over, popping up beside the boat for a rub on the nose.

Paul was just standing there, smiling at the couple enjoying Luna, when a big rubber tube quietly appeared right next to his boat, as chilling as a shark moving in over your shoulder. It was the edge of Ed's boat. Uh-oh.

"I saw you touching the whale," Ed said to the couple. They stood up, looking worried. Luna ducked under the boat and came up with his chin on the side of Ed's boat, seeming expectant. Ed ignored him.

Later, Paul recalled the moment. "They're saying we broke the wildlife act and saying we have to see your ID and you're going to be charged. All this, and I said, 'I never saw anyone touch the whale.' But maybe they had cameras."

The couple from Seattle looked petrified. He saw that they weren't exactly reaching fast for their IDs. Suddenly, he got worried. They had different last names. Maybe they were, well, on some kind of getaway weekend out here where nobody knew them. "And here they're going to be charged and maybe the cat's out of the bag."

Ed was writing everything down. Meanwhile, Luna rubbed his chin on *Rugged Point's* rubber tube, which squeaked, then went over to *Yabba-Dabba-Doo* and stuck his head up on the side of that boat and made a little raspberry noise. The humans weren't watching.

Paul wasn't happy. He'd taken these people out in a charter, and maybe he hadn't exactly explained that there was a chance that what they were doing was somehow against the law, though if you read the "Be Whale Wise" brochure, it didn't seem to be. "Here I was, trying to do a good deed," he told us, "and it all caves in."

So he said to Ed, just hoping it might help, "Let me see your badge."

Well, that was a moment. Everything paused, except for Luna, who gave a blast and a splash offstage. Ed looked around.

"I must have left it on my bedside table," Ed said.

The two Fisheries officers stopped taking notes.

"I can't charge you without my badge," Ed said. He started *Rugged Point's* motors and took off in a plume of wake.

Paul was skeptical about whether Ed had really been about to charge them with a crime. Maybe that was just an excuse. Maybe they had just been bluffing to scare him, and a badge number would have given Paul a way to complain.

He left Luna behind and took the couple back to Gold River. They seemed okay with that. But Paul wasn't.

Things were changing on Nootka Sound. For a while, this little community had not been in direct conflict with the scientists and the Fisheries officers in trying to figure out how to take care of this little whale. But now they were starting to become open adversaries, stalking around one another, feinting in one another's faces, with the beautiful little creature blowing rainbows in between them, just wanting to be a friend.

Paul kept going out on the water and playing with Luna. He had kids, dogs, paying guests, and grandchildren out there. His youngest granddaughter called herself "the Queen of the Whale Touchers."

"You always wish that you could communicate with wild animals like that," Paul said. "And when a wild animal actually comes and makes contact with you, it's an amazing thing."

Then one of the few charters he took to see Luna included two young women from Friday Harbor, Washington. They were, in fact, from the Center for Whale Research, the place where Astrid van Ginneken worked with Ken Balcomb. The two women wanted to see what was going on with Luna and take a report back to the center. But they didn't tell the Department of Fisheries and Oceans that they were there.

"Those girls from Friday Harbor were incognito," Paul said later. "They didn't want anyone to know where they were from."

It was another dazzling day. When Paul stopped and waited for the magic to begin, there was another boat there, too, with a family and a golden retriever. The big floppy dog wandered around on the boat as if he were the skipper checking to make sure everything was going okay and that the guests were happy. The dog looked mildly puzzled in its good-natured way.

The dog had a right to be puzzled. The people were mostly hanging over the side, sticking their arms and hands in a killer whale's mouth.

Over the previous few weeks, this had become the next great thing on Mooyah Bay: scratching Luna's tongue. No one knew how that had started, but probably someone who had seen trainers scratch orcas' tongues in theme parks gave it a try when Luna opened his mouth, and Luna caught on right away.

The women on Paul's boat seemed unsure of what to do. Should they be stern about this? Austere observers?

At one point, when it appeared that the people in the other boat were trying to break free from Luna's insistent attention, one of the women on Paul's boat called out, giving advice on what to do to encourage Luna to leave.

"His species is very tactile," she said. "Being alone, he wants anyone to rub him. So just don't touch him."

But then, a little later, Paul saw one of the women crying. She was sitting on one of *Yabba-Dabba-Doo*'s rails, her face running with tears.

Paul was stunned. What was this?

"I asked her why she was crying. She said, 'Whales aren't supposed to act like this. It's a baby and it misses its mother and family.'"

She cried and cried. Paul didn't know what to say.

A little later in the month, Paul went up to the Ridge and took down his whale-watching signs.

CHAPTER FOURTEEN

July 2002

G reat tides of salmon and steelhead trout come up Nootka Sound
to spawn in the rivers, and sportfishers from Canada and the
United States come out in hundreds of boats in pursuit. The summer
of 2002, they had a whale in their lives, too. He was a novelty, but he
was also a pest. One fisherman said it was like having the plague. If
people saw that you had Luna, they wouldn't come close because
they'd be afraid they might catch him from you.

On another one of those dazzling summer days on the sound, with
boats everywhere and Luna going from one to another, Marc Pakenham, who would later speak at that conference Suzanne and I attended, came up from where he lived in Victoria, at the south end of
the island, and went out with Ed Thorburn in his boat, *Rugged Point.*
Marc had previously worked with the Department of Fisheries and
Oceans as a community adviser. Now there was talk of setting up an
organization to try to control all the interaction between people and
Luna on Nootka Sound, and he was a candidate to run it.

"I like getting things done," Marc told us. "Working for government and getting things done seems to be a contradiction, but we
had a search-and-rescue background and responding in a hurry was
something that we had learned to do."

Marc brought his solemn, mournful face to Mooyah Bay and
watched Luna and the boats that he pursued and encountered. Then

Luna came over to *Rugged Point,* pushed on it, rolled over on his side, and looked Marc in the eye.

"I felt profoundly moved," he said later, "and profoundly sad for this whale. Because it was obvious to me that this whale was seeking some stimulus, some contact, something. And to stand on a boat, and look that whale in the eye, was profoundly moving. I thought, This whale is going to die with a boat strike, or someone is going to kill this whale. And that was where I got my motivation to kind of get it together and try to protect the whale."

Marc got things done. Ten days later, a truck towed another big inflatable boat up the long highway to Gold River. The Marine Mammal Monitoring Program, otherwise known as M3, which Marc ran, was coming to Nootka Sound, and change was coming with it.

Meanwhile, on the other side of Vancouver Island, the other little lost orca, Springer, the one seen near Seattle who was first thought to be Luna, was lost no more. After a remarkable effort undertaken by a number of organizations, including the Vancouver Aquarium, Springer was caught, penned up for about a month, then carried north in a fast catamaran, where she was put in another pen. When Northern Residents approached the pen and she responded with calls, she was released.

After a few uncertain days—nerve-racking to people like Lance Barrett-Lennard, who was deeply involved in the move—she connected with relatives, and the reunion was complete. There were estimates later that, including the in-kind donations of time and equipment, the whole effort had cost about a million dollars.

At almost exactly the same time, another change was happening, but it was not widely reported except among the members of the First Nations of the west coast of Vancouver Island, who are lumped together by their common ancestry and language as the Nuu-chah-nulth people.

It happened in late July, about a year after Luna was first seen in

Nootka Sound. One evening in the village of Tsaxana, near Gold River, Mike Maquinna, the chief of the Mowachaht/Muchalaht First Nations, hosted a dinner during a meeting of the Nuu-chah-nulth Tribal Council. The guests ate fish and turkey served by the Maquinna family. There was singing, and Jerry Jack made a speech in the Nuu-chah-nulth language. At the end of the dinner, Mike Maquinna also spoke.

"There has been a *kakawin* in our traditional territories for quite some time now," he said. "It is our family's wish that it be named after our dear father and from now on its name will be Tsu'xiit."

So the little whale, who had been called L-98, Luna, Patch, and Bruno, had yet another name. Each name had been given by a group or an individual, and each had its own idea about what, exactly, this extraordinary relationship between people and a whale was all about. Yet everyone who met Luna felt the same kind of thing, that strange combination of awe, fear, longing, and empathy. Everyone just attached different meanings to it, as if afraid to admit that they didn't understand it.

CHAPTER FIFTEEN

August 2002

Erin Hobbs and Michelle Kehler, two young women from Victoria, came to Gold River with the M3 stewardship program to keep people and Luna apart. So the first thing they did was go to Mooyah Bay to meet Luna.

Ed Thorburn and his enforcement partner took them out in his Zodiac. It was a flat, calm morning. *Rugged Point* was a fast boat, so they got to Mooyah Bay in about half an hour.

Ed stopped the boat somewhere between Anderson Point and Atrevida Point, and they just sat in the still water and waited.

"There was almost this pride about them," Michelle recalled later. "Just wait. Just wait and see."

It didn't take long. It was so calm that Michelle could see the white patches coming at them underwater. Luna did what Michelle later called "his *Jaws* thing." He came to the surface and swam with his body just below the surface, pushing a smooth dome of water above his head, his dorsal carving along in the water like the movie image of the shark.

"I think I was caught off guard by how close he was," Michelle said. "Right by the boat, here was a whale. Other whales are always going to keep their distance, but here he was coming right over, saying, Hey, how are you doing?"

On the boat, though, the two women didn't articulate their awe.

The mood became very professional, as if everyone, officers and recruits, were all conscious that they were there to prevent exactly this, not to revel in it. So while the little whale bobbed around the boat, spyhopping to look at the new people in it, giving it an occasional push, diving underneath, and making funny, disgusting noises, the officers gave solemn advice and the two women listened seriously.

"It was very practical," Michelle said. "It was very much just passing on knowledge." The main knowledge was in how to disengage from Luna. "It was just about making sure he was away from the prop," she explained, before a boat accelerated and got away from him. And it was also about why telling people to leave was a little tricky.

"We came up with a list," Ed told us later. "Well, how are we going to phrase this? So: No petting of the whale. No touching. No swimming with. No feeding. So we had that criteria. But it is a free country. So if the boat goes through, and they decide to stop in Mooyah Bay, and they are not in proximity of Luna, then what right do I have to tell them to get out of there? But what you don't have is the freedom to go and disturb a whale."

That was the extent of the training. They went to work.

The women were invited to stay at the Mooyah Bay logging camp. They moved into a house with the camp's caretaker. Michelle felt excited and optimistic. "We are going to work with a whale! We're going to have an impact! This is going to be incredible!"

It was the peak of the sportfishing season, and the water was crowded with mostly twenty-foot-long to twenty-six-foot-long outboard or inboard-outboard sportfishing boats with two to five people on board, who often stopped near Mooyah Bay to take a look at the whale.

"Okay, there's someone stopped in the zone! Let's go."

The boat would be there, with Luna cozied up to the side like someone leaning up against a bar for a drink and a conversation. He'd be getting a nose rub, maybe making a raspberry or a squeak with his blowhole. And up would come the Zodiac, with two young blond women wearing jackets that, somewhat inaccurately, identified them as working directly for the Department of Fisheries and Oceans. The Zodiac would sidle up next to the fishing boat, like a uniformed cop awkwardly trying to sidle up to the bar, too, and the charming women would smile.

Their statement was pleasant but official: "Hi, we're just coming to let you know about this whale. This is Luna, who is L-98, and he belongs to L Pod. They are very social, and so he's seeking social interaction at this point, and although we understand it is very exciting and you would like to interact with him, it is in his best interests if you don't."

It was all very cheerful and friendly. The people would be compliant and grateful.

"Oh, really, that's so interesting," they would say. "I hope he gets back with his family. Thank you so much for telling us. We'll go now."

In the evening, the two women would motor about four miles from Mooyah Bay to Critter Cove, the fishing resort owned and operated by Cameron and Catherine Forbes, and go to the restaurant for dinner. As soon as they walked in, they became stars.

"Somebody would come up to us," Michelle told us. "Because there we were, in the DFO jackets, obviously not from around there. Two young blond-haired girls, just happy to be there. So we would wind up talking to one person, but the entire restaurant would get quiet. It was like, What are they saying? What are they doing here? So it turned out to be a press conference every day."

All that innocence and goodwill didn't hold up too well. It turned out that some of the people were asking what the stewards' dining schedule was so they could go out and play with Luna while the two women were at supper.

"And then it was amazing the amount of boats that had engine troubles right in Mooyah Bay," Michelle said.

The two women got more stern. But something was happening that perhaps no one had expected, though Ed should have known it. Every time the women went to a boat that was engaged with Luna, they would have to distract Luna from that boat so it could zoom away. So then they'd have to connect with him themselves. They had to do exactly what they were trying to prevent. And that got absurdly complicated.

Once the stewards lured Luna away from a boat, Luna would be with them, and now they had to get away from him themselves. So there he'd be, and there they were.

"The other boat would take off, and we'd be stuck with him sometimes twenty minutes, and he would be turning us around in circles and that sort of thing."

So they were becoming part of his pattern of interactions. That was bad. And they were getting to know him. That was good. Or, wait a minute, which one was good?

"His behavior adapted to us," Michelle said later. "I watched it adapt on a daily basis. His relationship with me was different from his relationship with Erin. When he would come up to the boat, there was a lot of eye contact. It was very soft; it was very genuine. The energy was just different. Erin is very much more joking around, and he played out with her. He would spit at her. She would get water in the face. She would get all the gross stuff. She would get all the tail slaps, the pec slaps. The water pushed up against her.

"He never did that with me. And we are on the same boat. You know, like we are five feet apart. And he is exhibiting this behavior with her, and then he came over to my side, and was totally different with me. And I am convinced that he was reading the energy. We are different individuals. We have different energies. He played to that, for sure. And it was amazing to see."

So it became a relationship. But because the women were acutely afraid of dangers to Luna, every morning they were anxious. "Because he's a mammal," Michelle explained, "and if he does get a deep-enough prop cut, he is going to bleed out. So, yeah, concern every day. We were happy to see him every morning. Happy and not happy, if you know what I mean. Oh, I don't want to see you because I wish you were with your pod, but at the same time, Ahhh, you're still okay. That's great!"

Michelle thought about it a moment, then added another thought. "Yeah," she said. "Mixed emotions, all the time with him. All the time."

One cloudy day later in August, the two women were out on the water early. They were much more used to the place now. They had seen eagles patrolling the air and deer clambering around on the rocks right down by the shoreline. Once, they had even watched as a big black bear came down to the rocky shore at low tide and ate a starfish.

But Luna, too, had been learning things.

"At first, he really liked us," Michelle told us. "Because he thought we were another friend to play with. But you could see he was getting more and more anxious. He would get somebody, we would come, and he would come over and push us away, just say Get out of here! I have not had anyone to play with all day, you know. Get out of here! It was very much like we were taking his toys away from him."

On this cloudy day, one of the boats that stopped for Luna was a twenty-foot inboard-outboard with a canvas top. It had two men on it. As the women pulled up, Luna moved to the opposite side of the boat from them, and the larger of the two men, who wore a purple tank top with ATHLETICS DEPT on the front and carried a tiny camera, leaned over, with his back to the two women, taking photos of Luna as he bobbed up and down in the choppy water.

"This is the one that was on the news," Athletics Dept said over his shoulder. "The one that belongs in Washington?"

"This guy belongs with his pod, which is in the waters off the San Juan Islands," Michelle said, talking to Athletic Dept's back as he turned to shoot his photos. "He's of utmost importance to us."

Over the previous days, Michelle and Erin had changed their approach to boaters. "We weren't smiling so much. We'd have the video camera out. We were making sure that we used words like *prosecute,* words like *fines,* you know, 'one hundred thousand dollars,' et cetera. Because we needed to be more assertive."

So now, trying to get the attention of someone who was engaged with Luna but not with her, Michelle was assertive.

"This area that you're in right now is a no-stopping zone because of him."

That got Athletics Dept's attention. He turned, an expanse of belly preceding his face and his tiny camera.

"A no-stopping zone now?" He laughed. Michelle maintained the bluff. But her voice was a little uncertain.

"Yeah, we're in a no-stopping zone."

Athletics Dept left Luna and went over to the side of the boat near Michelle. She sat on the edge of the Zodiac and held on to the gunwale of the other boat as the two vessels bobbed together. Athletics Dept's friend, a bearded man in a T-shirt, stayed back in the shadows of the boat's canvas top.

"Are you going to do something with this one?" Athletics Dept said. "To relocate him?"

"Yeah," Michelle said, "we're going to cut down on the human interaction. Relocation? We're not sure. We're hoping his pod's going to come back up here. But it's not going to if people—"

"But it's been here for six months."

"—if people keep interacting. LUNA!"

Michelle shouted his name, all the exasperation of the conversation in her voice. She had to remain polite with these people, but with her old friend Luna, she could speak as she chose.

"Look at that goof!" Athletics Dept said.

Luna had come up between the two boats and was muscling them apart with his body. Michelle's arm was getting stretched between the two boats, and she had to lean far out from the Zodiac to maintain her hold on the other boat.

"So you're here just to keep an eye on this guy?" Athletics Dept said. "Nice job."

Luna pushed up between the boats again and gave a very wet exhale right in Michelle's face. Athletics Dept laughed again.

"Don't spit, you!" Michelle said to Luna. She was trying not to laugh.

Luna went down and came straight up beneath her and pushed his nose into her left armpit.

She refused to be distracted. She looked up at Athletics Dept. His tiny camera had almost vanished in his large hand.

"So, touching him—" she began valiantly, but she was interrupted by Luna, who wiggled his big nose in her armpit. "Luna, don't do that," she said parenthetically, then tried again. "Touching him is a hundred thousand bucks a pop right now."

Luna went back down in the water between the boats as if in mock amazement at the amount. Michelle looked up and gave Athletics Dept the best Ed Thorburnesque severe look she could manage.

"What?" Athletics Dept sounded incredulous. Michelle went on.

"And we're out here to make that happen."

Luna came up again and stuck his nose gently into her armpit. "Luna," she said, looking down at him. "You're not helping."

"Why doesn't somebody grab the thing and move it?" Athletics Dept said

"Because . . ." But she couldn't answer, because Luna came up again, moving the boats apart. "Don't push, Luna," she said.

But Luna planted his nose deep in her armpit and gave a mighty shove, half-lifting her off her seat on the Zodiac's tubes.

Michelle gave up gracefully and broke into laughter with Erin and the two men on the boat.

Luna, victorious, put his pec fin up against Athletics Dept's boat and shoved it away from Michelle.

"Unreal," Athletics Dept said.

This was what they did with Luna several times each day. They would argue over him with people, then they'd entice him away, and then they'd crank up the engine and leave him alone. There was a nickname for that. They called it "ditching him."

They didn't like ditching Luna. Neither did Ed, who did the same thing when he was on the water.

"I don't think he understood where we were coming from," Ed told us. "He would one day have all these people around and everything was great, and the next day, nothing! Because we would show up. That must have been pretty hard on Luna."

It was hard on the two women, too.

"It would just rip your heart out," Michelle said. "I don't want to be making your life miserable! But I know this is not good for you. Or at least I think it is not. Because, what do we know? I don't know that we know that."

CHAPTER SIXTEEN

April 2004

What was it that we did not know?

Suzanne and I were far from Nootka Sound. We hadn't seen Luna in person yet, but we had to go home for a while before heading back to Gold River to cover the end of the story. There were more interviews to do and there was Luna's capture and move to cover. And surely, before our work was finished, we would have to have at least one sight of the actual whale.

We lived on a small island just off the coast of the southern tip of Vancouver Island, on the edge of the waters where L Pod would soon show up at its summer home and meet again with its prodigal son. We were building our house there, and it wasn't finished. While it was being built, we lived in a three-room log house and went to the construction site to work on the house with the carpenters every day.

The pieces of Luna's story were coming more into focus. But a question lingered. Why did the Department of Fisheries and Oceans spend so much time, money, and effort trying to keep Luna and people apart? Why was that so important?

"Well, I think where the concern about fully engaging Luna socially came from," said Lance Barrett-Lennard, "was wound up in the notion that if he's going to be a wild whale again and find others of his social group and reintegrate, this relationship with humans isn't going to work."

A major cetacean scientist lived near us, just across the border, near Seattle. Her name was Toni Frohoff. She began her career as a biologist working with John Lilly, that legendary leader in the study of dolphin intelligence. Lilly's books made a huge stir with the proposition that dolphins were as intelligent as humans. The books led to the TV show *Flipper*, which described a dolphin as smart and helpful as Lassie, and to several films.

When Toni was in her early twenties, she helped care for two captive dolphins whom Lilly owned and was studying. She then went on to earn a Ph.D. and carve out a serious scientific career. Now she was studying the occasional dolphins and beluga whales in various parts of the world who got separated from their pods and interacted with humans, the same way Luna was interacting with people along Nootka Sound. She had written about these animals, which scientists called "solitary sociables," for the International Whaling Commission.

"You see in the media a lot of the really beautiful aspects of the human-dolphin interaction," she told us. "And in so many ways, that is the light side of it. But there is a very, very dark side. The dark side is the human side. In the short term, the interactions are satisfying to these animals. Our research has shown, and documentation has shown, that in the long run, the more interactions dolphins and whales have with people, the more likely they are to suffer injury and death."

Toni had seen the first news about the discovery of Luna in 2001. She was happy that he was alive but sad about where he was.

"When I heard that Luna was alone," she said, "it was kind of like my heart clunked. I was concerned because of the fact that Luna was so young, and Luna was alone. I mean, you are talking about orcas, who have such a unique bonded family unit, it is incredible. And their culture and their intelligence and all those things, and beyond that, are stupendous. But then to think of an orca alone, you know: Oh boy, this is going to be a tough one."

So the reasons to keep people and Luna apart made sense. We had accepted that effort simply as part of the story, as you would accept the principle that you shouldn't let a baby eat dirt. But as we learned more about orcas, there was a nagging question. What if preventing Luna from trying to get the companionship that he seemed to want so badly was not like keeping a baby from putting dirt in his mouth? What if it was more like refusing to give a baby affection?

"You're dealing with an animal for which, under normal circumstances, interaction is more important than food," said Lance Barrett-Lennard. "I would say killer whales have social needs as strong as those of humans. Perhaps more so. In fact, I think I'd stick my neck out and say that they really are stronger than humans'. I'm sure you could damage a whale psychologically by depriving it of contact. It presumably reflects their evolved survival strategy: that being part of a group is the way they prosper, and being single is not an option."

Toni Frohoff described the desperation she had seen in belugas and dolphins who were on their own but who saw humans as potential social contacts.

"We have even seen solitary bottlenose dolphins and beluga whales we studied practically strand themselves in their attempts to follow people," she said. "If I was going to anthropomorphize, it indicates to me a desperate situation, a sense of desperation, when you have an individual, an intelligent social individual, so desperate for companionship that he or she would risk life for that interaction."

Wasn't that need just like hunger? What if orcas have to have connections every day in order to be healthy? Many people believe solitary confinement of humans is torture, and studies show it creates both mental and physical health problems. What if solitude was as harmful—or perhaps even more so—to orcas?

What if Graeme had seen the peanut head in Luna? What if Luna had been emaciated and weak? No one would have said that food could wait until some indefinite time when he got back with his pod.

So if Luna needed companionship as much as food, why were his social needs less important than helping him find food? Why did some people think, in fact, that they were not needs at all; that they were optional for him? Everything he did—the risks he took, the determination he showed, the creative tricks he invented—showed how important connection was to him.

Why did people—even those like Lance Barrett-Lennard, who knew orcas' needs and who told us that he thought humans could have real social relationships with orcas—think social contact was something Luna could and should be denied, for days, weeks, months, years?

Yet this was what the Department of Fisheries and Oceans had decided to do. Many other people, including us, accepted that philosophy, because it was a thoroughly established idea and because it was framed as a compelling moral choice. If you really cared about Luna, this philosophy ran, you would selflessly smother your own longing to offer him company. If you gave him attention, it was self-indulgent. If you let your empathy take over your heart and your actions, you were weak. You should set it aside.

CHAPTER SEVENTEEN

September 2002

"This is not a watchable whale!"

The voice of authority came across the water. It was the voice of Louise Murgatroyd, from a different team of stewards, in the big black inflatable M3 boat. It was directed at another inflatable, a Zodiac model called an Explorer, loaded with five men and women with cameras. At the time, the Explorer was being shoved sidewise by a little whale whom everybody was watching.

It was late August. These stewards were both more experienced and more assertive. Erin and Michelle had been here for two ten-day shifts, and this was the second shift for Meghan Hanrahan and Louise, two other young women who had been hired to work as Luna stewards.

Meghan, who wrote some of the log entries for the second team, found herself swept into another world on Nootka Sound, in which numbers of days on the job didn't seem to be an accurate way to measure time.

"Time works differently here," she wrote. "It is set by the temperature and the tides, the size and number of fish being caught, the daily dinner special at Critter Cove, and the movements of the magical mammal that we are watching."

Now on a day of hard sunlight, high, thin clouds, and a choppy bay, the two women were trying to get the loaded Zodiac Explorer away from Luna, but it was a tense encounter.

The announcement to the boat was much more practiced and swift now. While Louise talked, Luna lay on his side, with his nose at the bow of the Explorer, as if pointedly ignoring the stewards. Some of the passengers seemed to be doing that, too.

"Folks, this is not a watchable whale," Louise said. "I need you to exit this area. Watching this whale or interacting with this whale can be subject to a hundred-thousand-dollar fine under the fisheries act."

Luna blew a big breath of mist right next to the boat and kept himself in front of the cameras. "We're hoping to reunite him with his pod," Louise said. "So I need you to exit this area as fast as you can."

"We just came out here," said one of the women in the boat, exasperated. "We were just cruising around." The other passengers were taking photos as fast as they could, since it was apparent their encounter with Luna would soon end.

"Well, there are notices all over the place. We're very serious about it."

"We haven't seen one notice."

The guy who was standing at the helm of the Explorer spoke up. "We won't touch her or anything."

Luna slipped under the inflatable and came up on the other side, still ignoring the stewards' Zodiac. He rolled on his side and looked up at the boat's passengers again.

"And I can't have you interacting," Louise said. "Sir?" Nothing happened for a moment. "Sir. I need you to exit immediately."

"Okay," the guy said, reaching for his throttle.

But then Luna got involved in the process. He was not exactly the stewards' ally. Now Louise had to change her authoritative tone.

"Hang on a second," she said. "We're just going to have to get him to come out from under your boat."

Later, Louise wrote in the log: "I think Luna is over us (though I suspect that none of us shall ever get over Luna)."

That afternoon, the two women talked with the Mowachaht/ Muchalaht First Nations elder Ray Williams, who lived with his wife at Yuquot. He came by in his boat and sat chatting about Luna to the two women for half an hour while they filmed him. They asked him about the story they had heard that Luna was there to mourn a dead chief, and Ray vaguely agreed but changed the subject, so they talked mostly about how people should be leaving Luna alone.

"We'd like to spend some more time with him," Louise wrote in the log that night. "It's what you need after a stressful morning of asserting authority about which you are uncertain."

Then Luna changed things again on Nootka Sound.

CHAPTER EIGHTEEN

September 2002

That summer, Ed had told *Uchuck III*'s crew that they couldn't stop the old ship in Mooyah Bay so Luna could come up alongside and entertain their passengers. And the stewards' message was taking hold. Fewer boats were stopping to see Luna in Mooyah Bay. Is that what made Luna change his tactics? Maybe. But for whatever reason, in September, Luna started hopping the wakes of the *Uchuck III* and other boats and riding them like a commuting hitchhiker all the way to the Gold River docks, where there were lots of boats and lots of people.

When Luna changed his approach, so did the weather. A chill wind blew down from the North Pacific and swept over Nootka Sound, and rain came—heavy, dark rain. The distant ridges disappeared in clouds and sheets of downpour. The afternoon winds did not build up the way they had when the days were hot. Instead, sporadic swirling gusts, shaped by the mountains as they carved into the higher body of the storm, swept down across the inlets and bays around Mooyah Bay and kicked up dark patches of choppy water, streaked with lines of spume.

Fortunately, the last shift of stewards to arrive, Kari Koski and Kristy Zeidner, volunteers from the United States, were well prepared.

"Kari and I both grew up in southeast Alaska," Kristy wrote in the log, "and the scenery, including the torrential downpour, pleasantly reminded us of home."

But pleasantries between people on the water were mostly over. During the course of the summer, tensions between the stewards and almost everyone else had grown and hardened. More people were inquiring about the stewards' eating schedule at Critter Cove, and more and more often when the women went up to a boat to tell its passengers and crew to leave, the stewards found that it was someone they had lectured before.

"It is continually frustrating," Louise wrote in her log before the shift change, "to learn that people still behave inappropriately even though they are well aware of what they are being asked to do, and which is only intended for the good of such a marvelous creature as Luna."

Sides were growing distinct. Because the stewards so passionately wanted to believe that they were helping Luna by trying to keep people away, they saw people who disobeyed them as selfish spectators interacting with Luna in spite of knowing it was bad for him. But others thought that since it seemed clear that Luna was desperate to get this interaction, why was it wrong to give him some company?

Kari Koski and Kristy Zeidner were not only used to this kind of weather and landscape, they were also experienced at interactions between stewards and whale watchers. Kari was in charge of the Soundwatch Boater Education Program on the U.S. side of the border, which existed to make sure people in boats kept their distance from wild whales. So she was no stranger to boaters' efforts to bend the rules. Kristy was an experienced intern with the same program, They were ready to deal with the people.

And they thought they were prepared for Luna, even when he showed up at the dock.

"We wanted to stay really far away from him," Kari Koski told us later, "and kind of monitor things, see what was happening with the boats."

It didn't exactly work out that way.

On their first full day, Kari and Kristy came into the Gold River docks on the big black Zodiac and were immediately hailed on the VHF radio from the *Uchuck III* by Fred Mather, who was bringing the ship into the dock.

"What are you doing? Where are you?" Fred said on the radio, sounding irritated, apparently thinking he was talking to women who had been here for weeks. "We need you to do your thing."

Kari and Kristy didn't know, exactly, what their thing was. Apparently, Fred expected them to get Luna away from the old freighter so that he could dock without worrying about him.

"When we approached, we saw Luna surfacing alongside them with a gaggle of passengers hanging over the side smiling and laughing," Kristy wrote in their log. "Luna was playing in the warm water that was discharging from their generator. He had his mouth open and was letting the water run over his head, mouth, and tongue."

The Zodiac approached the old freighter. The two women could hear Donna Schneider explaining on *Uchuck III*'s loudspeaker to the passengers that this was the stewardship boat and that the people in it were whale experts who knew all about orcas and how to handle Luna.

Hmm.

The two women in their Department of Fisheries and Oceans jackets and their big black Zodiac came up next to *Uchuck III,* looking about as competent and official as you could get. They had no idea what to do.

"We did our best at being professionals," Kristy wrote later in the log. "I splashed my hands in the water and snapped my fingers."

Luna, possibly, could tell that these women were not the same ones who made a habit of ditching him. So he didn't avoid their boat the way he had avoided the others. He came zipping right over and gave them a blast with his breath.

"And everyone's looking at us," Kari told us, "expecting us to do something miraculous."

"My heart was racing as he began rubbing against the side of the boat," Kristy wrote. "We knew we were way out of our league here and were clearly not the ones in charge of the situation. We were stuck in the middle of the Luna trap."

Kari, who operated boats daily down south, wasn't even comfortable running this one yet. But she managed to look like a seafarer as she slipped the boat into gear and motored slowly away from *Uchuck III,* leading Luna away. Both women turned away from *Uchuck III,* trying not to look as uncertain as they felt.

"Luna came up from below and began bumping our boat, hard," Kristy wrote, "and it was more than a little unnerving. Never had we experienced a wild killer whale behaving in such a manner."

So they just shut down the motors, let the Zodiac coast to a stop, and sat in the middle of the boat like a couple of prisoners, which in a way they were. They tried hard not to look at Luna, though for some of the time they couldn't help it.

"He pushed our boat around in circles," Kristy wrote, "spyhopping, blowing bubbles, tapping the side of the boat with his head, squeaking like a balloon releasing its air, tail slapping and making intent eye contact."

"It was pretty obvious from the get-go that this was not going to be a sustainable means of trying to prevent interactions," Kari told us, "because all we were doing was interacting with him in order to prevent more interaction."

Uchuck III was now tied up at the dock. The black Zodiac sat out on the water in the rain, with Luna hopping and splashing all around. For anyone watching from the dock, this would not have looked like a boat full of orca experts.

"We sat for a few minutes not quite knowing what to do," Kristy wrote in her log, "never having been in a situation quite like this before. It was comforting to us to talk to him. So we told him that he should really go home and that his mother was still alive and well and his family was missing him."

They tried to motor slowly away. He stuck right with them. Discouraged, they then moved the boat over next to a floating log, hoping that he might get interested in the log and let them get away. "He wasn't persuaded."

Finally, the two women tried a different tactic. They ignored what Luna was doing and just gradually accelerated until he could no longer keep up. They ditched him. It worked. They were on their way.

"We took off for Critter Cove," Kristy wrote that night, "feeling elated and saddened by the interactions. The whole situation here is so confusing."

What Kari saw was so much more intense than anything she had seen in her years watching people watch the Southern Residents that she wondered if the Department was fully aware of what it was trying to hold by the tail.

"DFO thought that if they just played it down, then no one would come and it would not be a big deal," she told us later. "But it's not that hard to get up to Gold River, and you can have an earth-shattering, mind-blowing animal-human connection experience, which people are really craving. I didn't feel that DFO at that time was being very realistic about how much people were going to be into this whale."

Kari had a dream one night that Luna was shot and killed because he was a nuisance. It put the women on edge. Then they had a scare and a lesson.

One day, two women showed up, paddling a canoe from the mouth of Gold River past the docks and out into the water. Suddenly, out of nowhere, Luna was beside them, blowing a tower of mist, looking as powerful as a truck. Kari and Kristy watched with concern. This could be deadly. But Luna, who showed so much power with bigger boats, just played gently with the canoe, pushing its nose around slowly.

Luna was strong enough to push a forty-foot log, to turn a thirty-foot sailboat in a circle, and to throw his two-thousand-pound body completely into the air, but when he came up to a canoe, he just pushed it gently to change the direction the women were going. Did he know he would risk their lives if he unbalanced them? Did he know the cold water, so comfortable to him, would be the death of them? Whatever he knew was unknowable to humans, but for whatever reason, he played gently with the canoe. He wasn't just seeking connection with people; he was somehow respecting the two-way care that maintaining this connection required.

But the women in the canoe were understandably terrified. So Kari and Kristy went out to meet them, and, as usual, enticed Luna away. That was enough whale canoeing for the paddlers. They turned and headed back to the dock. But Kari and Kristy couldn't ditch Luna, or he'd just go back to the slow-moving canoe. So they had to spend about forty minutes keeping him occupied before the canoe reached the shore.

"Everything I had done at that point, for the previous ten years, had been trying to keep people from having those types of encounters with whales," Kari told us. "And here's one that's seeking it out, and is it right to deny him all of that? But at the same time, it's putting people in a dangerous position and it's putting him in a dangerous position. I was really internally conflicted."

CHAPTER NINETEEN

February 2003

On February 7, there was fog up and down the coasts on both sides of Vancouver Island. There was a breath of frost at Gold River itself but not down at the docks. There was no rain, a relief in February.

Sandy Bohn, a young grandmother who worked at the office of a company that was starting to build fish farms in Nootka Sound, had her parents visiting from the town of Cumberland, on the east side of Vancouver Island. Sandy was a friendly, gregarious woman who smiled often.

"I am mesmerized by whales," she told us. "They're just absolutely amazing animals."

When Sandy was a child, her family went camping on the northeast coast of Vancouver Island, where the land breaks into a maze of islands, and narrow waterways wander, as if they have lost their way, deep into glacier-covered ranges where people seldom go. The strip of water that divides the big island from all the smaller ones is called Johnstone Strait. It's the summer home of the 250 orcas known as the Northern Residents.

Like Luna's community, the officially endangered Southern Residents, the Northerns eat only fish, but their calls are different, and they engage in what many scientists think is a unique cultural activity— they often rub themselves on the stones in the shallows at some of the gravel beaches on the islands. Sandy remembered being in a boat with her father, watching the orcas come up almost right beside her. "Their faces are just beautiful," she said. "There's so much intelligence there."

Back in January she had met Luna for the first time, down at the docks. She was vaguely aware of the signs that said you shouldn't interact with Luna, but she didn't think the government was taking the rules seriously.

"For a year and a half, people were doing it all the time and nothing was happening," she said. "So I just assumed that they were allowing it now."

She was wrong.

All through the fall and winter, memos had been flying—Ed Thorburn to Marilyn Joyce; Marilyn Joyce to John Ford and Graeme Ellis; Marilyn Joyce back to Ed. Marilyn's letters always referred to L-98, but not Ed's. He had abandoned the nickname Bruno, but he went back and forth between calling the whale L-98 and referring to him as Luna. Marilyn's letters were always in the tone of a wildlife manager; Ed's letters were about a friend.

"Relocating whales is not something we do as part of our business plan," Marilyn wrote.

"Luna does not seem happy," Ed wrote. "I see a sadness in his eyes."

Ed's e-mails grew more and more exasperated—but about people, not Luna. "Over the Christmas holidays Luna was a main attraction in Gold River at the government wharf. There were carloads from Campbell River and south but mostly locals with holiday guests. Reports were that for the most part petting is a major concern. . . . Luna is still growing and is in a good frame of mind these days. . . . I am sure he has those bad hair days but not that anybody has noticed."

There were certainly bad hair days for humans at the dock. Lorraine, the wife of the owner and chief pilot of Air Nootka, the charter seaplane service at Gold River, was particularly forceful in trying to get people to stop petting Luna at the dock.

"It's horrible," she told a newspaper. "I have gone down there and told them, 'You are only hurting the whale. His blood will be on your hands!' "

Sandy Bohn first stepped innocently into this growing tension on a January day when there were neither crowds nor observers at the dock. She found Luna next to the floats on the lower dock and spent about an hour with him. She just sat there on the planks, having one of those earth-shattering, mind-blowing animal-human connection experiences Kari Koski described.

"I swear," Sandy's husband, Roy, said to us, "if she could have got her arms around that thing, she would have."

Luna was as friendly as a retriever puppy. He lay in the water, looking at her. He put his chin up on the edge of the dock. She rubbed his nose, and then even his gums. And then—

"I was petting his nose and stuff and I thought, hmm, I wonder, so I put my hand there and he just opens his mouth. First of all, I just put my hand in a little bit, because you don't know what he's going to do, right? Then I just started my hand going farther down and scratching his tongue. His tongue is very raspy. But he is so gentle."

That time became one of the most special hours of her life. So, a few weeks later, on February 7, after her parents came to visit, she took them down to the docks to introduce them to the amazing being she had been talking about.

The morning fog had lifted, and you could see the mountains. Right opposite the Gold River docks, on the other side of the inlet, there is a wall of forested hillside, and off to the east a canyon opens and shows the mountains beyond. Now the distant mountains were fresh with new snow that went right up into the gray of the clouds and made the mountains look vast and mysterious. Down in the quiet water around the wooden docks, the little whale was just as mysterious, but a little less vast. He was sort of puttering around, checking out the people.

There were five people there when Sandy and her parents walked down the ramp to the floating docks. Some were standing and a couple of them knelt on the wood to be closer. None of them was petting Luna. It was just a little communal friendliness.

But up in an office above the dock, someone made a phone call.

Gold River has a small shopping center dominated by a grocery store. Constable Jacquie Olsen of the Royal Canadian Mounted Police (RCMP) was parked there. The call from the dock was relayed to her by radio.

She jumped in her vehicle. Someone who was watching as she zoomed off got worried. It looked as if there must have been a car accident somewhere.

But it wasn't an accident. It was entirely intentional. On the dock, Sandy and Luna were having another friendly connection.

"Well, he was just kind of floating there," she said. "And when I knelt down, he just sort of rolled over and had a look at me. And then I just put my hand out to pet his nose."

Luna's nose was in the water, and the water was, as usual, bitterly cold. But the little warm-blooded whale was not. Sandy was intent, kneeling there, her hand in the water, giving him an affectionate rub. She did not hear the police car roar into the parking lot above. She did not hear the door slam as Constable Olsen jumped out and strode toward the dock.

"His nose was kind of in the water," Sandy said, "and then he backed off so he could come straight up so he could open his mouth. But he didn't get a chance to open his mouth because of Constable Olsen."

The constable's voice arrived ahead of her. It was angry.

"You there, kneeling by the whale, get up off that dock right now!"

"So I stood up and was like, Oh, you must be talking to me."

Sandy was charged in court with "disturbing a whale." And she became part of history. The story was run all over the world, in newspapers that needed a funny anecdote or something fresh to put in "strangest news of the day" columns. GRANDMOTHER CHARGED WITH PETTING WHALE.

The law said you could be fined $100,000. Sandy wondered if their lawyer could get it down to $50,000. What would this do to her and Roy? Would they lose their home?

It didn't seem fair, to her, to be hit with this enormous fine after all those other people had been allowed to touch Luna. But more than that, she thought, it didn't seem fair to Luna to try to force him apart from the friends he had made over all this time in Nootka Sound.

"My thing was if that is the law, then when he first came into that bay, and first started approaching boats, there should have been something done about it then. Don't wait two years, till he thinks people in boats are his pod."

A date was set for a trial. A lawyer said she should just plead guilty.

"They want to make an example of you," he told her. "They'll fight you all the way."

It sure sounded that way. Jacquie Olsen was quoted in a newspaper. "I won't stop at one," she said. "I hope the message we're sending is clear."

There wasn't much Sandy could do except go to work every morning and wait for the interminable days and weeks to pass. Eventually, she would find out how much of her life would be ruined because she had been friendly to a whale.

CHAPTER TWENTY

February 2003

Far from Nootka Sound, on the west edge of San Juan Island, Ken Balcomb, at the Center for Whale Research, was thinking about the little lost whale, trying to figure out how to help him.

For over thirty years, the Southern Resident orcas had been Ken's whole preoccupation. But unlike John Ford and Graeme Ellis up at the Canadian Department of Fisheries and Oceans, his coauthors on the *Killer Whales* book, he had no direct management responsibility, so he didn't think like a manager. When Ken talked to us about the whales, he always seemed to be wondering on a very personal level what life was like for them, about the huge mystery of their seaborne lives that passed by right outside his door. He had carefully explored the surface clues that the whales had given him over the years, but the reality of their whole lives, which seemed so complex from just those clues, remained elusive and tantalizing.

"What they are giving you back is little bits of what is happening, not their full attention," he told us. "All of their attention is between themselves, doing what they do. But when you have one that occasionally comes out of the pod and checks you out and does this one-on-one thing, it's almost a universal feeling from the people side that there's a lot going on there. This is not just an animal looking with a blind stare and moving on. There's something in there that's beyond your puppy dog connections with creatures."

So that winter, Ken made a serious offer to the Department of Fisheries and Oceans. A major donor had just given a seventy-two-foot yacht worth $1.5 million to the Center for Whale Research to use for its work.

"And the owner felt that this would be a great way to start the use of the boat," Ken told us later. " 'Go up and save that little whale. I'll pay for that. Here's upward of a hundred grand to just go do it. Go up there and be there.' So I was trying to get DFO and John and Graeme up there."

Ken wrote a formal e-mail to John Ford on February 13, outlining the proposal to take the yacht and a support boat to Nootka Sound to monitor Luna and encourage him to follow, and to see if the two boats could eventually lead him back to L Pod. He offered two berths during the whole operation to the Department, and funds to pay for the whole thing.

"It was just this cosmic coincidence," Ken said. "Everything was coming into place. We were given a boat, a magnificent vessel, and money to do it. We just want to be there, we want to do a monitoring program, and I thought we'd do the Pied Piper approach: You know, play sounds of interest to him and sounds of his family. We'd allow him to travel with us for a while and we'd keep expanding the envelope of his range of travel, until by the summer we're down here. I was ready. I was going."

For the Department of Fisheries and Oceans, the proposal was a free chance to engage Luna and try to lead him back to his pod, while offering humans an opportunity to learn things that could not be learned any other way.

But Ken's proposal directly conflicted with the idea that had always been central to the management of Luna by the Department of Fisheries and Oceans, and which was the reason Sandy Bohn had been charged: that Luna would lose his wildness and his capacity to connect with his pod if he continued having interactions with people.

John Ford often talked about trying to keep Luna a wild whale, as if Luna's wildness depended upon his choice of friends, not his state of freedom. It was as if people could, in a sense, brainwash the wildness out of him.

To Ken, orcas had more capacity than that for choice and self-determination. So maybe Luna was choosing to seek human companions for the moment only because orcas weren't available. If Luna found his pod again, Ken thought, he would recognize his family, and the human relationships would fall away.

And to Ken, there was also a chance that if people worked more closely with Luna while helping him return to the pod, the little whale might offer people a window into the relationships between humans and other beings that the structures of our lives have closed.

"All my education and training and professional qualification as a scientist involve things you can measure, touch, somehow quantify," he said. "But there are these incomprehensibles almost, these things out there, where something's going on. Something's going on with the interconnectedness of a lot of life on this planet that we haven't really kept ourselves very well in touch with. But it's so big, I don't know how to approach it even, except by taking an opportunity to meet an animal in a natural environment, in its wild state. And then you have an opportunity for much more intimate contact and observation than ever before.

"If we are going to get at that big immeasurable thing out there, as to what are the connections in the species, I think Luna had it. He was just as curious about us as we were about him."

Ken sent off the letter with his proposal to the Department and waited for a reply.

CHAPTER TWENTY-ONE

March 2003

On a clear day in March, almost a month after Sandy Bohn had been charged with disturbing a whale, a group of men drove down to the docks with Fisheries officer Garth Sinclair and went out in *Rugged Point*. They carried a needle on a pole, attached to a syringe. They wanted some of Luna's blood.

The men were from the Vancouver Aquarium, the organization that had owned the first captive orca.

Thirty-nine years before, in 1964, the Vancouver Aquarium had commissioned an artist to kill an orca so the body could be used to create a sculpture for an aquarium facility. The artist and a crew set up a Norwegian harpoon gun on one of the islands near where Suzanne and I live. After weeks of waiting, orcas went past close enough, and they fired the gun.

The orca they hit was about fifteen feet long, about the same size as Luna was in 2003, so he was not much more than a baby. When he was hit, the harpoon went deep into his back, and he started to sink, apparently in shock. But two other orcas came up beside him and, between them, held him at the surface. The little orca began to breathe again and revived. But he was still attached, like a fish on a hook, to the harpoon and its rope.

The artist then took a rifle out in a boat and shot the whale several times. The orca still did not die. He thrashed around for a while, whistling so loudly that people over a hundred yards away could hear. Then, when it was clear that he could not get free from the harpoon, he grew calmer in the water.

The aquarium director flew out from Vancouver in a floatplane to look at the whale. The director decided to try to keep the whale alive. The artist and his crew started towing the little orca by the harpoon. The little whale apparently realized it couldn't get away and figured out how to reduce the pain. He turned and swam with the boat. The harpoon was still stuck in his back, but that made the rope slack and stopped the pulling.

This curious procession of the boat and its harpooned prey, moving along together as if they had had a fight but made up and were now tethered friends, went all the way to Vancouver, about twenty-five nautical miles to the north, across the choppy waters of Georgia Strait. Because the whale seemed so compliant on his leash, the crew named him "Hound Dog."

The trip took sixteen hours. The crew put the little orca first in a submerged dry dock, then in a mesh pen. Aquarium staff members gave him another name, because they mistakenly thought he was a female. They called him "Moby Doll."

Scientists and the public came to see Moby Doll and were impressed, but the whale refused to eat for fifty-five days. When he finally started eating, he consumed about two hundred pounds of fish a day. But he never fully recovered, and after eighty-seven days of captivity, he died.

Moby Doll was the first orca ever held in captivity, and his amazing qualities, seen by humans for only those last hard months of his life, started both a new appreciation for orcas and a new industry of catching and displaying the whales for entertainment.

For many humans, this was an exciting time of getting to know an extraordinary species. For Luna's ancestors and community, the sequence of events that started with the harpoon in Moby Doll's back was tragic. An unexpected source of terror, this capture for live display, had entered their lives. This culminated in brutal captures of orcas from the Southern Resident community in the late 1960s and 1970s. The captures of Southern Residents ended after a public outcry, but not the captivity. The business of catching orcas just moved to other places, such as Iceland, the Soviet Union, and Japan.

After Moby Doll, the Vancouver Aquarium got more orcas and kept at least one in captivity until 2001, when its last orca, an Icelandic whale nicknamed "Bjossa," was shipped away to SeaWorld in San Diego, where she soon died.

All the men who came to get blood from Luna for medical testing in the spring of 2003 had worked with captive orcas. And they all continued to work with captive cetaceans every day, since the aquarium still kept beluga whales and dolphins. The men were Clint Wright, an aquarium vice president; David Huff, the aquarium's veterinarian; Lance Barrett-Lennard, the orca scientist familiar to Luna from the "Happy Birthday" camera incident; and Brian Sheehan, a trainer with years of experience.

The report from that day tiptoed formally around the interaction that the four men in the boat gave Luna over the two days they spent trying to collect blood.

"The whale came to the boat immediately," the group's report read. "He adopted an upright approach with mouth open bobbing up and down less than a meter from the boat. . . . He solicited interaction by gently pushing on various team members who were sitting on the pontoons at the edge of the boat. . . . But we did not respond and thereby [did not] encourage such behaviour."

Officially, the men did not interact with Luna. When he nudged for interaction, they kept their hands to themselves. But when they started trying to get the blood, things changed. It was as if, in their minds, motivation made action different. If you were just trying to ease a lost whale's loneliness, it was not right to be friendly, but if you were trying to get blood out of him, friendly gestures were okay.

"By offering our hands, tapping the water, and occasional light touches to the head," they managed to get Luna beside the boat, with his dorsal fin sticking up next to them.

When the dorsal was close, David Huff whipped out his three-meter-long "extension set," a tube with a syringe to suck on one end and a hypodermic needle on the other. With Luna beside the boat, being distracted by the others up by his nose, Huff stuck the needle in Luna's dorsal fin. Ow.

"L-98 moved steadily away, pulling the needle out within a few seconds." A small drip of red came out of the black dorsal and slipped down toward the water, but the needle had not had enough time in the blood vessel it pierced to actually draw any useful amount of blood.

Luna then came back, "soliciting attention as before." But now a game of tag developed. Luna continued to come to the boat for attention, but at an angle that kept his dorsal fin just out of the team's reach. He didn't seem to want to give up the contact, but he figured out how to avoid the sting.

Over the four hours with Luna that day, the men managed to poke him with the needle twice from the boat and once at the dock. The needle never held in a blood vessel, so they did not get any blood.

The next day, they spent another four hours connecting with Luna beside the boat, this time trying different tactics, like moving the boat through the water while stroking Luna's side with a paddle to keep him close to the rubber tubes of the inflatable. Most of the time, Luna still managed to keep his dorsal out of reach, but they stung him three more times. Again, they got no blood.

But they got something else.

"I've studied whales in the wild for a couple of decades," Lance Barrett-Lennard told us later, "but I've never had that kind of contact in the wild as I did with Luna, so I think it was probably just as much of an emotional and surprising experience for me as it would be for anyone. So having Luna come along and approach me and be so interested right from square one, yeah, it set me back on my heels a bit."

Soon after the four men went back to Vancouver, Ed Thorburn wrote Marilyn Joyce another e-mail. In it, he requested that the blood-collection crew write up an "impact statement on human interaction."

This report was not to be a description of their visit and the eight hours they had interacted with Luna in their quest for his blood, nor anything about what this strange contact with a free whale who came to them by his own choice had meant to their experience. The report was to be used in the case against Sandy Bohn, to persuade the judge that the few minutes Sandy spent that day, offering her hands to Luna and giving him light touches, were so wrong that they were worth punishment that could ruin her life.

One dark and rainy day at the dock, a Gold River resident who occasionally worked as a stewardship volunteer, trying to reduce interaction, asked two of the fifty-four visitors she recorded that day where they had come from and why. The husband and wife said they had come from the town of Chilliwack, British Columbia, a drive of over seven hours if you timed the ferry just right, nine if the first ferry was full. They had driven all that way just to see Luna.

And how had they found out about him? They had seen the news story about the charges against Sandy Bohn. They thought that they absolutely had to see this friendly whale.

CHAPTER TWENTY-TWO

April 2003

The conference-call meeting of the scientific committee appointed by Marilyn Joyce was planned for late April, so on April 17, Ken Balcomb sent another proposal to John Ford. It was a request to work with Luna for a week with a smaller boat to find ways to train Luna to follow a boat with devices that would not be associated with other boats and lead him out of Nootka Sound, but not necessarily to try a full-out effort to return him to his pod.

"The stimuli currently envisioned . . . are: acoustic playbacks . . . moderate pressure water hose streaming, and brushing with inanimate objects (this is tree branches, etc). . . . The goal of the research/ training is to lead L-98 to expand his envelope of travel to include the ocean entrance to Nootka Sound, and perhaps farther south along the BC coast for opportunities to chance encounter with other Southern Resident killer whales." Once again, the costs would be covered by the Center for Whale Research.

Ken was a member of the scientific panel. The committee was initially made up of sixteen Canadian and U.S. orca scientists and managers. It included John Ford, Graeme Ellis, Lance Barrett-Lennard, Marilyn Joyce, Clint Wright, and Paul Spong, who ran OrcaLab, which studied the Northern Residents from an island off the west coast of Vancouver Island. They met via conference call in secret.

After the meeting, a summary led to this: "The panel has

recommended that a minimal intervention strategy be attempted. They feel that L-98 could be trained to follow a vessel, with appropriate stimulation and reinforcement. In this way, L-98 could be led out of the remote inlet, thereby having an increased opportunity to connect with his population 'naturally.' "

The thinking was that if Luna was led all the way to the busy area near Victoria and the San Juan Islands, he would be surrounded by crowds of boats most of the time, so that if he didn't connect up with the pod, the interaction problem would be far worse than it was in Nootka Sound. But if he were led only a short distance, to the area of the mouth of the sound, and spent more time there, he would be exposed to the open ocean and might have a much better chance of making contact with family members if they passed by during the winter. Thus the idea of leading him out only to the mouth of the sound seemed to be a useful solution.

From the wording of the recommendation, it seemed clear that the panel had suggested something very much like what Ken had offered to do. In many ways, it looked as if the panel of most of the orca experts in North America had endorsed his project.

On May 15, Marilyn wrote her immediate boss in the Department, a man named John Davis. He was the regional director general for the Pacific area. She reported that the United States National Oceanic and Atmospheric Administration, parent organization of the National Marine Fisheries Service, "agrees with the panel's assessment and would be supportive of the proposed plan. They have offered support, [in] the way of staff input, advice, and assistance, if we require."

The process of consulting with the experts had run its course. A conservative recommendation had been made that at last took some action to try to resolve a situation that many of the people on Nootka Sound saw as a crisis. As Kari Koski had written at the end of the first year's difficult stewardship, trying to keep Luna and people apart simply didn't work. Everyone was looking forward to trying something different.

Dr. John Davis was an expert in the management of salmon. He had been involved in the past with the successful lamprey-reduction program in the Great Lakes, which led to salmon-run recovery. Davis often saw the resident orcas being followed by whale-watching boats, and he didn't like what he saw. He made his decision and wrote back.

The boats around the whales, he wrote, looked like "flies around the water buffalo." This apparently gave him such distaste for human interaction with whales that he overruled the science panel and shot the recommendation down.

"The boat training to me," he wrote, "is more likely to produce a negative outcome in terms of boat familiarity." The solution, he wrote, as if it was a fresh idea, would be to "leave things alone, post signs, issue notices, and inform the public about the necessity to stay away from the animal in Nootka Sound."

That same week, Sandy Bohn went to court.

"The fisheries guys and the RCMP made it seem like we were going to trial for murder," Sandy's husband, Roy, told us. "Four lawyers and all these books! But the judge was good. He knew she was just being made an example of."

She agreed to plead guilty. She was fined seventy-four dollars, plus costs, making it an even one hundred dollars. There would be no enormous fine. She and Roy would be okay.

After that, there were more articles in newspapers around the country and in various places throughout the world: "Woman Fined for Petting Whale." And more people read the articles and learned about Luna and decided they would go up to Gold River to try to see this amazing whale.

And how did Sandy feel? Did she regret what had happened?

"No," she said. "It was the best hundred dollars I ever spent."

CHAPTER TWENTY-THREE

July 2003

When Maria Chantelle Tucker arrived in Gold River, the summer afternoon wind was howling up the inlet. Boats thrashed around in the windblown chop at the dock. About fifty people milled around, looking at Luna. A volunteer met her at the top of the ramp down to the dock and handed her a clipboard.

"Good luck," said the volunteer. "You're going to need it."

Beside the dock, where a sloping wall of rocks led down to the water from the parking lot, a man was putting a kayak in the water. In the two-seat kayak was the man's young daughter, perhaps nine or ten years old. And Luna, whom Chantelle knew until that moment only from photographs, was rubbing against a skiff out by the dock, looking for someone to befriend.

"The first minute we got there it was mayhem," said Chantelle, who uses her middle name. "It was absolutely insane. I thought, Oh, my God! There are people everywhere!"

This was not exactly what had been in her dream back in February.

Chantelle Tucker takes action on her dreams. In February 2003, she had had a dream. "It was basically a dock, some boats, and a killer whale, stuck between the boats. And they were just floating there." It had seemed relatively peaceful.

But she knew about Luna, and the dream haunted her. So she found out about Marc Pakenham and called him. He signed her up, and in July she went to Gold River to work as part of the Luna Stewardship Project with another woman from Victoria, Rachael Griffin.

Rachael was a quiet woman with training in biology and a careful scientific personality. She came to Nootka Sound equipped with a hydrophone, a recorder, and headphones. A crew from the Department of Fisheries and Oceans had come up earlier and had played some L Pod calls to Luna, but Luna had been largely unresponsive, and the crew had gone away, wondering if he was mute or deaf. Rachael's approach was a little different. She didn't try to make him call; she just listened. And perhaps as a result, she was the first to record calls from Luna that characteristically resembled those made by others in his pod.

So the two women made a useful team—Chantelle was a dreamer, seeking emotional meaning on the edges of the mystical, and Rachael was equipped by training and nature as a scientist, trying to pry knowledge out of observation and detail.

Rachael had served an earlier shift with the Luna Stewardship Project, so she knew roughly what to expect. But when they arrived that day, both described the scene as mayhem.

All these years, Chantelle had been thinking about orcas, how beautiful they are, how smart, how magical, how special it would be to be close to one. And now she was here, right next to an orca who was trying to befriend humans, and she didn't even have time to look at him. What focused her attention were this man and child about to set out into Luna's sea in a very small boat. If they got in trouble with Luna because of their misjudgment in tempting his playfulness with too small a boat, Luna would be the one to pay.

She clambered down the rocks. The man had been having an argument with the volunteers who had been there. But somehow

Chantelle was more authoritative. She said something like "We can't have you going out there. It's not safe."

The kayaker gave up. He took the boat out of the water, put it on his car, and drove away.

But there was no relief. "It just went from one situation into another," Chantelle said. "Into another, into another, into another. When one situation ended, there was somebody else."

Before Chantelle went to Gold River, she said, Marc Pakenham had told her what to do.

"Marc just said go up there and ankle-bite if you have to." She didn't know what that meant, exactly, but she tried to live up to what it sounded like: that she should be aggressive.

The two women lived in a travel trailer a few yards back from the water's edge, beside the road leading up to Gold River. The trailer looked small enough to be towed by a motorcycle. No, by a bicycle. When Suzanne and I saw it later, it was hard to imagine one child being able to stretch out inside it. But two full-grown women had to live in there.

When Marc Pakenham first asked Rachael Griffin to work in Gold River as a Luna steward, several weeks before Chantelle got there, Rachael drove north from Victoria in her own car. She went straight through Gold River and down to the docks about half an hour ahead of Marc. When he didn't show up, she decided to drive back up the hill to town to get something to eat.

On the way up, she saw Marc's car coming down and stopped. Marc, seeing that she was driving away from the docks, made an assumption.

"You saw the trailer and you're leaving?" he asked her.

"No, no, no."

Rachael was tougher than that. So was Chantelle. They put up with it. What bothered all the stewardship women who used the trailer that year was not the cramped space, or the leaks when it rained, or the large variety of insects that seemed to have resident-manager status. What bothered them was the chaos around Luna.

"I feel like we're dropped inside of a fireball that was already burning and we were left to fend our way to safety," Chantelle wrote in one of her daily log reports. "We fear for Luna's future and freedom and want to see him grow up as we grow older and not in an aquarium. Anything is better than that because Luna is a survivor, a fighter, a clown; a compassionate, rambunctious, and very loving being."

CHAPTER TWENTY-FOUR

September 2003

Layers of cloud shrouded the hills along the edge of Muchalat Inlet. Showers swept past, making the water dark with the disturbance of rain, but shafts of sunlight wandered among the columns of drizzle like searchlights looking for Luna. Patches of shining water blossomed and faded under the shifting gaze.

It was September 7. Chantelle and Rachael recorded their arrival from the trailer to the dock, a commute of about thirty seconds, at 9:00 A.M., and described the unsettled weather as "Sunny and rainy."

For a while, the day was almost peaceful. The numbers of visitors to the dock had dropped off as the summer waned, so Rachael had the chance to put her hydrophone in the water and listen quietly to Luna's clicks as he played with a boat fender.

Then one of the Air Nootka planes came in, a de Havilland Otter with a big, rumbling World War II–era engine, and tied up at the air-taxi dock. Luna went over to this new toy. He started pushing the spring-centered water rudders on the plane's floats with his nose.

The peaceful day had suddenly turned bad. Chantelle and Rachael watched, unable to do anything. The policy this year was not to engage Luna intentionally to lead him away from events like this.

"It's a very bad situation," Chantelle said to a German couple standing nearby. "These guys have to fly in and out of here, and he's not making anything any easier."

"I've never heard of such a behavior," said the German man.

Grant Howatt, the owner of Air Nootka, came out of his office. Angry, he yelled at Chantelle and Rachael. "Why don't you guys get your boat and lead him out of here instead of taking pictures?" he said. "He's just going to wreck that! That's worth a bundle of money."

But engagement wasn't part of their mandate. So they looked on helplessly.

Lorraine, Grant's wife, came out, too, and shouted, much louder, like a teacher trying to get a daydreaming student's attention: "Chantelle!"

Chantelle was baffled about what to do. It was Sunday, but she called Ed Thorburn on the phone. She had his home number in Campbell River.

And the mandate changed.

"He said, 'Do everything in your power to get that animal off the seaplane.' He said, 'If you have to touch him, do it. Because if he does not stop . . .' I don't know if I want to say it. But the word came up. He was going to have to face a decision."

The word, when used by Marilyn Joyce, was *euthanasia*. In the more straightforward words Ed used, if Luna didn't stop doing this kind of thing with the seaplanes, the Department might have to shoot him.

Chantelle and Rachael took their black Zodiac over to the seaplane and lured Luna away by splashing their own fender in the water. He followed, but when they tried to lead him far away, he scooted back to the docks. But at least he didn't return to the plane.

The sky darkened and it began to rain. Luna played peacefully with a fender on a boat.

Most of the people who had come to see Luna had left. But in the rain, another vehicle drove into the parking area. In it were Ed and Garth Sinclair. Ed had driven up from home, an hour and a half away.

"What was I supposed to do about this?" Chantelle recalled

asking. She and Rachael stood with the two Fisheries officers on the dock, doing crisis management on the fly, while Luna played with the fender below them.

"At that moment in time, I broke down," Chantelle told us. "I had tears. I said, 'I am leaving. I can't do this. I can't be here, and be part of this, and watch this animal die.' And we were the only ones to deal with it. I was really torn, and I did not know what to think or feel."

Ed must have realized right then that he had to do something to give these two hardworking but frustrated women some hope, or his team would collapse.

"Those two girls were working so hard," he told us later. "They would work fourteen or fifteen hours a day, seven days a week. Living in an eight-foot trailer! They were thinking of the whale before anything else, including their own comfort, their own safety. But it was not helping."

So he dropped a bombshell.

"This is confidential," he said quietly to just the two women. "He is going to be moved."

Silence. What?

Ed said that a decision had been made and that Luna was going to be moved back to his pod. He couldn't discuss it further and they had to keep it confidential. But he had new instructions for them.

"He basically said, 'We are changing everything,' " Chantelle said. " 'You are going to go down to the boat and spend a lot of time with him. You're going to talk with him; you are going to play with him.' He said, 'I want this whale to become familiar with this boat.' They said that they were going to make the announcement to move him, and for now, all we had to do was just to get to know him. And Luna would feel safe with us."

The two women got on the boat, still almost in shock.

"Luna is back at the gov't dock rubbing up boats," Rachael wrote in the log, "so I lure him over to the M3 with a buoy and drag it over his back repeatedly while I talk and whistle to him."

Luna followed the moving fender with his mouth and made little noises that sounded like a combination of a cry and a hum. He seemed at ease, but the stewards weren't. They were doing something they should have enjoyed doing, because they loved Luna, but they were torn. It was so much against what they had been told was good for him that it bewildered and worried them.

And what kind of example were they giving to the public? Now that the rain had stopped, people were again gathering on and above the dock, watching Luna. And what they were watching was the two stewards, who had just been telling them how bad it was to play with Luna, now playing with Luna.

"Many onlookers at this point," Rachael wrote in the log. "God only knows what they are thinking. DFO is on the scene to educate onlookers, and what are we doing?"

And what on earth had happened that had changed everything so fast, from John Davis's decision in the middle of May to this?

Back in May, John Davis's decision to put up signs was first supported by a raft of press releases explaining it and justifying it. The Department's complex press releases mentioned the scientific panel but played down its recommendations. This apparent lack of Department engagement with Luna's situation didn't suit people who cared about Luna. So along came the argument of fear.

The *Victoria Times Colonist* published an essay by Paul Spong of OrcaLab titled "Is Luna Headed for Disaster?"

"In my view," Paul wrote, "a plan must be put together as a matter of urgency which would give Luna a chance he deserves to find his way home."

Marc Pakenham started voicing the melancholy that seemed always present in his face.

"Luna is either going to be injured or killed by a boat," he told a reporter, "or someone will recommend he be taken into captivity for his aggressive behavior."

A new urgency filled the air. Reports from Nootka Sound grew more scary. Four people spent the night being pushed around in their boat and couldn't get to the dock. Luna had broken a sailboat's rudder.

Then the owner of Canada's only marine park that held orcas, Marineland of Niagara Falls, wrote a solicitous message to the Department, requesting a meeting with the Fisheries minister and expressing great concern for Luna's welfare. "Continuing this lifestyle could well lead to Luna's demise and I would hate to see that happen."

Marilyn Joyce wrote a message back, saying that Marineland didn't need to go through the minister; it could just make contact directly with her. She then asked another Department official in Ottawa for guidance on how to legally handle Luna's transfer to an aquarium either in Canada or the United States.

Meanwhile, thousands were signing a petition demanding that Luna be reunited with his pod. And a Campbell River woman named Gail Laurie, working with an Internet expert from the Canadian prairies named Ryan Lejbak, started a Web site called Reunite Luna, which gathered advocates by the thousands.

"We have a river running through Saskatoon that's about as wide as a street," Ryan told us, "so we don't have any whales there. I am the self-appointed Saskatchewan expert on orcas right now."

The response to the Web site surprised and delighted him.

"The Reunite Luna Web site brought people together from all over the world; from England, Japan, Africa, every continent, people put effort into reuniting Luna. That was the moon shot for these people. It was them sending rockets to the moon."

In mid-July, the Earth Island Institute and several other conservation groups sent a fax to the Department: "It is our belief that DFO's refusal to come to the aid of this whale is causing needless suffering caused by social isolation. . . . Direct reintroduction of Luna to his pod is the most promising path to his survival."

"There was a tremendous amount of political pressure coming from all kinds of NGOs, conservation groups, whale enthusiasts," Marilyn told us. " 'Move this whale! Take him home to his mother! It is not fair! It is not fair!' People would write to me and say, 'I just want to spit on you!' "

In late July, Jacquie Olsen, the same RCMP constable who had charged Sandy Bohn with her notorious crime, wrote a personal note to Marilyn Joyce, also urging action. "There's been talk heard from some of the locals, and [on] more than a few occasions, [that] the whale is a nuisance and that he should just be shot. . . . You need to know that L-98 is polarizing this community."

Then, at the end of July, John Davis stepped in again. Although virtually all the major concerns being expressed by the onslaught of letters and phone calls to the Department were about Luna's loneliness and threats to him, Davis focused the fear differently. He described the main concern as Luna's danger to humans.

"As you can see . . . the whale is getting more and more active and there are concerns about safety of people in the Gold River area. . . . I have asked our staff to prepare pros and cons on several options."

The options quickly became three, as announced by a PR person later.

"One is to leave the animal where it is, keeping an eye on it. The other is to move it to a facility like an aquarium. And the other one is to reunite it with its family."

Ken Balcomb later pointed out that the minimal-interaction recommendation, the one product of all those scientists working together, was not included in the options the Department chose to consider. Ken thought that idea was still the simplest solution. Luna was not, in fact, all that far from the waters his family often wandered, not in terms of how much sea an orca can cross in a day.

"The option of dedicated efforts to modify his behavior in situ has not been rigorously attempted," Ken wrote in an e-mail to some of the scientists. "Don't get me wrong, this has been much fun and stimulating, but Luna is still in the sound and his family is still just a left turn and 120 miles away much of the time. That is about 50 hours of what we call 'slow travel.'"

Ken couldn't resist taking a shot at the elaborate process that had resulted in the recommendation that had been rejected both then and now.

"If the current round of talking is as productive as the last one," he wrote, "maybe we can do this again next year."

Behind the scenes, the decision was established long before the choices were even floated in public. On July 31, an updated action plan was sent to John Davis to be signed. The action plan chose one of the three options. It recommended that Luna be captured and moved back to his pod, with the option that he be caught again and sent into permanent captivity should the pod not take him back.

Davis was supportive of this plan, perhaps because he somehow thought catching Luna, keeping him in a pen for a week, then carrying him around in a truck would not involve as much human interaction as leading him south in the sea. On August 12, he sent a fax to the assistant deputy minister for Fisheries in Ottawa. It contained an approval letter from the Pacific regional director of Fisheries Management, Don Radford. That letter had a slightly different rationale for the costly effort: "Also," Radford wrote at the end of his letter, "demonstrating some effort was made to reunite L-98 with its pod would make captivity a more publicly palatable option if that is the ultimate outcome."

The decision was signed off on by the Department on September 4.

Then, several days after that decision was made, the Department announced it would reconvene the scientific panel to help it make a decision. The Department put out a news release: "DFO has not made a decision at this time, but is prepared to consider reintroduction if the panel can present options to deal with possible risks."

At the same time, a man in the office of the Fisheries and Oceans minister in Ottawa sent a private message that solidified the decision that the Department had just announced in public that it had not made. "[The minister] is keen that you get on with moving the beast if the US agrees."

When Ed told Chantelle and Rachael that Luna was going to be moved, he was accurate in letting them know that the decision had been made. But he had to require that the two women keep it quiet, because the Department itself was saying something different to the public. So when the two women went back out that evening to carry out their new instructions—to get Luna familiar with the boat so it could be involved in Luna's capture—they could not tell the people who were watching the purpose of what they were doing.

In the evening, the clouds diminished and the sun came out. Late sunlight on trees reflected by the calming water made the surface of the inlet look green and golden. In their Zodiac, the two women were doing something they could not have imagined six months before, something that was in conflict with everything they had been told about what Luna needed.

As they waited, Luna came to the boat, splashing gently but seeming very large. They talked to him, but for all his size and the intelligence they understood all orcas had, they talked to him in baby talk.

"Good boy, Luna," Rachael said. "Good boy."

"You are pretty, aren't you?" Chantelle said. "Yes, you're a pretty whale. And you just stay away from Air Nootka, okay?"

"Yeah, good boy, Luna," Rachael said.

"Stay far away from the airplane," Chantelle said. "Airplane is bad."

Luna rolled over on his back and stuck his head under the boat, put his pectoral fin up against its edge, and pushed a little, splashing the water with his tail. Chantelle started to talk to him again in a baby-talk singsong voice: "You have to stay away from airplane rudders, you understand? You're grounded."

Chantelle suddenly found herself watching all this in her mind from a distance.

"We had gotten so used to him, but at that moment in time, I popped out, and I went, 'Wow, this is really weird. This is bizarre.' I remember thinking, I am never going to be able to forget this. This is so out there. It is beyond anything I've ever dreamed of. Like, how could this have ever happened? How did it happen that I am here, nursing a killer whale with a fender? And it is looking up at me? With direct eye contact?"

Luna pushed the boat with his head underneath it, then rolled over again on his side, and his eye came up out of the water. Chantelle looked down at him, and he looked up at her.

"You stay close to this boat, all right?" she said to him. "And your life will be okay."

CHAPTER TWENTY-FIVE

October 2003

In October, the rains came early to Vancouver Island, with the force and authority of a monsoon. Chantelle and Rachael had gone back to doggedly trying to keep Luna and people apart. The idea of training him to hang out with the boat had faded almost immediately. Ed Thorburn had thought at the time that a move was imminent, so he had wanted to prepare, but he'd been wrong. The Department had, instead, waited until October to publicly announce that it would entertain proposals to move Luna.

But it also announced that it wouldn't pay for the move. It was asking for volunteers. Organizations applied, but none had enough money to conduct a full capture and relocation, which was much more complicated and would cost much more money than Ken Balcomb's idea would have. But Ken's idea wasn't on the table.

Time passed, and what to do with Luna seemed stalemated. So internal memos started circulating about just grabbing him and sending him straight to an aquarium, with no stop to see if he'd connect with his pod.

"Should no groups come forward, and DFO is left 'holding the bag' so to speak," wrote Nancy Fowler, a Department communications specialist in Ottawa, "the communications roll-out pertaining to a live capture and captivity of the whale would need to be stick-handled delicately in a highly emotionally charged environment."

The Ottawa offices didn't seem particularly empathetic toward

Luna. After all, this agency regulated and authorized the mass killing of harp seal pups on Canada's east coast and the taking of beluga whales and narwhals and even endangered bowhead whales by
the Inuit in the Arctic. Now it was being asked to treat a single lone
orca child as if he mattered.

Way out there on the West Coast, there was Ed Thorburn, a severe
enforcement officer, sending tender notes to his many bosses about
Luna's moods and loneliness. And what did they think of that? Possibly not much. In the capital city, far from any sea, Nancy Fowler
signed an e-mail "cheers to a Luna-Free weekend."

On the coast, the rain hammered everyone with walls of falling
water. But Chantelle and Rachael, magnificent in their persistence
and love, kept climbing out of that little trailer to go down to the dock
every day. They, too, felt tender toward Luna and were fiercely protective of their young whale, who was so innocent and so unknowing
of all the words about him that flew back and forth among the humans.

The rain soaked the bed in the trailer and shorted out an outdoor
socket on the Air Nootka building that Chantelle and Rachael used
to run a heater in their cramped and damp quarters. They used a
blow-dryer on an extension cord to dry the outdoor socket, and it
worked again. In the chilly nights, Chantelle had a series of dreams
in which she saw Luna's body lying on the upper dock.

"This creates a sense of panic and confusion," Rachael wrote in
the daily log. "Chantelle is not 100% sure that Luna will be safe during his move."

Chantelle happened to be in the Air Nootka office when a news
story came on the TV, announcing that the Department had authorized
its people to kill Luna if he didn't successfully reunite with his pod.

"I am disgusted with the TV, the situation," Chantelle wrote, "and
leave the room." Chantelle's loyalty was not to a Department that
might kill Luna. "I will stand in front of him before that ever happens."

Marilyn Joyce and John Ford drove the long road to Gold River and met with Chief Mike Maquinna at the offices of the Mowachaht/ Muchalaht First Nations. Maquinna had been saying again that the band would oppose any move of Luna, and Ed had been writing insistent notes to Marilyn, saying that she should meet with him.

Ed's notes of the event said that Maquinna talked "of the spiritual and cultural connection to the whale, and about his late father." Marilyn Joyce, he wrote, "explains that the whale is a danger—to himself and to the public."

After the meeting, Marilyn and John went out on the water and found Luna in a bay opposite Gold River. He porpoised by the bow and splashed everyone on board.

When they came back, Marilyn and Chantelle talked, and Chantelle wrote in the log: "She asks us to get more hazard handouts photocopied to hand out to people attempting to [go] onto the water."

When Marilyn Joyce left the two women to their thankless, impossible, love-driven work, Chantelle gave her a handful of chocolate bars.

Would she have done that if she could have read a memo Marilyn sent to Ottawa about the same time? Marilyn had often said in interviews that she did not want to see Luna sent to a tank, but she sounded different in a draft memo for another Ottawa official: "Approaches other than capture and placement in a long-term captive facility will likely require significant and ongoing contributions of staff time and money. This will mean that work on other important initiatives, such as the Marine Mammal regulations, which would benefit the species as a whole, will be adversely affected."

And she didn't talk to Chantelle about something else she wrote in a draft for the same memo. It would have made all their work to stop interaction seem wasted: "It is felt that habituation to people and boats is extensive and there is little downside to proactively interacting with the whale." The note appears to have been deleted from later drafts. Perhaps it was too honest.

CHAPTER TWENTY-SIX

April 2004

The old log house in which Suzanne and I lived while we were building our home was about a mile and a half from the lot where the new building was. As we worked on the house, waiting to hear when the capture of Luna was scheduled and we should go back to Gold River, we kept working to make a bunch of lumber into a home.

Almost every day, we would walk or jog along an old path to go to work on the new house. The path led near a long cliff that dropped straight off to stones and a beach. Once, I started jogging down to the house site but forgot something and had to turn back when I had gotten part of the way there. Our two golden retrievers, Max and Maple, had gone with me and had ranged out into the forest, but when I came home, only Max followed. Maple had disappeared.

I called and called, and she didn't come back. What had happened? Had she fallen over the cliff? There would be no chance of survival there. Had she become entangled in the old fences that littered the island, where sheep farmers had once made paddocks? She would be hard to find. I came home and didn't see her anywhere, and suddenly everything in my heart was about this one animal, with whom I shared no language, no thoughts, but something else that seemed terribly important but was very hard to describe even when it went missing.

Many years before, when I was still in school, I read the book *Ring of Bright Water*, about a man who loved a river otter, which was killed, then loved another one. At the time, millions of people read the book, and it was credited with changing human attitudes toward otters, which before the book were seen as vermin.

When I read the book, I was captivated, like everyone else, with the idyllic stories the author, Gavin Maxwell, told of his life on the northwest coast of Scotland, near the island of Skye, and how he shared it with the otters. It gave me dreams of landscapes beyond my knowledge, and of friendships I wished to find among the other kinds of lives on the Earth.

In a way, there was an otter in the Luna story, as well. Graeme Ellis, who was so cynical about the relationships that people felt they had with Luna, had an otter in his own life. When he was a teenager, Graeme found an orphaned river otter cub and raised it. River otters are smart, playful, and energetic. The otter was semi-wild; he'd go in and out of Graeme's boat and grew up playing with humans instead of with other otters. Graeme named the otter Tarka. The name came from a novel about a river otter who had to fend for himself—and defend himself—in the wild and among humans and their dogs.

But then Tarka started playing with schoolkids, and conservation officers came around.

"He never hurt anyone," Graeme told us. "He never bit anyone. The conservation officers were obviously covering their butts, because you're not supposed to be interacting with wildlife. They were doing their job, but they said he had to go to an aquarium, or be taken off and dumped somewhere."

Graeme couldn't face sending Tarka to a tank, where his freedom would come down to a few cubic feet of display and a few gallons of soiled water. So he found a place to leave him where he could have both people and wildness. It was on an island called Lasqueti, a long wooded island in the middle of Georgia Strait, west of Vancouver. Lasqueti is a wild place, where people go to live outside the cozy embrace of conformity.

So Graeme took Tarka to Lasqueti and turned him loose in the care of a family that lived on the island. He told the family how to live with this little cherished critter with his quizzical look and his eager eyes.

"I spoke to them about what was appropriate," Graeme said. "He was not to go in a house. They are amazingly bright little animals, and the family just loved him. And I thought, This is great. He's got kids, the beach; he can get his own food where he can be safe."

While we talked to Graeme about this, on a warm spring afternoon on the lawn at his house on a small island about fifty miles from ours, the phone started ringing. He knew the call was about a gray whale that had become stranded earlier that day near Vancouver and was being hosed down by a fire department to keep it wet until the tide came up again. The people who were trying to save the gray were calling for advice or to tell Graeme the end of the story, and he knew he'd be on the phone for a while. So he didn't mince the punch line of his own Tarka story.

"So anyway," he said, reaching for the phone, "he got into the guy's chicken coop, and the guy shot him."

There is a six-line section of a long poem, "Lament for Lost Paradise," written by a British poet, Kathleen Raine, that I find haunting. In the 1980s, I'd often see those six lines in articles or essays about the environment. I first encountered the poem during a winter ship's journey from South America to Antarctica in August 1985. The journey was wonderful because it was real exploration—and it was terrible for the death in it.

The seal biologists on board were shooting seals. They were killing both crabeater seals, relatively small Antarctic seals, and the larger leopard seals who preyed on penguins and crabeaters. Many of the crabeaters were pregnant females. They were on ice floes and could not get away, and they seldom even tried when the big steel wall of the ship came crunching across the flat world they lived in. They didn't move, and suddenly something from above the wall reached out and stung them to death.

The point of the work was to dissect them; no one knew what they ate all winter, because no ship had done what the ship we were on did. The team killed eighty-five seals. Only twelve had food in their bellies.

The guy with the dissection knife was as cheerful as a butcher. I took a photo of him holding a seal's steaming heart high in the air, pouring blood straight from it into a beaker. *Smithsonian* magazine, which had sent me on that assignment, too, didn't publish the picture. But even now I don't have to find the slide to recall exactly how it looked.

But I also remember the guy with the rifle, who would sometimes weep when the blood he brought forth sprayed the ice.

It was on that ship that I read the six lines from Kathleen Raine's long poem:

Because I see these mountains they are brought low,
Because I drink these waters they are bitter,
Because I tread these black rocks they are barren,
Because I have found these islands they are lost;
Upon seal and seabird dreaming their innocent world
My shadow has fallen.

Many years after that Antarctic journey, I found out that Kathleen Raine was in love with Gavin Maxwell, who wrote *Ring of Bright Water.* She considered him the love of her life. The title of the book came from one of her poems.

They spent one night together, and the love she wanted was not consummated. He was gay. In her memoirs, she wrote that after that one night, she spent all the rest of the nights of her life alone.

There was worse to come. When she was at the home where he lived with the otters, she and Maxwell had some kind of fight, and she went outside and stood beside a rowan tree and cursed him: "Let Gavin suffer in this place, as I am suffering now."

I do not believe in the supernatural part of curses, but I can understand the effect those kinds of things may have on one's own mind and one's choices. Raine believed that she ruined Maxwell's life with that curse; and soon after, life for him indeed crashed and ebbed in that place. His first otter was killed; then a few years later the cottage beside the rowan tree burned to the ground, and his second, most-cherished otter died in the flames. Maxwell died soon after, and so did the rowan tree.

Taking the blame, Kathleen Raine later wrote, "Being what I am/ What could I do but wrong?"

Those words, too, might seem to fit what humans often do to animals. Maybe that is why Graeme Ellis, with the loss of Tarka as one of his foundation stories, could see no good in the people who were trying so clumsily to befriend the lonely orca of Nootka Sound. Being what we humans are, what else could we do but wrong?

But I don't think it's that simple. Kathleen Raine didn't acknowledge the hard tumult that Maxwell's life had always contained, before her and after her, which probably brought on the pain at its ending more inevitably than her words. She assumed more power than she actually had. With that curious human combination of arrogance and abject guilt, she assumed she could summon nature to her bidding and tell it to accomplish her curse.

Maybe we humans are too arrogant both in our claim to mastery of the Earth and in the completeness of our self-contempt when we look at our destructiveness. And regarding ourselves as evil is at worst an excuse, which allows us to evade the responsibility of choice. If we assume we are evil, then why bother trying to do anything good? Why bother to try to make things better for a lost and lonely whale?

That Antarctic journey I was on led us into tough territory on the way home.

Heading south, we were beaten up by a storm that hit over ninety knots and made the pack ice a weird heaving sea of white with no chop on it, as if the prairies of winter Kansas had come loose in the wind and were washing up against the Rockies. The ship made it south across the Antarctic Circle, which was symbolic but placid, then turned north toward home. But then we saw one final devastating thing. When we stopped at the United States base near the Antarctic Peninsula, we stumbled on something that made our own seal slaughter seem relatively humane.

A group of leopard seals, predators unique to the Antarctic, with muscled, flexible necks that can crack a penguin like a whip and can toss a crabeater seal clear out of the water, had chased about a hundred of the crabeaters up on a couple of acres of solid ice in a cove. The leopard seals were gradually tearing the living crabeaters to bits. When we were there, the leopard seals were in the water and the surviving crabeaters were up on the ice, but the crabeaters were terribly wounded, often with flippers gone and great gashes in their sides, and the ice was splotched all over with red.

I walked among the wounded with a couple of the seal scientists, including the guy who had wept. They had never seen anything like this. While we watched, half a dozen leopard seals patrolled the ice edge, back and forth, back and forth, and it was easy to feel the fear that rose around us like the vapor drifting up from the breathing and the blood. Leopard seals, too, cast a shadow.

That day on our island when I was worried about our dog Maple, there was a commotion outside. I went to the door, and there was Maple, panting, exhausted. Eventually, talking to people who had seen her, we figured out what she had done. She had run ahead of me on the trail, and, apparently thinking I had gone ahead of her while she was in the forest, she had raced the whole distance to the house site, looking for me. When she got there, I wasn't there. So she had raced back.

She came in and lay down near us and panted for an hour.

After that, whenever I went jogging on the island and she ran ahead, she would always look back and check to make sure I was still there.

Gavin Maxwell forgave the curse, or never believed in it. When he published his book, long after Kathleen Raine spoke the words that brought more suffering to her than to him, he chose the title for the story of his beloved otters from one of her poems. He put the poem, which was about love, at the book's beginning.

We all cast our own shadows and choose where they fall, and the lives of men and women and otters and dogs and whales are linked forever across the reaches of time. We distance ourselves from them with our hunger for flesh, or our carelessness, or our cruelty. But what of the forces that bind us together?

CHAPTER TWENTY-SEVEN

April 2004

On a gray afternoon on Nootka Sound, we pumped up our red inflatable on a gravel beach at a place called Tuta Marina, across Hanna Channel from Mooyah Bay.

The idea was to take the little Zodiac across a couple of miles of water from a gravel launching ramp to a point of land where, we'd been told, we might get a glimpse of Luna as he chased salmon in the bay. But this was the first time we'd ventured out into open water instead of hugging the shore. We wanted to be sure we didn't encounter Luna on the way. We didn't want to break the rules against making contact.

"If you go faster'n seven and a half knots," said Larry Andrews, owner of Tuta Marina, "he won't be able to catch you." Larry was a member of the Mowachaht/Muchalaht First Nations.

The little Zodiac had a fifteen-horsepower motor and went about eighteen knots flat out. That should take care of it easily, Larry told us. "If you go out to Anderson Point," Larry said, "and climb up on the rocks there, you'll probably see him eventually. He likes to hang out near there."

We left the docks at Tuta and dashed across the water. The Zodiac slapped little waves, and the fifteen-horsepower outboard howled. Seven knots was way behind me; I'd passed that speed in the first thirty yards. We danced on the skin of the sea, with a bare froth of a wake behind us and a mist of spray on each side. Our speed made me feel good and safe. Then I looked west and saw a small white plume a long way off.

"He's there!" I shouted to Suzanne. A sharp stir of uncertainty went through me. This whale was so famous that to see his solitary little tuft of white in the distance suddenly made something real that had seemed legendary. I was glad that we were going to have a chance to see him, but I was also glad that we were going fast enough to stay away from him. I didn't want to get in trouble. And I wasn't quite sure what it would be like in this very small boat if we met him up close.

So just to be completely safe about it, I changed course to port, to steer a good way around where he had blown that distant little tower of mist.

We were moving light and fast. Anderson Point grew closer, a dome of mossy rock and a few fir trees tufted up on top. We'd be there in about two minutes, I figured.

Then, right there to starboard, only fifty feet away, a black-and-white torpedo flashed into the air, going our way, and hit the sea in a burst of opening silver water and flying light.

Boom!

This was disturbing. How had this whale gone from being a distant white plume to something big and powerful and swift over such a long distance in such a short time?

I could not quite believe this. This whale, who allegedly couldn't go faster than seven and a half knots, did not look like a whale going at that speed right now. In that wild splash, it looked to my widening eyes as if he was going about fifty knots, right there in the open water.

This whale really wanted to meet us. This wasn't some fawn tiptoeing through the grass toward an apple in my hand, or a duck paddling shyly up for a piece of bread. This guy blew breath like a steam locomotive and made a splash like a truck hitting a flood. He was coming our way like the wrath—or the gift—of God.

I cranked the throttle of the outboard to make it go faster, but it was going full out. This was everything we could do to keep away. What was going to happen now?

We raced on toward Anderson Point. For a tiny boat, we were flying. But Luna caught us.

The entire world exploded in our faces. Suddenly, there was not just one vessel racing across the surface, but two in tight formation, flinging water everywhere. But the second boat was actually a broad blue-black back blowing a tower of spray right next to the starboard edge of our boat, and a curved dorsal fin carving the sea into a flying wake that leaped into our faces. The sound of a breath blasted out and blasted in. *Pfoosh! Hshooop!* Splash! Gone!

At eighteen knots, he had come up so precisely close to the boat that his skin had slid right along the skin of the starboard-side flotation tube. But he had just brushed against it. I could feel his touch in the motion of the boat, but I didn't have to correct for it.

Then it was over. The rocks of Anderson Point loomed ahead, and Suzanne had to shout at me because I was so wet and dazzled that I didn't see a reef that made the water green right in front of us. I yanked the boat around to starboard, cut the motor, and ran the bow up on the stony edge of the point. We clambered out, tied the bow line to a log, and rushed up the rocks to look.

Everything was still. Little waves lapped at the rocks. We couldn't see anything out there but shiny gray water and distant mountains. Was what had happened real?

Then, about twenty meters out from the stone, Luna came up and rolled slowly over on his side, showing white patches and his long white belly sideways in the water. He was looking up at us. He lay there and looked for a long moment, then rolled over and went back underwater. After a few seconds, he came up again, heading back out toward the wider water. A few minutes later, we saw a couple of salmon leap in desperation as he chased them just under the surface.

But in that moment in the boat, when we had been touched by

this swift, hot life from the sea, so driven toward us by his clear intention, it seemed to me that something had been shattered. Human beings and wild creatures do not connect. But he had connected.

There's a wall, built of fear and respect, that normally stands between humans and wild beings. Humans sometimes try to get through it, with our pets, our domestic animals, our bird-watching, even our bears. But this wall does not seem to break in spite of all the pressure of our intention.

But when a life out there on the other side of the wall, a life from true wildness, that state of being we can barely comprehend, comes back the other way, to us, it breaks more than just a wall or a membrane. It is like the breaking of the law of gravity, or the speed of light, one of those immutable, established pieces of one's understanding of the world that cannot be moved. It seems to require so much energy that it is theoretically impossible, except for the moment in which it happens.

That night, after we drove back to Gold River, my memory tried to make sense of this, because it felt more significant than I thought it should.

My mind thinks in pictures long before it gets around to words, so I am always trying to interpret things to myself that first appear in my head as colors or shapes or detailed images that look like the real words but are not geography lessons. So as I grappled with the visual shapes in my head that tried to frame a meaning that escaped me, the metaphors changed, like a butterfly turning to a lion in a dream.

In memory, it seemed to be more than just a wall that Luna had smashed or leaped over. It was as if he had brought us some kind of glass container that I thought had held one kind of thing but, when it was broken, turned out to hold something different. It was as if in one breath he had blown the molten sea into a hollow shape by the force of his determination, filled that globe with urgency, then exploded it in our faces. At first, it was just a globe full of air, but when it burst, it seemed to release a color that I didn't know existed.

He came up and blew the globe and then smashed it into fragments that were cold on the skin of our faces, and the color I couldn't describe flooded out into the world and into our eyes in a flash, and then in a flash disappeared.

But it didn't quite disappear. It was gone and I couldn't remember what it had looked like, but it changed the shade of everything.

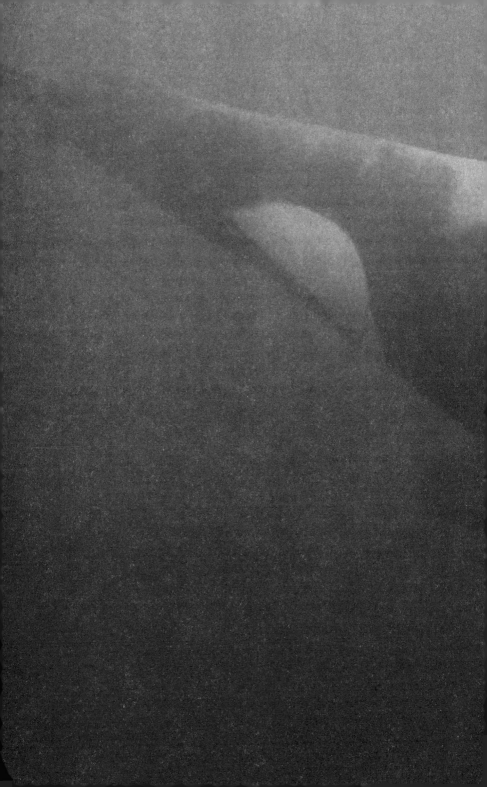

Part Two

~~~~~

SAVING LUNA

CHAPTER TWENTY-EIGHT

May 2004

We went down to the Gold River docks one morning in early May. Luna wasn't in sight. From there, you could see the big wharf on pilings about a quarter of a mile to the west, where the ships used to land at the pulp mill. Things were happening over there. A pickup was moving down the wharf slowly. A crane was moving into place. There were rumors that Luna was going to be captured the next week, but we already knew they weren't true. Everyone was still waiting to see if L Pod would come by and pick up its wayward child on its own.

In California, my father was going farther away. My mother asked him if he had a message for me, and he just said, "It's perfect." It was one of those messages that can mean anything or nothing but that your persistent but unrequited faith in life insists that you take as meaning everything.

Nine months before, long after the Alzheimer's had stolen a lot of him, but not all, he had put on the Anglican priest's cassock, surplice, and collar he had worn so often and had joined in holy matrimony my daughter from my first marriage and her slender, kind new husband. Relieving my mother's fears, he had remembered every line and every gesture, like a great horse running the race one last time.

When he woke up the next morning, he was bewildered. He kept saying, "I don't know what I am supposed to do now. I don't know what I am supposed to do." It was as if the God he had believed in so faithfully had finally released him from responsibility and had given him permission to go easy now. I wanted to say to him, "Just rest, Dad. You have done it all; you have fulfilled your promise to the world, to all of us: You have done your best." I believed that, but I did not say it. It would not have helped.

He had been an artist all his life. He had given his professional life, without salary, to a religious organization, for which he made films, but when he retired, he brought his watercolors out and made another career painting beautiful landscapes with those trembling hands that made clear lines. Now, after the wedding, he intended to go home and paint a picture of the wedding site, the way he had done for many others. But when he got home, all he painted was a wash of blue sky, and that was it. It was his last painting. It was perfect.

For me, still held by the awareness of that precious life that ebbed, everything in Gold River seemed fraught with grandeur and threat, of being mortal yet alive. Tides and choices seemed mighty, and the little whale, who carried such vibrant life but who was also soon to leave the sound, seemed, in his way, just a disappearing spirit, too.

I found myself attached to the people of this small town, so beat-up, so fragile, and suddenly so beatified in ways they hardly recognized by the appearance of this life, and to the Mowachaht/ Muchalaht people, in their own little group of families trapped by poverty and aimlessness in the village in the hills above Gold River, who were seeking the reassurance of being honored by the supernatural. Over the past months, the chief, Mike Maquinna, had often been quoted in the press as opposing Luna's move. His mantra was, "Let nature take its course. Leave the whale alone."

Sometimes when he gave interviews on the subject, Mike Maquinna put a deadline on the band's engagement with Luna, pointing out that the celebration of his father's life—a huge potlatch—would take place sometime in 2005, by tradition four years after Ambrose Maquinna's death, and Luna should stay in Nootka Sound at least until then.

The Department didn't seem likely to wait, and my daydreams were already turning Luna into legend. Long after Luna was taken away in that truck, I thought, people would tell grand and grander stories, and an old woman would say to unbelievers, "I touched Luna when I was a little girl." And it would seem to later generations that this could not really have happened at all, that it was all an amazing fairy tale built out of longing.

Ed Thorburn had been checking in with Luna regularly. Ed seemed to be very careful about what he wrote in his reports. He would not write that he got close to Luna, but he would describe how Luna's breath smelled, and he couldn't have detected that unless he'd been within the cone of blasted mist that Luna blew.

One day in May, Ed went out to see Luna and get his measurements for the design of the sling that would lift the orca out of the water and into the truck. As usual, when Ed stopped, Luna came right over.

Luna was very quiet around the Zodiac that day. Ed reported later about a relaxed little whale, just lying beside the boat, letting Ed and his partner lean over and take the measurements.

Luna was still a very small orca. He was fourteen feet long, compared to the thirty feet that he could become as an adult, and he was between nineteen and twenty-one inches across the area of his underside, which humans would think of as his chest, between his two pectoral fins. His dorsal fin, still in the curved shape like the female orcas' dorsal—the shape that juvenile males have before their fins grow upright as they reach adulthood—was twenty-two inches tall.

This was a special moment for Ed. He had always been okay

with looking in Luna's eyes, but when people had leaned over and patted Luna's nose or rubbed his belly, that was too far, and Ed never did that. Until that day.

"Today," he wrote, "is the first time I touched him."

For Ed, giving Luna passage back to his family was the only hope. Ed saw the troubles with seaplanes and sailboats as indications that Luna could no longer stay in Nootka Sound and keep away from trouble or harm.

"The bottom line was to get Luna back with his pod," he said. "I mean, however it was done, either by road or by sea, I didn't care. As long as he was given that opportunity."

And he hated the idea of Luna's going to an aquarium.

"Other than a couple of aquariums," he said, "nobody wants to see that. That would destroy me. I have warned the Department: If all efforts aren't made to make this relocation a success, and it goes that way, there's going to be blood in the water."

So getting Luna back with his family was the same for him as it was for the people who had signed up on the Reunite Luna Web site. It was Ed's moon shot, perhaps one of the great hopes of his career: a gift to a whale.

CHAPTER TWENTY-NINE

May 2004

Under a flat, gray, overcast sky, the long coastline of Vancouver Island opened out ahead of the small plane with a spaciousness that you could not see from the surface. The sea below was disheveled by northwest winds. How on earth would we be able to detect whales in that wilderness of whitecaps and windblown spray?

We were in the small Cessna that I have used for many years to help with travel and research for much of the writing I have done for the *Smithsonian* and *National Geographic* magazines. Now I was flying us north to try to help find Luna's family.

The two options for the attempt at a reunion were known, with striking originality, as plan A and plan B. Since Luna's family, L Pod, had not been seen yet this year, plan A was to try to keep an eye out for them. If they were seen near Nootka Sound, the idea was to have Ed lead Luna out to meet them. Most people preferred plan A and hoped it would succeed, because there were shadows in plan B, the plan to capture him and move him by truck.

Getting Luna into the net pen that was to be his trap raised uncertainties. A technique that might have been called "plan B (3)" involved lassoing his tail and dragging him into the net pen. People like Paul Spong thought Luna could get hurt if he fought the rope. In addition, if Luna was caught in the net pen, a satellite tracking device was to be attached to his dorsal fin with bolts that would go right through the fin, and there were a lot of opponents who argued that this could result in a dangerous infection, since major blood vessels run through orcas' dorsals. The costs of plan B were estimated at $628,900.

So everyone was asked to help keep a lookout for L Pod.

One of the watchers was a Texan, Keith Wood, who had a sailboat called *ANON,* which stood for Keith's NGO, Act Now for Ocean Natives. Keith had sailed up the coast and had anchored in Friendly Cove at Yuquot. Every day on which the weather was reasonable, Keith sailed out of Friendly Cove into the Pacific, put a hydrophone down, and listened.

Suzanne and I, too, got involved in looking for L Pod. We did not see this assignment as controversial. The story, though more complicated than we had expected, was still simply about a united effort by humans to help a lost whale, just like the story of Springer. In the past, I had often worked with scientists, doing grunt work or flying for photography missions or to provide transportation; it helped them, and it helped me get insights for the stories.

So every few days, or when we heard of whale sightings, we would find ourselves longing to help Luna in some way. So we'd hop in the airplane and fly north. And every time, the same phenomenon would happen. We'd start out eager, excited about the overarching perspective that a plane could provide, then we would get there.

As we dropped closer to the sea, a familiar sense of ludicrous reality seeped into the cockpit. What on earth were we thinking? Beneath us and out to infinity stretched an expanse of windswept water that was absurdly vast, in which swells and surface chop marched past below us in endlessly repeated patterns of gray textures, splotched with flecks of white. Each fleck was brighter than the spout of an orca, and each shadow of a wave was longer than an orca's back and fin.

But we were there, so we looked. L pod might be close to shore, so we looked there. Or the whales might be farther out, fishing along a well-known reef, so we went there. One small reef with breakers looked exactly like breaching whales in the distance. Nope. Black rock.

We tried to make the pattern our eyes took across the sea systematic, but that made us bug-eyed. Finally, under our wistful gaze, the sea became an implacable enemy, an expanse of wicked whale camouflage, a bland face of deception rolling past beneath, heedlessly concealing our little whale friend's lifeline to contentment and survival. How dare the great sea be so heartless? At that point of ridiculous personification of a completely inanimate large body of water, it was time to leave and fly home.

We worked on our house but kept close to the cell phone and the Internet to find out if there was news, waiting until once more the itch grew in us to fly over that impenetrable sea and try to spy out the secrets that might save Luna.

CHAPTER THIRTY

May 2004

On May 18, we were back in Gold River, drawn north again by an assault of rumors, by stories of conflict, and by a lack of real facts. In the morning, I went to the Department office in town for some information related to another flight we planned to take that afternoon, in our rather excessive optimism of what we might find.

I went in the main door but stopped at the inner door to Ed's office. It was full of people. I sat down to wait.

In between our flight over the implacable sea and this morning's visit, things had changed. Trust was evaporating. We no longer found this to be just a good-natured story about people getting together to help a little whale.

First, we found out that the Department was planning to cut off all independent journalistic access to the site where Luna was to be captured and monitored in the pen. The place where all this was going to happen was hugely roomy; there was a large wharf right next to the capture pen, so it wasn't about the constraints of space. It appeared to be about hiding things.

That question was hanging in the air, and the question of whether Luna would be sent to an aquarium had come up again. We mostly thought that rumor was persistent because it so perfectly fed paranoia, with its image of heavy-handed government selling a precious child into slavery. But it turned out that there was substance, too.

Most of the people at the Department and at the Vancouver Aquarium seemed to believe that any reunion attempt wasn't likely to work. And if it didn't, the tank was the place he'd go.

"Most of us were not convinced that it would be successful," John Ford told us later. "Some people have a blind faith that there is absolutely no question that it'll work. But a lot of us, who actually know these animals in great detail, from studying them in an aquarium setting to studying them in the wild, were not so certain."

The e-mails buzzing through the Department's offices showed an organization that seemed eager just to be done with this animal, and that captivity was seen as much more palatable in secret than in public. And a careful look at the plan revealed a possibility that the Department was setting Luna up for a fall.

In giving reasons for the capture, Marilyn Joyce never said it was being done to help Luna. It was always about human safety. Luna, she said, was becoming dangerous to people on Nootka Sound, so the move was being undertaken entirely for the purpose of ensuring public safety.

But that didn't make a lot of sense. Against the advice of several of the members of the scientific panel, the Department was planning to move Luna to the Victoria area at what many of the scientists thought was a very bad time—in late June, just in time for the active boating season. In summer, that area is one of the busiest recreational boating areas in the world. So how did it make sense to move a whale that the Department claimed was a danger to humans to a place where the whale would have far more humans per square mile to endanger?

What the Department was doing only made sense if it had already been decided that the best place—or perhaps what its scientists and policymakers thought was the inevitable place—for Luna was an aquarium tank. In that case, it made sense that the people making these decisions were willing to increase the odds of interaction, so one would happen quickly and give them the excuse to take Luna away forever. And John Davis made it clear in a memo that Luna would not be given much time after his release. He used a negative word that made Luna's character part of the story: "We must be able to react quickly if the animal persists in aberrant behaviour in southern waters—there cannot be a protracted 'wait and see and hope he gets better' situation where the animal and the public are put at risk."

So in some ways, if the Department had that underlying expectation that Luna was inevitably bound for captivity, you could think of the entire $628,900 as being spent on a public-relations gimmick, as one Department official had said before, in order to "make captivity a more publicly palatable option."

The public had no idea that this was happening. The general understanding was that all Luna needed was a bus trip home and everything would finally work out for him. That's why people wrote checks and raised money.

One of the people who answered that call to help Luna was a five-year-old girl from the Victoria area named Katie Lewis, who sold pictures she drew of Luna to the public. She raised over four hundred dollars for the reunion.

But on the same day on which Marilyn Joyce was being reminded to write Katie a thank-you note, the owner of Marineland of Niagara Falls followed up on Marilyn's invitation to write her directly. He sent a fax: "We believe the likelihood of a successful reunion is extremely slim and we do not want to see the public or the whale put at further risk."

There was interest from across the border, too. A little later, one of Marilyn's advisers back in Ottawa wrote a colleague, asking about a document called a "non-detriment finding," otherwise known as an NDF, from the organization called CITES, the Convention on International Trade in Endangered Species of Wild Fauna and Flora.

"Robert," the memo read, "please confirm if the CITES Scientific Authority is prepared to issue an NDF for the export of Luna to the US."

Apparently, Marilyn Joyce went ahead and thanked Katie Lewis, who had so much faith that her government was going to help Luna get back to his family.

From Ed's office, I went down the hall to wait, sat down next to a bulletin board, and thought about my father. Time passed. For a while, I looked at a sign on the door of a meeting room that might also have been used as a courtroom. It said NO WEAPONS, NO CAMERAS, NO RECORDERS. I sat there some more and tried to figure out what the real story about Luna was.

There was something powerful going on here. Luna's need to make contact seemed so shocking and wonderful that just a glance from him threw people into amazement, euphoria, mysticism, love, defensiveness, shock, or fear. For some reason, Luna captured people's attention and made them respond in fundamental ways.

It was not, in my mind, like the cultural power of whale and wolf that First Nations mystics saw and I didn't. It wasn't the scientific momentum and political power that drove the animal-management policies of the Department of Fisheries and Oceans. It was some kind of emotional power that made people do things that might threaten their own comfort and safety for the sake of another being and made them feel exalted and brave and good even when they broke the law. There was something here that had emotional majesty. It was something we hungered for just as much as Luna did.

NO WEAPONS, NO CAMERAS, NO RECORDERS. I was sick of reading that. It sounded like the Department's rules on the capture wharf. I got up and read the bulletin board instead of the sign. That didn't help much.

On the board there was a picture of a child, a young girl of about eleven. It was a poster about the terrors of child prostitution. The girl had big eyes and was looking straight at the camera. Someone who had stood at this bulletin board recently had pulled one of the thumbtacks out of the board and had stuck it in the girl's eye.

The door opened down the hall. The meeting in Ed's office had apparently ended. I went in. There was Clint Wright, the Vancouver Aquarium vice president, who was in charge of the capture operation. I thought it was a chance to address what seemed to be unnecessary secrecy at the site. So I gave him a short speech about honesty in journalism and the old saw that "if it looks like you're hiding something, people think you are."

I should have known that wouldn't work. Usually, the people you use it on actually are hiding something. So what was the point?

Clint Wright gave me a look that said, Who is this guy? I felt the air fill with a kind of gas in which my argument about the virtues of frankness sounded squeaky.

When I was done, Clint said that the crew didn't give out details, in order to protect people and whales. "There are things that if we announced them," he said, "we'd have people protesting."

I thought, Yeah, I'm sure you would. But I didn't say it.

CHAPTER THIRTY-ONE

May 2004

Then there was news.

Southern Resident whales, Luna's community, had been seen only about fifty air miles south along the coast, near the district of Tofino. Paul Spong called Ed, saying it was K Pod and L Pod—positive identification.

Ed's mind lit up with possibilities. L Pod was just around the corner, at least in terms of a species that can easily cover one hundred nautical miles a day.

For Ed Thorburn, this moment must have been dazzling. Maybe he could just put a fender on a rope behind the boat and lead Luna straight out of the mouth of Nootka Sound, then turn left and start for home.

At 6:30 the next morning, he was on the phone to Marilyn Joyce. "Discussed the lead down to Tofino," his notes read. "My boat can do it. The big question is would L-98 follow 20–22 hrs. I'm not at all sure. I am willing to try. Would need a support vessel, etc."

Marilyn did not say no. Ed called his enforcement partner, Greg Rusel, and told him to prepare for an overnight on the boat. He called a backup enforcement officer to come to Nootka Sound, as well.

This must have been the sweetest of hopes for Ed. What lovely symmetry and justice! Here he was, the man who had probably known Luna the best, whose heart Luna had won so easily and completely, now in a position to just slip away with his young friend behind him and lead him back to that connection with family that he needed so much.

Ed must have visualized that moment of reunion. When I heard about the possibility, I did.

It would happen quickly, maybe in a maze of big swells and white-caps, or maybe in the smooth shelter of a bay behind a point. Either way, the pod would appear almost without notice. Suddenly, the sea would be filled with tall dorsal fins and the sounds of breathing, and backs like locomotives would rise from the sea.

And suddenly, just like that, the story of the whale who made friends with people would be swept into history, and the little whale who had been poofing up thin plumes into the whaleless air of Mooyah Bay would sail blithely away, swept up in a ghostly armada of lifted breath, into a long, safe life with the ones who had nurtured his beginnings and would now be his companions forever.

And, of course, I daydreamed of this young whale breaching, giving Ed one last splash of his tail, and then disappearing, without looking back. Ah! Beauty!

At 8:33 in the morning, Ed called his enforcement boss.

At 8:56, he talked again to Marilyn. He wanted to know if this was actually feasible. What about getting Coast Guard support? And what if they didn't find the whales in Tofino? Would they continue down the coast all the way to Victoria, to the place where they were going to take him by truck? Would that work?

At 10:07, Marilyn Joyce called again. She said if there was confirmation that this was L Pod, they would look at this. John Ford suggested that Ed give a trial run, leading Luna to the mouth anyway.

What a moment! Here, all of a sudden, the whole Department was looking seriously at having Ed lead Luna south in his twenty-four-foot-long Zodiac, in a plan being thrown together in a matter of hours.

If it happened, then without a lot of fanfare and after only about two or three days of Ed's being Luna's companion, the whole thing would be completed. There would be no net pen, no bolted satellite tag, no blood work, no long and frightening truck ride, and no bill for $628,900. There would just be a humane, slow run down the coast, with eye contact when Luna wanted it and stops to go fishing as needed, just a bit of kindness from a man who had always given Luna that glance of contact when it mattered.

To Ed, it must have seemed natural, like nature taking its course.

It all seemed to depend on whether L Pod would be seen near Tofino again, or, better yet, farther up the coast toward Nootka Sound. Or had the pod turned south and taken the chance away?

A day passed. Ed and Clint Wright went out to Mooyah Bay to see how easy it would be to lead Luna, though Ed already knew.

It was easy. And as usual, Luna did something new. Ed led him along with a blue fender on a rope, like a golden retriever on a lead. Luna scooted along behind the boat as it moved at seven or eight knots. As he surfed the wake right behind the boat, he lifted his tail clear out of the water, and held it there.

Without his tail in the water, Luna seemed to have no propulsion system, but he kept going, right behind the boat. He must have been using the wake to sweep him along—some combination of the shape of the wake and the strength of his pectoral fins alone helped him keep up with the boat. But Ed couldn't figure out how.

"His tail was in the air," Ed said later. "Out of the water. And he was going seven knots. I don't know how you could do it, but he was doing it."

Another day passed. Ed waited. Luna played and ate fish, and didn't know that everyone was waiting for his family to decide.

CHAPTER THIRTY-TWO

May 2004

We ran the bow of our Zodiac up on the rocks at Anderson Point and got out and sat with our dogs on the moss in steady rain. We looked for Luna. The water was gray and folded into wrinkles from the wind. We couldn't see him anywhere.

After about an hour of watching, we zipped across the channel and around a little point of land to Tuta Marina, where a friend named Lisa Larsson sat in her elderly little wooden boat, *Henrietta*. If Luna wasn't around and Lisa had a cabin to dry out in, why not?

The dark bare-wood floats at the marina were ancient, and some of them had missing boards on their sides. A couple of the floats listed alarmingly; it was an adventure to explore their outer reaches, particularly on slippery days in the rain. *Henrietta* was tied up at one of the more secure floats halfway out the marina, just past the scale-flaked fish-cleaning station. Lisa came out with her braids tucked into a hooded jacket and invited us in. As she had been doing for two months, she was listening for Luna's calls on a hydrophone.

L Pod had not opened the door for Ed Thorburn to take Luna home. After the big family's appearance near Tofino, it had disappeared from anyone's sight, and Ed's great hope to lead Luna to his family had faded for the moment.

But plan A was still in play, and out at Yuquot, Keith Wood kept sailing out with his hydrophones in the water, hoping for that crowd of whale calls to come seeping into his speakers like a child's mother calling across the fences from far away. The family had vanished, but it was on the move. It could show up at Luna's doorstep at any moment.

Lisa was thirty-seven and came from Sweden, but she had done twelve years of audio monitoring and analysis for Paul Spong with the Northern Resident orcas on the northeast end of Vancouver Island. Paul had received a grant from the Department to monitor Luna and his calls that spring, and Lisa had come up in *Henrietta,* a long, lean wooden boat that chugged along on a tiny diesel engine but was big enough to live in.

Lisa was boiling eggs, so the windows were fogged up. It made the place warm and cozy, as if the fog were on the outside. We brought Lisa muffins from Gold River, which made her eyes brighten. She was the kind of person whose eyes light up almost literally; she could look solemn and very focused on her work with a recorder and headphones, but when something happened that made her happy, whether it was muffins or the first day's calls from Luna, her face immediately became a beacon of delight.

Lisa never approached Luna or touched him, but most days she heard him clicking and whistling right inside her head on her headphones, and she felt as close to him as did people who were out on the water every day. She said she thought of herself as his nanny. It was as if he were a completely different form of life to her than he was to us. She lived in his other world, in many ways his more real world, shaped more by sound than sight.

"We don't even understand how well they hear," she said. "It is a totally different way. I mean we can't even imagine how it is to be a whale. We have to expand our minds to even comprehend how it is for them."

Orcas filter incoming sound through high-quality fat in their lower jaws, and this appears to give them abilities to distinguish sound and where it comes from in ways humans probably can't visualize.

And they make sounds with both their blowholes and through nasal mechanisms in their heads. Yet something about what Lisa heard carried stories of emotion that she felt she could recognize, maybe in the same ways that Ed saw loneliness in Luna's eyes. Was this just human imagination carrying them away, or was it more?

"I feel much closer to a whale when I hear him than when I see him," Lisa said. "Some calls are more urgent, and some are goofy. Especially when you can hear him and see what he's doing. This one time, I hear this rising call, and right when it ends, he comes out of the water and breaches. And you see that kind of connection: He makes a rising call as he is on his way up."

One day she was listening while she watched Luna playing with sea lions. He was dashing around with them—sometimes chasing them, and sometimes letting them chase him, like a kids' game of tag.

"He was whistling and he was imitating them, like doing this little—" She made a barking noise, then laughed. "I could hear the sea lions at the same time, and I thought, Oh, my gosh, that is not the sea lion. That must be him! And then sometimes, when he only makes one call every forty minutes for a while, it is a different intensity, as if he is just wanting to hear his own voice. On some days, he is just quiet. And we don't know why."

She spoke of him with a happy familiarity.

"He's like a street-kid whale," she said. "He has to survive by himself. It's not a normal childhood for him, so he has to be really strong just to survive."

Her hydrophone was in the water at the shoreline, but it was connected to a small FM broadcast station with a range of about a mile. So sometimes she would take the receiver high up on a hillside above Tuta Marina, on a brushy clear-cut that had been logged only five or ten years before, where she could see all of Mooyah Bay. There she could watch for Luna with a spotting scope, while at the same time she recorded his calls.

Up on the hill, she had a blue tarp strung between some chest-high cedar saplings, so she could crawl under this awning in the sun or rain and sit there listening. If she started to hear Luna, she would emerge with her spotting scope and try to match actions and calls.

We had visited her there before. It was a lovely scene up on that hillside, with a solitary young woman standing on a tree stump, looking out over the joined waters by Mooyah Bay at a young whale, his voice sounding wistful, or eager, or urgent in her ears, her mind reaching out toward his life with bright eyes he could not see.

She looked through the logbook for us, sketching out recent history. "Sometimes he makes a few calls, and then he is quiet. Or like on the twenty-first, he was calling for three hours nonstop. Not even foraging. Just lying on his back, calling. He is calling out, just the hopefulness, the life, the joy, the positiveness of him. He just doesn't give up. If only there would be a response."

Lisa had run into other forms of life on the hillside while she listened to a whale. Eagles drifted across, giving their typical wimpy little chirps. Once or twice, a wolf howled. The most troubling visitors were bears. But Lisa had a secret weapon. She was not just familiar with her own language.

So when a big black bear came shambling into her camp one day, she spoke to him briefly in English, which didn't seem to make any difference, then in Swedish. Nope. So she tried Finnish.

"It's the loudest language I know," she told us later. "I don't know that much Finnish, but I just said, Hello, Bear! *Hei, karhu!*"

That stopped the bear.

"His ears go straight up, and it was like, Oh, this is weird."

The bear turned and ran.

The people who seemed to believe most strongly that Luna should be kept away from humans were the ones who watched from far away or people who had come here from the outside—people like

Suzanne and me and Lisa. To us, it seemed more than just a scientific concept; it was a moral issue. It seemed to be all wrapped up in ideals and beliefs and driven by that power of emotion that seemed to run through everything about Luna on Nootka Sound.

For me, it was as if the determination we had not to meet or engage with Luna was strong because the longing we had to give him what he seemed to want was also strong. Our denial of that longing was so intense that our success at keeping away from him made us feel tempered by self-sacrifice. It was, in many ways, a very complicated set of emotions. The first response one had to his apparent need was a personal longing to try to ease it. On top of that, though, we would layer the information we had that human contact could be dangerous to him, as well as the Department's clear instructions to keep clear.

But that wasn't enough to make us decide to turn our backs on a young whale's entreaties for company. Maybe much more important, there was a different tide of emotion that came from within our society and troubled me even while I yielded to it. It was the idea that the longing to help that engulfed me when I perceived Luna's loneliness was in itself a form of weakness. Empathy itself was seen as soft, unmanly, childish, self-indulgent. In the corporate world and even in biology, a display of empathy was not seen as strength of character.

So we would be strong. Lisa, Suzanne, and I sometimes played a game among the three of us, a kind of theological test of the toughness of our characters: "If you were out on Mooyah Bay in the fog and no one could see you, and Luna came up to you and put his head on the side of the boat, would you touch him or not?" Each of us said, "Of course not."

But I guessed that Lisa, like Suzanne and me, was probably conflicted in her heart. Lisa said fiercely that Luna should be left alone, but she talked warmly about the relationships that Luna had made with the people who befriended him when he first got to Nootka Sound.

"I totally understand the people here," she said. "They have seen him since he was small, they have been connecting with him, and whales are amazing. I think the love for him they might have is more profound in a way, because they have seen him as a kid growing up and surviving—and greeting them every time they come up to him. I mean, that is wonderful! How many creatures do that?"

So in spite of thinking that people should be kept away from Luna, she also couldn't help feeling awe at what happened when there was contact across that wall.

"You can see in people when they have been affected by a whale," she said. "It is something that he gives, that happy presence in the moment. It's funny, all those guys working at the dock, you can tell, they are all— Yeah, he has touched many hearts, that's for sure."

Like Ed Thorburn, who probably had felt intense empathy for Luna for as long as anyone, Lisa turned her own concern toward hoping for a family reunion. She was particularly eager that the pod would come by and meet Luna on its own, because she did not like the plan to bolt a satellite tag to his dorsal fin.

"That love is what he has been giving," she said. "So that is all we should give back. Nothing painful. Nothing that we wouldn't want done to us. What gives us a right to do that to him?"

When we sat in the cabin of *Henrietta* that day, Lisa told us an odd story. Six orcas had been seen a few days before near the mouth of Nootka Sound. Everyone had assumed that they were transients, the meat-eating kind that Luna would always avoid. But no one had been close enough to take identification photos. So all anybody knew for sure was that some kind of orcas had been close.

There was a little burst of wishfulness. What if L Pod had gone north, out of sight, after it was seen to the south of Nootka Sound?

What if that small group was a foraging subgroup of the larger pod? What if, what if?

That same day—Lisa found out later, looking at her logs—at about the same time that the other orcas were seen, Luna's calls had changed.

From the hill, Lisa could see Luna near Anderson Point, at the edge of the arm of water called Zuciarte Channel, which leads directly to the mouth of Nootka Sound. While Lisa watched and listened, Luna's calls became very unusual.

"The calls were kind of higher pitch," Lisa said. "It sounded like he was really impatient, like he didn't have time to give the whole call. They were urgent, impatient calls."

When she told the story, there was a chill of missed possibility in the air. Had Luna faintly heard calls he recognized? Had he been desperately trying to call back? If so, his calls had not been heard—or answered.

CHAPTER THIRTY-THREE

May 2004

Afew days later, I came back toward the Gold River docks from Mooyah Bay in a wind-conflicted sea, in the strange light made by heavy cloud cover and bursts of sunlight and the raging shine of rough water. The light made the sound and its mountains into a cathedral full of radiance and gloom, the kind of place where a man in a surplice like my father used to wear could give a sermon about sin and redemption that you would remember forever, for the weather as well as for the words.

We had driven out to Tuta Marina, but Luna hadn't been there, so I had left Suzanne to drive back and took the little Zodiac back to Gold River the wet way.

We'd been up on the hillside at Lisa's observation camp, talking with her. She had looked and listened for a little whale who was not there, then mused on how much more ancient whales are than humans.

"They have been in the oceans millions of years longer than we have been on Earth," she said. "It is like, we can't accept that. That is what I find. There is a dead stop and you can't go beyond it somehow, and that is why we can't really understand."

This difficulty didn't stop us from wondering, though. Whales are descended from land mammals that eased themselves back into the sea about fifty million years ago, long before the species that led to humans began to emerge. Since then, they had evolved into very different animals from us, dependent on sound for many of the things we do with sight. When you thought about that history, it seemed impossible that they could have anything in common with this upstart, upright creature that had to get so burdened with equipment in order to do anything with water that it appeared to be allergic to it.

And yet, though we had been so long apart in the flow of time, and were separated further in the great division of the planet into earth and sea, we offered something familiar enough in our gaze, in our presence—in something—that a lone orca could seek in us a way to ease his loneliness. And when our eyes connected, the same thing could happen to us.

"We know they have this awareness," Lisa said. "We can sense it, you know, their presence." She paused to think about it. "I mean, they kind of look through your otherness at you."

As I got closer to the docks, after a lumpy trip in the Zodiac, I rode three-foot waves blown my way before a twenty-five-knot wind. As I came in, a hard wind eddied down off the mountainside as if born of the fierce light up there. It hit the water and threw every whitecap back in the waves' faces, kicking spray into the air. I rode the Zodiac straight into the weird light and the crazy winds, every wave a spout ahead of me. But when the real whale put me on his back, I didn't expect him.

I arrived at the docks going fast, right up to the edge of the lower floats. Suddenly, I was no longer going in the direction in which I was pointed. Then I heard his breath.

He looked small at first, because not much of him was out of the water. He was pushing me from the port side to the starboard. I kept driving the boat, but Luna didn't appear to approve of my direction.

I looked over the side at his broad, dark back. There was his blowhole, with its muscular flap closed tightly. For some reason, it seemed strikingly larger and more complex than I had thought. I guess I had imagined it to be a simple hinged flap, like the lid on a kettle. But here was a strong, firm thing with a complex fit of flesh to flesh, much bigger than I had expected. As I was looking, in that moment's burst of wonder, it opened and blew a blast of fishy mist in my face.

I blinked, and Luna's back passed across my view. His black, shining skin, with the patches of white going down into the water, looked amber through water stained by the incoming river.

I looked up toward his head. With a shock, I saw what looked like a stream of dark red blood in the water. Oh no! I must have wounded him with my prop, I thought. Then he turned and came back to give the Zodiac a little shove sideways, and I saw what it was. As he pushed me around, Luna was holding a strip of red-brown cedar bark in his teeth. It hung out of the side of his mouth like a droopy thin cigar. What a little thug!

He kept pushing.

"Don't do that, Luna," I said.

I think I had expected that Luna would be less independent than this. Maybe the way we relate to domestic animals makes us expect domesticity in all other lives. Humans get out of the car to feed bears, and that is definitely a move made in error. So maybe I didn't expect him to be as alive, as intentional, and as self-confident as he seemed to be right now. This felt like a meeting between two similarly free individuals, both disposed to be friendly, but whose immediate goals did not exactly coincide.

You could suggest all kinds of metaphors about what was happening, about wildness and human intervention, about the planet being, in reality, far less in our control than we think, about our fates being more simple to divert than we may wish. But this whale was not a metaphor at all; he was a force of life distilled out of the sea, big, strong, curious, willful. It was hard to accept that level of awareness and intention in something that did not look in any way human.

Then he picked up the stern of the boat and lifted until the outboard was right out of the water.

The motor raced. I pressed my thumb on the shutdown switch. It stopped.

He put the boat down. I looked around. Luna had pushed me toward the dock. I was passing right next to the rail of a moored logging company's tin boat, called *Koprino Wind*. I grabbed the rail and vaulted up onto the deck like a rattled pirate, clutching my bow line. I tied it off to a cleat on *Koprino Wind*.

Suzanne had arrived a few minutes before. She came down to the lower docks and we both stood there and watched our boat jumping around.

Without me, the Zodiac was acting even more lively than it had been with me in it. It was moving back and forth, spinning around, with the bow up, with the stern up. We watched for a while, then started walking up the dock.

Nearby, two people were working on their boat, an aluminum gillnetter with a big spool but no net. They were Rick and Sheila Millard, who had known Luna from the beginning. We hadn't met them before. They smiled at us, looking amused at my stunned eyes.

"We've known him since he was the size of a dolphin," Rick said. "He's a member of the family."

There was another guy down on the dock, an eager, friendly man with a shaven head. I didn't know him, either.

"We're not supposed to be down here on the lower dock," I said to him. "We should probably go up onshore."

It turned out that he was another curious link to Luna's history. He was Ryan Lejbak, the cofounder of the Reunite Luna Web site, visiting from the Canadian prairies. He had been instrumental in pushing the Department to attempt the reunion.

He introduced himself and shook my hand. He had just come out from Saskatchewan, and this was the first time he'd ever seen Luna. He had the good grace to be sheepish that I had found him on the lower docks, where he knew he wasn't supposed to be.

For just a moment, the group of us stood on the dock and watched as Luna played with the Zodiac, pushing it back and forth on its bow line beside *Koprino Wind*. We were five people from all over the place, but all of us were bound up, in our intense but different ways, with the life of the little whale who had come so far across the wilderness of time and the sea to look through our otherness at us and tell us stories of redemption and sin.

CHAPTER THIRTY-FOUR

June 2004

The phone rang in our house, where we'd gone for a couple of days. The capture and move process would get under way soon, and we needed to get some errands done before going up to Gold River for what would probably be the last time.

Suzanne answered. It was Paul Spong, from OrcaLab, the place that employed Lisa Larsson. Soon Suzanne was writing on a piece of paper: "48 22.263, 122 59.615."

There were latitude and longitude readings. L Pod had been seen near San Juan Island, south of Victoria.

I found the spot on the chart, and we flew out to see what we could.

It was a day of very low tides. There were mud flats near some of the islands, and tidal rips churning the water. But out where the whales were, the water was still.

They came into view subtly but with a kind of inexorable force, gradually surfacing. Once we noticed one, we saw twenty, then more. They were like what their bow waves resembled, a steady flow of life, edging gradually across the surface. They were slow blooms of white on the surface, and a shadowy mix of black and greenish patches underwater, in small groups spread well apart, all moving north toward the coast of San Juan Island.

The whole pod had arrived. Without doubt, it had now ceased its winter wanderings and had come back for the summer. There was no longer any chance that it would show up near Nootka Sound. This meant that the capture, the truck ride, and the bolt in the fin were almost inevitable for Luna. After all that we had come to know about the situation, both its dangers and the possible hidden agendas, this was not happy news.

"You forgot Luna," Suzanne said, as if to the whales below us. "Silly Luna."

The appearance of L Pod, with such majestic deliberation, began a hard chapter in Luna's life—one everyone hoped would be brief—of fear, imprisonment, and pain. It might also mean the joy of an eventual reunion, but for now that was eclipsed by the fact that a much easier and perhaps safer route to that reunion was now drifting away.

"Silly Luna," Suzanne said again to L Pod below us. "You forgot him."

We finished our errands and rushed back to Gold River. There had been another change. The Department announced that a landing floatplane had missed hitting Luna by a couple of feet. It was all over the press.

It was, in fact, not a very realistic story. Ed Thorburn and Clint Wright said they saw it from the pulp mill dock, where the net pen was being finished. The span between that dock and the area where the floatplanes landed was far too distant to gauge distance accurately across flat water, so any blow or appearance of a fin within hundreds of feet of a plane could be interpreted as either a near miss or perfectly safe, as one chose. When I went in to the offices of Air Nootka, Grant Howatt was disgusted with the story. "Didn't happen," he said.

Over the previous weeks, a lot of lobbying had developed to try to get the Department to keep waiting for the chance L Pod might come up the coast close enough for Ed to lead Luna out. But Ed, along with everyone else in the Department, was convinced that the capture had to happen now that the crews had gathered and the payrolls were adding up like taxi meters running berserk. So, conveniently, Luna suddenly became more dangerous. He could have caused a crash! We have to get him moved!

The next day, we heard that the Department had picked a date to do the capture. Though there was no official proclamation, the date chosen was Monday, June 14.

Marilyn Joyce did an interview with a reporter from a Vancouver Island television station. His name was Jonathan Bartlett, and he was good at what he did. For this one, he needed all his persistence.

Marilyn talked first about how the plan to move Luna came about entirely because there was a safety issue for humans. Then Jonathan asked his key question.

"The other question a lot of people have," he said, "is what if it doesn't work? What if Luna doesn't want to go with his pod or the pod doesn't want him?"

"Right," Marilyn said, and started in on a useful, long-winded answer. "And I think that is something that has been the subject of debate for many of us now since Luna showed up here. There's no certainty in whether or not Luna will go back to the pod or [if] they're going to accept him. I think we all understand that. We hope that this will give Luna the best opportunity to be with his pod, to stay as a wild whale, and at the same time mitigate that public risk. I think we'll just have to take one step at a time here."

That was it—concluding remarks. Something faintly like a smile crossed her face. Was she hoping that little red light on the camera would go off? It didn't.

Jonathan wasn't buying it. He tried again: "And what is his future if it doesn't work?"

Marilyn, too, tried again. But what she was trying to do and what Jonathan was trying to do were two different things.

"Well," she said. "Our focus at this point is on the post release, and that's really going to be the telling time for us, to have as many measures in place to keep boats, people away from him. NOAA, the

National Marine Fisheries Service with the U.S. is leading that part of the program, so we'll have a number of boats tracking Luna. We'll have boats on the water that are providing some education and making people stay away. We'll also look at ways to keep him out of some of these sensitive zones, give him the most time."

A diversion. Was it a successful diversion? No.

"But what is his future if he's not willing to go with his pod?" Jonathan was going to have to utter the word he had been hearing all over town already. "Is his future likely an aquarium?"

"Well," Marilyn said, giving up but apparently trying to put enough padding around the word so it wouldn't stand out, "if he doesn't go with his pod, but he's not causing the same kind of public risk, then, you know, we're quite prepared to leave him out there as a wild whale, just behaving a bit differently than what we're used to. If he is a public risk then we're obviously going to follow up with some sort of contingency plan, and we're looking at options. Placement in an aquarium is one of those options that we obviously have to consider. At the end of the day it really will depend on a number of the circumstances, just how much of a danger he is."

On the U.S. side, there had been a public meeting at the Seattle Aquarium to describe the plan. It was marked by the same kind of mutual praise that we had heard at the meeting back at Orcas Island. But near the end of the meeting, a speaker got up at the back of the room. He was Ben White, who had begun his activist career when he infiltrated the Ku Klux Klan for a high school project. Later, he became known for putting protestors at the 1999 World Trade Organization in sea-turtle costumes during what became known as "the Battle of Seattle."

Sending Luna to an aquarium under any circumstances, he said, would be a betrayal of those who had donated to the reunion effort. "So you have all these people who are eager for this whale to be reunited with the family, who might be snookered."

His question was direct. "Can anyone at DFO or NMFS promise

me that this whale will not, under any condition, be put in captivity or be killed?"

Brent Norberg, regional marine mammal coordinator for the National Marine Fisheries Service, answered. Like Marilyn, he avoided using the word *captivity*. While Marilyn watched impassively from a nearby chair, he made the familiar assertion that these two organizations, which had planned every detail and contingency of the capture and release itself, were not actively planning the details of what would happen if things did not work out well after Luna was released.

"I think we've been clear from the beginning," he said, "that the path that we take with respect to decision making we want to leave open until the point that we get there."

In his speech leading up to the question, White suggested that there were rumors that an anonymous donor, a marine park, had offered a large sum of money to "facilitate the process" of moving Luna to its tanks.

That sounded like a conspiracy theory when I heard it, but it turned out that it may well have been true. We were later told the same thing, very unexpectedly and with no prompting, by one of the world's most accomplished professional dolphin wranglers, Jeff Foster, of Global Research and Rescue, who regularly managed dolphins and orcas for captive facilities. Foster, interviewed by Suzanne, told her that the organization that made the offer was Six Flags Marine World of Vallejo, California, which had a lone female orca, nicknamed "Shouka," who had been bred in captivity.

"There were rumors around Gold River that he was worth fifty million," Suzanne said to Foster.

"No," Foster said. "Five. Five."

"So," Suzanne asked him, "would one of the captive facilities have paid that kind of money for him?"

"Absolutely," Foster said. "Absolutely. Yes. But you know, this is the other thing. You make a trade-off. You say, 'Okay, the value of this animal is,' so you put the money back into research. And that's what Six Flags was going to do. They were going to put one million into research into whales in Puget Sound, and in Canada, for the next five years."

Maybe that was why the Department was trying to find out what sort of permits it needed to export Luna to the United States. For people who didn't think there was much chance of Luna actually getting back with his pod, the idea of having a huge new source of funding for research on the rest of the wild orcas might have had some influence on their planning. It might even have made them feel that Luna's continued life in the wild was actively impeding their work.

In the Department plan to catch Luna, Jeff Foster and his crew were to be hired to wrangle him.

Meanwhile, up in Gold River, Luna was helping the crews build the net pen. The little rascal kept going right up to the net pen itself, where he played with the construction crew. He was also fond of the Jacuzzi blast of his future captors' little jet boat. As they buzzed around, tying up loose ends, he'd stick his big blunt nose right into the jet and lash his tail against the force of it. At times, he pressed so hard against the jet that it behaved like a garden hose with a thumb on it and blasted water straight into the air, creating a fine, soaking rain for the people building the net that would hold him.

Each day the workers would eventually ask Ed to lead Luna away. Ed was happy to do this, because his instructions were to train Luna to follow his boat. Ed's eventual job was to lead Luna into the pen, at which point the gate would be closed and Luna would be trapped.

"But, you know, that is a lot of credibility I'm going to lose with him," Ed had told us when we interviewed him. "I mean, I know that. But I know it's for his own good."

"Are you going to feel guilty about that?" Suzanne asked.

"Well, you bet. I feel guilty now, and I haven't even done it yet. But I would rather have him back with his pod."

CHAPTER THIRTY-FIVE

June 2004

On June 12, it rained. It really rained. On the west coast of Vancouver Island, the weather is often like a baby. When it's sunny, it can be sweet and charming, but when it rains, it doesn't just weep. It cries as if at the world's end.

As the rain poured, we rode *Uchuck III* west toward Yuquot, the place James Cook had called Friendly Cove. The ship cruised at twelve knots through the rain. We passed fish farms, logging camps, Anderson Point, Tuta Marina, and the hillside where Lisa had her outpost camp, where she had spoken Finnish to bears.

She wasn't there, though. Luna had been spending most of his time around the Gold River docks, so Lisa had moved to the steep hill next to the pulp mill and put her hydrophone in the water at a small dock near the mill that Ed also used for *Rugged Point*. This had an unexpected benefit; now when you came down to the docks with your car or a portable FM, you could dial in her frequency at the end of the broadcast spectrum and maybe hear Luna directly, in real time.

Because of the geography, you couldn't get to the hillside by road from Gold River; you had to go by boat. Lisa rowed over in *Henrietta*'s dinghy. We also helped her sometimes with our Zodiac. This gave us an idea. The hill overlooked the old ship's wharf at the pulp mill, where the net pen was being built. The pen was on the opposite side of the wharf from the community docks, so you couldn't see it from there, but the hill gave anyone who climbed it a perfect view.

So, a few weeks before, long before the tensions had developed, we had asked Ed Thorburn if he'd mind if we watched the capture from that hillside, too, and he said he thought it would be fine. We didn't ask again. We just climbed the hill and put up our own tent, waiting for the moment.

Uchuck III made several stops along the way to drop off the equipment and supplies it was carrying. Finally, the ship developed a new restlessness as the edge of a long swell from the sea met it at the sound's mouth. Then we turned into the shelter of the cove.

Keith Wood's sailboat, *ANON,* was anchored in the bay. We had talked with him often over the past months, and now we met him up at the home of the last First Nations residents at Yuquot, Ray Williams and his wife, Terry.

Keith walked with us across the field that lay in the embrace of the curve of land, toward the hill at the windward side. We wanted to watch the breakers roll, and to talk. Keith had logged 310 hours of sailing time over the past month, listening for L Pod. This would probably be our farewell to Keith, because in only a day or two, the capture would happen and Luna would be trucked away.

We walked together on a narrow path through the hedge of blackberry bushes at the south edge of the grass basin that used to hold the village of Yuquot. The rain and mist made it a somber place, and we all felt melancholy.

Only a few months before, when the Department had announced that it would support Luna's reunion, there had been a wide celebration by people of different backgrounds, politics, and geography. And now the serious effort at a reunion was about to start. Everyone should have been thrilled. But something had happened to that good mood.

We walked across the basin through long, wet grass toward the hill that broke the waves. We could hear the breakers rushing up the gravel beach before we climbed the grassy bank to see them. They sounded like gusts of wind. Keith looked bedraggled. His hair was soaked. Rain dripped down his face.

"It's like a funeral on the Irish moors," he said.

Uchuck III went back toward Gold River across a stretch of open sea that led to Zuciarte Channel. The gale drove a six-foot swell and heavy chop toward the mountains and whipped the crests off the waves in little spouts of spume. It looked like the waves I had ridden in the Zodiac a few days before, but bigger.

I found myself daydreaming that the gray backs of the waves were materializing into black and white, turning into the army of L Pod, and suddenly we were surrounded by a host of orca soldiers blasting their muscular breath into the sky, marching down the storm to rescue their lost child from the confusion of human beings.

CHAPTER THIRTY-SIX

June 2004

In trying to figure out what we needed to understand and describe this story, it seemed to Suzanne and me that the Mowachaht/ Muchalaht band was peripheral to the actual events because it didn't look as if the band was going to take any action to either oppose the capture or support it. But the spiritual idea that the First Nations had about Luna, like everything about the little whale, showed the passionate way humans reacted to this extraordinary relationship that none of us could really understand.

There had been a partial solution to the lack of an independent journalist at the capture site. Under pressure, Marilyn Joyce agreed to allow the Mowachaht/Muchalaht people to have a reporter and videographer on the dock to observe. The reporter would be David Wiwchar, a fine journalist who wrote for a First Nations newspaper, and the videographer would be a man hired by a Seattle organization that had actively lobbied for the reunion attempt. This wasn't exactly nonpartisan independence, but at least it was a presence that was not on the Department's payroll.

Suzanne and I kept trying to get a full magazine-style interview with Mike Maquinna, but we didn't get more than a few words. One afternoon while the crowds of technicians and whale people were arriving from all over the Pacific coast of North America, we saw Mike down by the dock, on his way back from a TV interview.

Suzanne asked him what they were going to do, and he gave a slow grin. "We're calling up a big storm," he said, "so they'll run out of money and go away."

The next day was Monday, June 14, the date originally selected for Luna's capture. But the net wasn't ready.

That morning, we and other journalists were invited by the Department to look at the capture site. We were led past the guards and out onto the wharf. It was old and massive. The deck was concrete. Sailors who came in on the big ships before 1999 had painted insignias and names on the concrete to mark their fleeting presence: *Infanta* '94; *Tern Arrow; Harefield; Iris Arrow,* Nassau, 08-05-98.

It was like the names prisoners leave behind: statements of existence in the halls of memory. The crew of a ship named *Westfield* had covered parts of the wharf with the names of the sailors who had worked in its engine room and galley, so names of men that sounded like a roster of all the hard, poor places on the planet would be under the wheels of the truck that would soon roll past with Luna in its belly: Macatangay, Sabado, Flor, Valido, Capinto, Melo, Alcazaren. Some of the painters had drawn images—a big Mickey Mouse was one of them, with letters stuck in his teeth.

No orcas were painted on the dock. No one was going to have to put Luna down in paint in order to remember him.

On the water beside the dock, men were hooking weights that looked like large cannonballs to the edges of nets held in place by cylindrical floats. Someone else was washing more loose netting on a dock float with a fire hose. The net pen was eighty feet in diameter.

Our time was up at the capture dock. We were sent back to the government docks. Luna soon appeared, following a fishing boat, and dazzled the electronic eyes of half a dozen TV cameras. In the middle of this wandered members of the public, some of whom rushed down to the lower docks and splashed their hands urgently in the water to try to get Luna to come to them.

Over by *Uchuck III,* Sean Mather, who was skipper when Donna

Schneider first saw Luna, was doing an interview. He was asked why people would continue to break rules that were printed on signs right in front of them in order to see or touch Luna.

"It's because he's awesome," Sean said. "He's like Everest. You'll never get a chance to do this again."

In the afternoon, Luna left the docks to play with two little dozer boats that were working in the log-booming ground nearby. The public drifted away. The reporters and TV people all migrated to the Ridge for dinner. The news for the day was over.

We didn't go to the Ridge that evening. We went back to the docks. It was still light enough to see what Luna was doing. And we found out that the news for the day was not over after all.

It was a dry evening with a high overcast. The water was dark with the reflections of the clouds and the forested mountains. Both the water and the forests were greenish blue in the evening stillness. The water shimmered as the day's ripples faded.

Two First Nations canoes were out there on the water beyond the docks. They were full of men and women with paddles. The canoes were right next to each other, and in the twilight, the red paint of their insides looked like the color of blood. The paddles were upright, and the boats were not moving. The people were singing. Luna was with them.

Whoa! We stopped the car right in front of a NO PARKING sign and jumped out. What was this? What was going on? The Department made announcements of what it was going to do, and the press was attuned to that. The First Nations didn't make announcements. Or maybe nobody had asked.

We were on the dock by ourselves. We set up our tripods and started to film. We had no clue what this was about, but we thought we should at least record it. Then Suzanne saw something even more unexpected.

"Ed's at the front," she said.

"What?"

I looked at the bow of the canoe to our left. There was Ed Thorburn, sitting in the bow with a paddle, in his uniform. Luna came up beside him and blew mist in his face. Ed had a small smile on his face.

I could think of only one reason that Ed would participate in public interaction with Luna. Ed must have agreed with the First Nations members that if they didn't oppose the move, they could go out on the water and say good-bye. So, I thought, to show their respect and to symbolize what this apparently represented—the healing of the rift between them and the Department—they had invited him along.

"It's a ceremony," I whispered to Suzanne. In the still air, we could hear the singing, and Luna's breathing. The songs were wordless chanting, sung by the men to the slow beat of hand drums. The voices and the rhythm of the drums floated out across the water and echoed faintly back from the distant cliffs. It all seemed wrapped in symbolism and reverence. I whispered, as I might in a church, "It's farewell."

They sang song after song to Luna. We watched with the telephoto lenses of our cameras. Luna kept popping up beside the boats to touch outstretched hands or paddles. Once, when Ed paused in his paddling and held his paddle horizontal for a moment, as if in thought, Luna came up and gave the paddle a little push, and there was clearly a look of pleasure on Ed's severe face.

"Getting some good shots?" said a loud voice behind us. It was Grant Howatt, the owner of Air Nootka.

"It's incredible," Suzanne said.

"Do you know what's happening here?" I asked Grant. "You know, with Ed sitting in front like that?"

"I saw that," Grant said. "Maybe now they'll use the canoes to lead him into the pen. That would make a lot of sense."

Out on the water, the paddlers focused on Luna. The songs drifted across the calming waters, sounding like an elegy to a long-gone past.

Nootka Sound is made up of many winding inlets between mountains that rise abruptly to over 7,000 feet. Luna stayed within the labyrinth of relatively enclosed waters, which made it impossible for him to hear the calls of other whales who might have been passing by in the open sea.

Luna's characteristic plume of breath in still air. The plume was beautiful, but what was more striking when you were close to Luna was the sound of his breathing, so urgent and, to us mammals, so poignantly familiar.

Luna seemed to love the energy of ships and smaller boats on the move. He would ride the rough water behind outboards and surf the wake near ships like this one, the *Uchuck III*, a sight that the passengers loved.

No one was immune to Luna when he sought contact with people. "Humans were really the only social animals around," one scientist said. "That explains his motivation." Some people tried to stay away from him, while others got down close to the water, mesmerized by his presence.

Luna was barely a toddler of a whale when he showed up in Nootka Sound, but even a baby orca is an impressive sight up close, and some people were afraid when he approached seeking contact.

Keith Wood, a software engineer from Texas who came north in a sailboat to try to help Luna get back with his family, used hydrophones and a remote satellite dish to broadcast Luna's calls on the Internet.

People using their boats in Gold River could not escape Luna's attention, but they didn't know what was the right thing to do. Many, like this woman, chose to watch but keep a distance and not reach over to touch Luna. He often seemed content just to make eye contact and rub against the boat, or to play with bilge water being pumped out.

Luna's ability to show up unexpectedly near boats created a dilemma for people like us who knew humans could be both a solution and a problem for Luna. For a long time, we tried to get away from situations like this, and even to avoid looking him in the eye. But his efforts to make contact continued, and eventually we came to believe that some kind of contact should be intentionally—and carefully—offered.

Luna and younger people seemed fascinated with one another. One scientist who was working to keep people and Luna apart admitted, "If I was a ten-year-old kid or a fifteen-year-old kid, you would have to kill me to keep me away from that whale." *(Photo by Fred Lazuk)*

Luna's eagerness to approach boats took about six or eight months to develop fully, but after he grew accustomed to seeking social contact from people on their metal or fiberglass vessels, he would approach almost anyone who stopped nearby.

The power of the engines humans brought into Luna's sea seemed to be particularly fascinating to him. He sometimes appeared to try to pry his way into outboards, and sometimes he actually managed to lift the cover off the outboard on the Mowachaht/Muchalaht patrol boat.

Luna seemed fascinated with running water. He played with small hoses or full-out blasting fire hoses that some boat crews would put over the side for him.

When Luna looked at people, his gaze did not seem exotic or sterile. People perceived thought there. A scientist called Luna's eyes contemplative, and Donna Schneider, the cook on the *Uchuck III*, said that when she looked in Luna's eyes, "I could not breathe."

When the Canadian Department of Fisheries and Oceans tried to capture Luna to carry him south and attempt to reunite him with his family, the crew managed to entice him into the net pen for about eleven minutes but did not close the gate.

Like a lone stranger approaching a foreign shore, Luna swims toward the towering structures of the closed mill at Gold River. This was part of his regular neighborhood.

When the Canadian Department of Fisheries and Oceans tried to capture Luna for an attempt at a reunion with his family or eventually to possibly send him to an aquarium, the Mowachaht/Muchalaht people launched their canoes to intervene.

Across the species barrier, a hand reaches out in friendship to Luna. Somehow both the people on one side and the whale on the other seemed to find these momentary, haphazard touches full of meaning.

Jamie James, the Mowachaht/Muchalaht fisheries manager, quietly established a strong bond with Luna. Jamie's natural gentleness and patience apparently appealed to Luna, and the little whale seemed most relaxed when Jamie was around.

Ed Thorburn, caught between his sympathy for Luna's apparent loneliness and the scientists who said the whale should be left alone for his own good, worked hard to try to keep people and Luna apart, often in vain.

Eugene Amos, a member of the Mowachaht/Muchalaht First Nations, had a way of laughing even when he was serious. During the First Nations action against Luna's capture, he wielded a paddle as effectively as his carving blade.

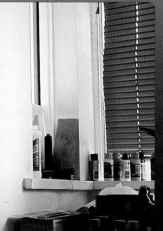

Sandy Bohn, a resident of Gold River, was charged with a crime called "disturbing a whale" when she petted Luna at the dock. She believed Luna needed the attention. Although the potential fine was as much as $100,000, the judge fined her $100, which she called "the best hundred dollars I ever spent."

PUBLIC NOTICE

It is illegal to disturb any marine mammal in Canada (Section 7, Marine Mammal Regulations). Disturbance includes attempting to attract, touch, feed or throw objects at any mammal. Violators face potential fines of up to $100,000

Although Luna appears to wear a grin as he plays, orcas' faces are so thick with blubber that they are not expressive. But to many scientists and other people, orcas appear able to both experience emotions and perceive them in others as part of their fundamentally social lives.

Luna stayed with the canoes all the way back to the launching ramp, much farther into shallow water than he usually went. Finally, he turned gracefully away into the depths. His white patches seemed to dissolve in the darkening water, the last light going out of the day.

Ed Thorburn got out and walked up the dock, shaking hands with some of the men and women. He stopped to ask me to please make a copy for him of what we had filmed. That meant a lot, he said.

The men and women in the canoes unloaded paddles and life jackets slowly, as if still transfixed by the experience. One of the women came walking up the ramp with a child. I overheard her say, "You will remember this all the rest of your life." She wasn't telling him what to do; she was telling him what she knew.

Most of the people got out of the canoes and walked up the ramp to the shore. But Mike Maquinna and one other man, whose name was Kelly John, remained sitting in the back of one of the canoes. Mike was wearing his trademark New York Yankees baseball cap.

Kelly John brushed at his eyes for a moment. Mike just sat there, elbows on his knees, looking straight ahead, his large face impassive. Kelly got up and started to get ready to leave the canoe. Mike stayed where he was sitting. Kelly gave Mike an affectionate pat on his back and waited for him.

After Mike finally left the canoe and walked up to the road, the group gradually reassembled in a small cluster at the top of the launching ramp. Two of them brought hand drums. They started to sing again.

There were fewer than twenty people, including five kids who hung around the edges. I recognized Jerry Jack, a large man leaning on a paddle, the guy who had talked to Ambrose Maquinna about coming back as a *kakawin*. Eugene Amos was there, with flowing salt-and-pepper hair and goatee. Mike Maquinna came up from the boat and sat on a log near Eugene. Mike slapped his knee softly along with the beat of the drum, but he didn't join in the singing.

The high overcast started to shred away in the drying air. A little breeze picked up, and a few sparks of late sunlight fluttered into the brightening evening. Against the towering mountains behind, this group of family and friends looked like a tiny remnant of an ancient group that had lived here once in abundance, now clustered together for bare survival, singing ancient songs. They were oddly like L Pod, Luna's family. The whales, too, were a tiny remnant of an ancient greatness, a family of survivors that had been decimated by captures and killings, poisoned by debris humans have fed to their world as waste, scarred by sonar, starved by the fading of the salmon, still singing songs to the past.

I was not sure how all this fit the story that I would soon be wrapping up, except in symbolic ways. Watching the Mowachaht/Muchalaht people here, less than half a mile from the industrial operation that would soon scoop Luna up and carry him away, I realized that it was impossible for these few to do anything to get in the way. No wonder they had taken the chance to honor the whale and their lost chief in their own way with Ed. They had chosen a gentle way to let Luna go.

When they finished singing, Suzanne and I talked to one of the group, a young man with a tiny ponytail, who had led some of the songs.

"I feel all filled up," he said. "Like after a feast."

Late than night, after the day had ebbed out of the sky over Nootka Sound, Lisa Larsson listened to Luna's calls on the hydrophone. He was not calling the same way as he had been the night before.

"For two hours, between ten and twelve, he was making special calls," she told us later. "It was more low-key, more varied. I remember thinking, This is new. It was like he was singing himself."

CHAPTER THIRTY-SEVEN

June 2004

The story of Luna had taken a turn into deeper waters than we had expected when we came here to cover it. I wasn't sure what our editors at *Smithsonian* magazine were going to think about the little "humans helping animals" story that now had turned into something else. I wasn't sure what I could tell them it had become.

Here we had a huge government presence, a tiny group of First Nations, and a community that had been mostly in favor of the move but was not so sure now because the Department didn't seem forthright. Cameron Forbes was irritated by the secrecy about the captivity option, the kind of secret that any community learns to pry out when strangers come to town.

"A lot of people involved with the whale project would stop out here," Cameron said one day at his resort on the sound, "and you just got the sense that it was all smoke and mirrors. There were just too many unanswered questions, and everyone kind of knew that once he went in a net, he was going to SeaWorld or to another form of captivity. So I think even people who would not have minded that just got put off that the government was lying to them and treating people like morons."

On the day before capture day, Suzanne ran into one of the crew members of *Uchuck III*.

"I hope somebody has the balls," he said, "to cut the net."

The actual capture was not expected to take long. Luna had practically caught himself in the net pen already, playing around it while it was being built. Nobody thought it was going to be difficult for Ed to lead him inside. Then, once Luna was locked in the pen, which we expected would take just a few hours, Luna would be kept there for several days for blood tests to make sure he wasn't carrying a disease back to his family. He would then be hoisted in the truck and carried south. The journalists would go away after he was caught and would then come back for the truck ride and his release into southern waters.

Our plan was to stay around watching, wherever Luna was, even if we had to sit on that hillside for days. We'd then follow the truck and wait for Luna's release to L Pod.

Our whole article was still built around that moment of wonderful reunion that was going to be its culmination. But now, like so many people here, we had doubts that it would ever happen. We weren't even sure that what the Department announced about the process was completely true.

About all we knew for sure about this story was that Luna was an extraordinary character, driven by what looked like a hunger for social contact, and that when he directed that hunger toward humans, people responded with strong emotions of their own but disagreed fundamentally about what it all meant, why it was happening, and what should be done about Luna.

So all Suzanne and I could do was to follow this story through to whatever happened in the next few days. To us, now, it looked less like it would end with a great moment in the ocean and more like it would end with a sad one in an aquarium. But we'd be here for either.

The Mowachaht/Muchalaht people had a barbecue that night down by the water. They slow-barbecued salmon split open on wooden frames planted in the ground next to bonfires. A group of men stood in a circle, wearing shorts, T-shirts, and baseball caps, banging on hand drums and singing. The air was full of the aroma of wood smoke and cooking salmon.

Most North American First Nations groups seem to have a free way with ceremony that takes some things very seriously but some not seriously at all. So when Mike Maquinna started to make a speech, he sat directly in front of a little beige building labeled PAT-TIE'S PORTABLE POTTIES. Nobody seemed to care about that.

The press didn't care about any of it. Most of the reporters didn't seem to be concerned enough about the First Nations factor to come down to the barbecue site. Mike had said nonconfrontational things. He had explained that while the band members sang to Luna from the canoes, they had just been warning him to stay away.

"We told him that he needed to be away from here and go to a safer place," he had told us earlier that day when we got a short press-type interview on camera. "That was yesterday, and today we still see him around. So if he is going to get captured, we also told him that he needs to be strong."

When we had asked Mike if the band was planning to resist the capture, he said the same things to us as he had to everyone else.

"We can't really answer that at this time," he said. "We are not prepared for it. We weren't prepared for it. As time comes closer to it, the anxiety level is up. If there is going to be a move, then our hope after this is that he comes back this way."

That was not exactly confrontational. It did not even hint at road blockades or direct protest, the kinds of things that had taken place in other parts of Canada when First Nations groups had been provoked. So the press, once again, saw that the news day was over. Almost everyone was up at the Ridge for dinner or at their motels getting ready for the capture event that would begin the next morning.

But for us, the barbecue was at least atmosphere, and might be something more.

The atmosphere was pleasant. There was still salmon-scented

smoke in the air as Mike started talking to his little group. At first, he just sat in his chair in front of Pattie's Potty and began to speak.

"We have two canoes," he said. "We're going to do the same thing as yesterday, give other people a chance to go out tonight. But tomorrow we are going to need the men."

Most of the people at the barbecue, perhaps as many as fifty, had gathered around.

"They are going to have to be strong out there. Be tough." A long pause. He looked around. "You can either camp here or be here at six in the morning. Be out on the water."

He stayed sitting. He paused for a long time. Twenty seconds. Thirty seconds. It seemed that he had finished. He looked around again. A few people began to talk quietly. He seemed to be grappling with his own mind, looking hard at individuals or just into space. Ambrose, his father, had been beloved, but Mike was not seen the same way. He did not speak the ancient language. He was a new generation and had the loyalty from people that came with the position. But did he have the leadership?

He took off his Yankees hat, ran his hand across his hair, shook his head hard, and ran his hand through his hair again. Then he put the cap back on. He was still silent. Finally, after over a minute of silence, he said, "I want you guys to know this." Another ten seconds of silence.

He stood up. His voice got louder.

"We are a people who are very proud. Of who we are, and where we come from. And there are people that are out there who want to do something, to take something away from us that we know belongs here, that has made a choice to be here. And they want to take that away."

Someone came out of Pattie's and went off to the side to listen. Mike looked around at the group.

"When we go out there tonight, and tomorrow," he went on, "you think of yourselves. Be respectful and be mindful of yourselves.

And to the whale. It's not about us. It's not about us here. It's about the whale. Tsu'xiit."

He looked back and forth across the small group. On a chain around his neck he wore a medallion, a small bright image of the original chief Maquinna, the one who, some stories of the time have it, met James Cook in 1778. That chief had been friendly then, but later in that history, once the trade in sea otter fur became intense and sometimes bitter, Maquinna's people attacked an English ship, killed most of the crew, and took one as a slave. In the image, Chief Maquinna wore a conical woven-willow hat known here as a "Maquinna hat."

"It's not games anymore," Mike said. "Be serious. And be respectful. All this time, I have been answering questions from these media people: What are you going to do? Are you going to confront them?"

He looked around the group. There were a couple of kids playing in the background, but everyone else was listening.

"That's all they're looking for," he said. "Some kind of confrontation, between us and them. They are trying to make this about us. It is not us. It is Tsu'xiit, the whale."

He stood, taking in the group, the men in their shorts and baseball caps, the women in slacks and jeans and T-shirts, the children playing. It was such a small group that he could single out each one and look in his or her face. It seemed that he might say something more. But he didn't.

He nodded to Jerry Jack, who started to organize people to go out in the canoes in the twilight and sing to Luna. Mike Maquinna sat down, folded his hands in front of him, and stared ahead of him at the ground. People moved around him, but they left him alone. Finally, someone brought over his young grandson. Mike held the little boy in his arms as the people walked past to go and see Luna.

The sun moved off the mountains and the inlet grew still. The canoes went out on the water, and again the Mowachaht/ Muchalaht people said to Luna, "Do not stay here. Go to a safer place."

CHAPTER THIRTY-EIGHT

June 2004

It was June 16, the day of capture. As the morning brightened, a cool wind came down the canyons from the mountains and swept the calm off the face of Nootka Sound.

Suzanne and I were up early that morning and went right to the docks. At 7:00 A.M., things seemed completely asleep. We got in our little red Zodiac with Max and Maple and headed over to the hill where Lisa's monitoring station was. Suzanne had water and lunch, and together we took one load of stuff up the hill to the tent. I left her and the dogs there to watch and went back to the docks to see what else was going on.

Not much was expected yet. The previous day, Clint Wright had told a press gathering that it would probably not be an early start. First, he said, they would orient some of the people who were arriving that night to the net pen.

"Then we'll start probably leading him around, and just see how he reacts." He had been asked what the chances of success were. He had laughed. He wouldn't give odds on how things would work out after Luna was released, but, he said, "In terms of getting him into the pen, I would say ninety-nine percent."

"How will you find him tomorrow?" someone had asked. Clint had laughed. After all the time Luna had spent playing with the people who had been building the pens, this did not seem difficult. "Hopefully," Clint said, "he'll find us."

So the press didn't rush down to the dock that morning. They waited in the breakfast room at the Ridge motel or down by their satellite trucks for an announcement that the capture process had begun.

Given how quiet things were, I planned to go back up to town and fill the boat's portable gas tank, which was low.

But then I looked out on the water again.

Uh-oh.

I was wrong about the morning. I was wrong about having time to get fuel. I had been wrong two nights before when I had thought the Mowachaht/Muchalaht people were having a farewell ceremony. They had not been saying good-bye to Luna. They had been saying hello.

When the sun climbed over the mountains to shine full on Nootka Sound that morning, it did not find Ed Thorburn leading Luna into the pen. It found two canoes loaded with First Nations men and women, paddling west. And the little orca, their symbol of truth and justice in the sea, was going with them. When I looked out there, they were already in the distance.

I ran down to where our boat was moored, put my uncomfortably light gas tank and camera in the boat, and headed out toward the canoes.

What on earth was going to happen now? This wasn't exactly a confrontation, but it was not what anyone had expected. And I had a personal worry. I had to follow this, but if it went on for a while, my boat would run out of gas.

By 8:30, I was even with the canoes. They were rafted together, in a kind of makeshift catamaran, very solid in the water. Luna was right there, his black fin popping up right next to first one side of the canoes and then the other.

The First Nations' fisheries patrol boat was there, too. It was called *Wi-hut-suh-nup*. It was carrying a French-Canadian film crew and other photographers. The Department had told the press to maintain a minimum of one hundred meters away from Luna at all times, but *Wi-hut-suh-nup* was right next to the canoes, and all the cameras were running.

I approached this little procession, but when I got close, Luna left the canoes and came zipping over to see me. He gave me a blast of fishy breath and a contemplative eyeball. That wasn't good. I did not want to be a participant in this newsy moment. So I turned the boat and moved farther away, and Luna went back to the canoes.

The east wind blew. The men in the canoes reached down into the red-painted belly of one of the canoes and pulled out a sail made of a green tarp attached to five horizontal stays. When they unfurled it, their canoes looked like a Chinese junk.

The sail filled with the east wind and drove the canoe to the west, past a forested hump of rock called Victor Island. I pulled the boat up to the rocks there, set up a tripod on the rocks, and filmed the canoes and their entourage sailing past.

Things happened slowly, but nothing seemed slow. The air around the canoes and the little tin boat was electric. Nobody knew what was going to happen when the Department came out and noticed that its whale was gone.

As the morning wore on, Ed did not appear. Suzanne, up on the hill where the action was not, did not feel electricity. It was the Hill of Boredom. She watched the net pen, and occasionally something happened. A jet boat moved into the open net gate, then was hoisted out of the water by a crane. Then it was put back in the water by the crane. Ed Thorburn's boat came out and supervised the placement of a long line of logs, linked by chain, which blocked off the capture area from the rest of the sound. There were several vehicles on the wharf and about six people.

The sun rose in the sky. Flies buzzed around Suzanne's face. The dogs slept, then got up and came to her for a moment of attention, then curled up and went back to sleep.

Eugene Amos was one of the paddlers that morning.

"The number-one priority was just to keep him away from the pen at that point in time," he told us later. "And somewhere along the line, it dawned on us, that, my God, we are fighting for his freedom! We are fighting for his . . . at the time it seemed like for his very life."

The paddlers had no specific plan to take Luna anywhere.

"The feeling was that we are just going to keep going," Eugene said. "We will see where we are at the end of the day. I think that one of the objectives was to introduce him to parts of our Mowachaht/ Muchalaht territory."

The east wind died and the daily inflow from the ocean began. The men in the canoes put down the sail and went back to their paddles. My boat's gas supply was getting lower. I wished I had a sail.

Then an odd thing happened.

As the little group moved into the Mooyah Bay area, Luna, who had been a relatively calm companion beside the canoes for all these miles, became spectacularly energetic. He started jumping clear out of the water and slapping his tail and pectoral fins. He made huge splashes, and the paddlers cheered.

What was he doing? What was there about this particular piece of geography that seemed so special to him that he appeared to be trying to communicate something about it to the humans to whom he had become so attached for this day? This had been his chosen territory for almost three full years now, the place to which he always returned, and where he often lived exclusively for weeks at a time. It was the closest thing to what we would think of as a home. And now he was doing something different and spectacular, only in this place.

There were no answers to this. But the questions were compelling. He wasn't just going off and jumping elsewhere in Mooyah

Bay. He was doing all this stuff right around the canoes, so it must have had something to do with his connection to the people as well as his connection to the place. But there was no way to know what he meant.

For just a moment, for me, this shifted the feel of this story away from all this complicated human conflict. Luna was expressing something about what this place was to him, and he was expressing it to us. When I thought about it, this seemed to be a reminder that this whole history wasn't ours.

It belonged to him. His actions, his intentions, his determination, you could even say his choices, had driven all the events of the past three years. After all this time, we had lots of ideas about what humans thought about him, but we knew almost nothing about what he thought about himself, except that he needed company.

It was early afternoon. The canoes were heading for Yuquot, the Mowachaht/Muchalaht's ancient home. Another First Nations boat had joined the procession, and I had saved gas by tying up alongside it for a couple of hours as it followed the canoes. But now I had to leave, or I would certainly run out on the way back.

I drove the Zodiac apart from the entourage, then stopped for a moment just to watch the little group of boats move slowly away around the corner of Bligh Island to the west. Luna lifted his tail and gave a little slap. Someone reached out and caressed the top of his head. When I had talked to the French-Canadian reporter earlier, he had said, "I have never seen such a gentle kidnapping."

I turned the Zodiac around and raced back to pluck Suzanne and the dogs off the Hill of Boredom and go back to Gold River. The spectacular image of a young wild orca following the colorful canoes would be all over the world in newspapers and on television tomorrow. But what was the Department going to do now?

CHAPTER THIRTY-NINE

June 2004

What the Department did first was daring and spectacular. Ed Thorburn took Lisa Larsson's hydrophone out of the water so that she couldn't hear Luna's calls.

For some reason, the Department thought Lisa was helping the First Nations. Over the months, Lisa had become our friend, and we knew this wasn't true. But the false theory grew into an idea that Lisa was sitting up on her hilltop with headphones, keeping track not of Luna, but of the comings and goings of Ed's boat. The theory was that she was relaying that information to the First Nations by radio. So Ed went to the dock in the early morning and pulled the hydrophone out of the water.

Lisa was furious. She considered herself a careful scientific worker, and this would interrupt her work of monitoring and recording Luna.

Meanwhile, the person hired to be the band's official videographer had to go back to Seattle. Unexpectedly, Suzanne was signed up to replace him. It happened when several people, including David Wiwchar, the reporter for the First Nations newspaper, realized that there would no longer be someone with a video camera to fill the position. Suzanne volunteered, with the provision that her main purpose would be to provide footage to anyone else in the press who wanted it.

We got up at 6:00 A.M. and I took Suzanne to the capture facility, which she could now get into because of her new position. And I went down to the dock and headed back out in our Zodiac—with enough fuel this time.

The first thing Suzanne did when she got into the wharf where the capture facility was located was try to find out about Lisa's hydrophone.

She got the runaround. No one knew anything about any hydrophones. Suzanne went out on the wharf, where she heard someone at the net say, "I have an hour's worth of sewing." She saw Jeff Foster down on the water by the net pen, wearing a shirt that said DOLPHIN RESCUE TEAM. She asked someone carrying an oxygen tank and an air regulator if he was an underwater guy. He said, "Only if things go south." Someone lowered a camera on a rope into the net pen and kept asking someone else, "Do you see fish?"

Suzanne ran into David Wiwchar, the reporter. The two of them walked down to the floats where the hydrophone had been. It was sitting there in a bucket, still connected to its electronic cables, happily transmitting to Lisa the intimate sounds of two gallons of the sea. They took the hydrophone out of the bucket. They plopped it in the water by the dock. The cable snaked away down into the darkness. They walked away. Luna was back on the air.

That morning had begun early for Ed Thorburn. Footage we saw later showed that at 6:45 A.M., *Rugged Point* had arrived at Yuquot. The two First Nations canoes were tied up at the shoreline, empty. There was also a sailboat in the cove. On the bow of the sailboat, a man was winching up an anchor by hand. Ed drove *Rugged Point* over to the sailboat.

"Good morning!" Ed shouted to the sailor. He sounded like a shy person looking for his dog. "Have you, ah, seen the whale around?"

"No."

There was another sailboat farther out in the mouth of the

sound, and the people on board called Ed on the radio. Luna was with them as they headed out to sea.

But as the sailboat crossed the area where the open ocean narrowed between two points of land, Luna left the sailboat and swam back into the sound.

So Ed put a fender in the water on a rope for Luna to play with and started to lead his old friend back toward the pen, over twenty nautical miles away. But when Ed got to Mooyah Bay on the way back, Luna dropped off his boat in that familiar joining of passages, did some fishing, and didn't seem interested in going any farther.

And the canoes showed up again, towed over from Yuquot by *Wi-hut-suh-nup*.

Until then, there had been no direct confrontation between the Department and the First Nations. But after the kidnapping, things were different. The press had handed a victory, even though it had not been contested, to the Mowachaht/Muchalaht people, and things had changed on Nootka Sound.

"That first day, we knew we were in trouble," Ed said. "So that was when we decided, This is now a totally different story. We had a job to do, and we planned to do it."

But now, with the success of that first day all over newspapers and TV broadcasts in Canada, the Mowachaht/Muchalaht people felt the same way.

"Tsu'xiit is *kakawin*," Eugene Amos told us. "He is the wolf of the sea, and we hold him in the highest regard. Our relationship is very deep, very special. I have a great love for that mammal. I would put my life on the line for his protection. No questions asked. I would do it."

Eugene was in one of the canoes that second morning when they were first towed to Mooyah Bay from Yuquot by *Wi-hut-suh-nup*. The two canoes were still tied together, making a stable but heavy platform. There weren't as many paddlers—whom the men in the canoes called "pullers"—as there had been the day before, but there were enough to keep the canoes moving. The pullers hit the gun-wales of the canoes with their paddles and sang traditional songs, and Luna joined them.

But Ed now had reinforcements. A boat that looked just like his had joined him. With that other boat, Ed approached the two canoes. He used the loudspeakers mounted on the cabin roof over his head.

"Members in the traditional canoes," he said, "we ask you not to interfere with this operation. The traditional canoes: Do not interfere with this operation."

The men in the canoes did not even look at him. A young man in the back, a strong kid of twenty-one named Wayne Lavoie, who was assuming some of the leadership, shouted, "Keep paddling, boys," and began to sing in a voice that carried to the far shore.

On the surface, what the First Nations were doing didn't seem to have a specific strategy. But Mike Maquinna's idea of how to meet the Department's dramatically superior force soon turned out to be clear and planned.

"We had the upper hand right from the start," Mike Maquinna told us later. "Because, first off, we weren't the ones who were wearing the bulletproof vests."

The press did exactly what Mike expected. The big black-and-gray Zodiacs looked so threatening, with their huge outboards, their blocky partial cabins, their radar domes, and their armed and vested men, that some of us started talking about them among ourselves as the "Darth Vader boats." Against them, the old dugout canoes with the men in their bright T-shirts or bare chests made a ragged but appealing underdog.

In other places in Canada, First Nations groups had come across as threatening and dangerous when they blockaded roads or bridges in their confrontations over political issues. But this was not like that. Mike Maquinna seemed determined to maintain that difference.

"The media people were perhaps wanting to get something from us that we were going to be confrontational," he told us later. "But that was not the case. I said to the pullers that all we were doing was practicing our culture, as we had been doing in our history for thousands of years. I told them that if they felt that things were going to get out of hand, or escalate into a confrontation, if they were yelled at or goaded into it, I just told them to sing louder."

So the sound of what was, in fact, confrontation in all but name was just the bark of Ed's loudspeaker and the sound of men's voices singing across the water.

Eugene was in the front of the starboard-side canoe, working just as hard as all the rest, though he was twice the age of most of the other men. He was shirtless and looked scrawny, pulling his paddle hard, his chest shiny with sweat, nodding a greeting to Luna when the little whale came up beside him and blew a spout of mist.

"It is amazing," he said later, "the hours you can put in, or the rush that you get when you're all pumped up and the adrenaline is going. It's just amazing. And it's amazing when we think as one, and work as one, and paddle as one, how powerful we are."

So as the day moved into afternoon in that remote little joining of waters, Ed Thorburn, the man who had been Luna's friend since the beginning, found himself in a fight, which wasn't a fight, over what Luna's life was going to become, and Ed was losing. In mid-afternoon, after Luna had played enthusiastically with every boat he could find in Mooyah Bay, without going anywhere with anyone, Ed called off the fight for the day. The decision had really been Luna's.

CHAPTER FORTY

June 2004

The Department did not continue its operation over the weekend. Marilyn Joyce called it a "temporary stand-down." To Eugene Amos, who always thought about the feel as well as the meaning of words, that word *stand-down,* made him think of the military. "It reminds me of an army in a hostile country," he said, and laughed.

During the long, bright Thursday evening after Luna had decided to stay in Mooyah Bay, Mike Maquinna took Marilyn Joyce out to Yuquot in *First Citizen,* the boat used by Maxi's Water Taxi.

"It was a wonderful experience," Marilyn Joyce told the press the next day, to the whirring sound of many rolled eyeballs; it was difficult to believe that statement mirrored her true thoughts.

When Marilyn came back, somebody had sent a message to the bosses in Ottawa: "A mutually respectful personal relationship between Chief Maquinna and Marilyn Joyce DFO has been developed."

But that wasn't really what Marilyn was feeling. The reality was that Mike told her where he stood, and she got it. She was frank enough with us later.

"I think in a sense," she said, "maybe there was a genuine understanding that I was wanting to look for solutions here. And I think he genuinely really considered all the options. And he came back and he said, 'No, I cannot agree. I have thought about this, and [what] my instinct is telling me is no.' And I said, 'Well, that is fine. I won't ar- gue with you. I won't try to convince you. Your belief is your be- lief.' I think, by that point, the issue was that it had gone too far."

Mike remembers it a little differently, but with the same out- come. He remembered sitting with Marilyn on one of the benches above the gravel beach, which looked out at the north wind, where the breakers rushed up the stones. While they sat there, Mike said something to her that one of his daughters had said to him a few days before.

"We live in a place where our people are used to having bears in the fields and deer walking on our trails," he said to her. "We live in a place where people are used to playing with their kids with eagles flying above us, and a wolf walking on the beach. And a whale in our midst."

As Mike remembered it, Marilyn knew then that he was telling her there would be no agreement.

"She was sorry about what I had said to her, because that was the indication that nature needs to take its course. She was disappointed in that, and her body language showed that. And we didn't discuss it anymore. She put her head down."

That weekend, at Uptown Cappuccino, Remi Charette was all worked up.

"They should leave that whale here! They got mad cow disease. They got mad chicken disease. Now they want to kill the whale!"

Another Gold River friend of ours, who had been strongly in favor of the reunion attempt until she saw the way it was being handled, was disappointed and furious. "I would rather pour cyanide down that poor whale's throat than see him go to an aquarium."

Then Monday came, the twenty-first of June. The stand-down was over.

I stood in the Zodiac, braced by the bow line and the throttle, racing out across still water. It was a lovely morning, but for some reason, that day, that perfect, windless day, filled me with dread that I couldn't place.

Each side in this fight believed that what it was doing was the only way to save Luna. But there was something that didn't connect here. I had a sense of a gap in perceptions and understanding that opened an empty space in my awareness, like a depth of sea into which I could stare as long as I wanted but in which I would never be able to see what mattered.

All this human fighting over Luna seemed narcissistic, self-referential, and overconfident on the part of all of us. What did we really know? There were times that it felt as if we were all children playing with stuffed whale toys on the bed.

When I thought about Luna looking at us, I thought of two things. First, from the experiences of trainers with captive orcas and the stories the stewards told, it seemed evident that Luna could detect and recognize individuals. Second, in spite of Luna's awareness of individuals, it also seemed likely that when Luna looked at us, he would not detect our differences of culture. We'd be individuals to him, but all that other superstructure of our lives would be beyond his view and interest. Those very things that built the conflict between us in which he was the central figure would not matter to him. He wouldn't even see them. What mattered to him about us was something else.

But though the political fight may have been irrelevant to him, in practical terms the conflict mattered to Luna's life. So my dread was a fear that we were all missing the point, and that if we continued to miss it, whatever actions we took could turn out to be folly, and he would be swept away by our mistakes.

But what *was* the point? Clearly, I was missing it, too. My fear was not just that we were missing it but also that maybe it was easily visible and we were making choices that helped us to avoid looking at it. I was scared that maybe the real point of all this was hugely, clearly, obviously visible, if we could only just shift our view.

I wished there was a way to make that shift. Maybe if we could see what mattered to him about us, we could see what should matter to us about him.

Such were the thoughts of a journalist zipping along alone in a little red Zodiac on a flat calm day on Muchalat Inlet in Nootka Sound, heading for a human conflict between Darth Vader boats and red-throated canoes over a black-and-white whale.

But I never found the conflict that day. Nobody found Luna. The whole day was an aimless wandering around for everybody, with patches of fog on the water supplanted in the afternoon by fierce inflow winds. Our whale was elusive.

Not long before almost everybody bagged it and went in for the day, I sat by myself in a misty bay where Luna wasn't. But I hadn't been there more than fifteen minutes when Ed's Darth Vader boat appeared. He had radar, which I didn't have, and he'd seen my echo, which made his eyes narrow and his face more severe.

"What are you doing here?" he said, his voice full of suspicion, the same kind of suspicion that no doubt had led to him pulling Lisa's hydrophones out of the water. Ed was a thoughtful guy, but I now had a clear impression that he believed he was trying to save Luna's life, and once he settled on the position that the capture was necessary, he took it seriously. I think that those who did not share his direction were no longer his friends.

But I was just drifting there in the Zodiac, with my handheld VHF radio resting on my camera bag, scanning automatically through frequencies, listening for action that wasn't happening.

"I'm just sitting here trying to figure out what's going on," I said.

That was the utter truth, on every possible level.

CHAPTER FORTY-ONE

June 2004

At 7:00 A.M. on Tuesday morning, June 22, the early sun hammered on banks of fog and low cloud out near Anderson Point, just west of Mooyah Bay. It made an eerie lightscape of mist, shadows, and dazzling breaks, in which three Darth Vader boats and one canoe maneuvered to get Luna's attention.

In the Mowachaht/Muchalaht canoe, the twenty-one-year-old puller, Wayne Lavoie, filmed the action with a little video camera in his right hand while he held his paddle in his left. On Ed's boat, a crewman filmed Wayne filming him.

Their films recorded a narrow window of blazing sunlight to the southwest, an overcast of dark gray low overhead, and silhouettes of Vader boats and pullers against patches of water that shone and patches that looked as deep as night. In that mixed light, the single canoe moved between two of the Vader boats, with the third Vader boat right behind it.

A man in one of the Vader boats shouted at the pullers, not using the loudspeaker: "If you don't stop now, you will be in violation of the Fisheries Act!" His voice was loud and the boat was very close to the canoe. The fact that he was shouting almost in the pullers' faces was far more provocative than if he had been using the loudspeaker, because it held more personal animosity. But the men in the canoe paid no attention. They didn't even look at him.

In the canoe, Wayne Lavoie shouted, "Keep paddling, boys," and went back to singing and filming. Luna came up beside him, upside down, cruising along with the motion of the canoe.

"Way to be, Tsu'xiit," Wayne shouted. "Way to be, Tsu'xiit."

But there was tension in his voice. It was a moment of intimidation. The three Darth Vader boats were each within a few meters of the canoe. They loomed over the pullers. The armed men looked chilling. In two of the boats, men walked forward to bow lockers and removed small lockboxes, which they took back to their cockpits. The pullers might be excused if they thought that the men were preparing weapons or ammunition.

"They're going to board us, boys," Wayne said. He started to sing again, and the others joined him. But their voices were tight.

"My hands are all shaky," Wayne said to the puller next to him. The picture shot by his video camera wobbled. He said it again. "My hands are all shaky." One of the older men, Sam Johnson, who was sitting in the stern wearing a woven Maquinna hat, said to him, "Just relax. Relax and paddle."

They paddled and they sang. They didn't relax. The three Vader boats crowded in.

Did the fact that the pullers just sang make it impossible for the Darth Vader team to make arrests? Or was it all just bluff anyway?

Either way, nothing happened. The moment passed. The three boats dropped back.

But not long after that, the three Vader boats passed the canoe again, and Luna went over to Ed. The three boats, now roped together, moved off faster than the canoe could follow.

So at a little before 9:00 A.M., as I reached a passage just east of Mooyah Bay in the red Zodiac, the Darth Vader boats were far ahead of the canoe and pulling away.

I put the Zodiac up on the rock shoreline at a place called Kleeptee, where some men were working on a logging camp, and got out with my tripod.

The Vader phalanx came rolling along, and the canoe was so distant behind them that I had to use my telephoto lens just to pick out the shapes of individuals. But then Luna messed things up for Ed. There was a lone boom boat pushing logs around at the Kleeptee log sort, and Luna decided to go over there and play Bruno for a while.

He slipped under the boom sticks into the log pond and trucked around with the boat while it worked, giving an extra push on a log here and there. The three Darth Vader boats waited outside the boom sticks, vapor rising from their idling engines like the smoke of Ed's impatience. Pretty soon, I could see the flash of the paddles in the canoe as it drew closer.

Finally, Ed got the guy driving the boom boat to bring Luna outside the log pond to his boat, and the three Darth Vader boats took off again for Gold River.

While I was at Kleeptee, Suzanne was back at the campground waiting for *Wi-hut-suh-nup* to take her out there herself. Once the confrontations had begun, the Department quickly closed the wharf to her and ended the official First Nations' videographer position. But Suzanne was invited aboard *Wi-hut-suh-nup*.

When *Wi-hut-suh-nup* came to the campground from a crew change, Eugene got off the boat with blood-blistered hands. He laughed and said to Suzanne, "They call me Osama bin Paddlin."

Out on the inlet, Ed and the Darth Vader boats were steaming toward Gold River, but Luna, the most social being on the water that day, took another detour so he could say hello to a prawn-fishing boat called *Sun Dog*.

The canoes went up the port side of the boat, and I went up the starboard side, trying to stay out of the picture. But Ed, coming back to try to pick up Luna again, saw me and yelled at me.

"Michael, you're within five hundred meters!"

"No, I'm not," I said, zipping away. "Not right now."

But the canoe had Luna, and Ed turned his attention from me. The pullers turned the canoe west again, to lead Luna farther from the pen, and went around the rocky edges of another island into a narrower passage that led west to Mooyah Bay.

That familiar inflow wind had picked up and was blowing about twenty-five knots. The canoe faced into it. It was brutal for the pullers, with the whitecaps blowing at them and the Darth Vader boats all over them, trying to get Luna away. But they kept paddling and singing, and Luna stayed with them.

"That was impressive," Ed told us later. "I mean, we really were impressed by their determination. And that was when it solidified to me that they were not going to go away. If this went on for three or four days, would they get tired and go home? Not a chance."

But Ed wasn't going away, either. And then things went spectacularly his way.

The canoes led Luna almost four miles back toward Yuquot. But then Mr. Social Whale took a detour to visit another prawn-fishing boat, around a corner of an island from the canoes. Ed went to the prawn boat and asked it to continue south for a couple of miles, and its skipper said okay. Once the boat had led Luna far enough from the canoe that Ed figured the pullers couldn't see what was going on, he picked Luna up with a fender behind a two-boat Vader phalanx and started back toward Gold River.

He was on his way. He called the command post at the pulp mill.

"I estimated that it would take us three hours to lead him back," he said.

He was wrong. After all this back-and-forth, what the press called a "Tug of Whale," suddenly getting Luna to the capture facility was the simplest thing in the world.

"It took much less time," Ed said. "I could not believe how fast we were going. We sped up a little bit, and Luna kept up. And a little bit more and Luna kept up. We were probably doing ten knots."

The sun shone on Ed, the inflow wind was behind him, the

waves drove him forward, and Luna tucked in behind the boats and rode the wake all the way in. At 2:45 in the afternoon, Lisa looked down from her mountain camp and saw two boats bouncing slowly through the lines of windblown waves, with Luna beside them, coming in. The pen was just a few hundred yards away.

CHAPTER FORTY-TWO

June 2004

I had driven the Zodiac back earlier. After watching what looked like a developing stalemate out in the wind by Mooyah Bay, I had guessed that there wasn't going to be much more news that day, so I came in to give some video to a journalist. Wrong again. Suzanne and I were standing at the dock when we heard a reporter say, "They're here. They're leading him into the pen right now."

We had questions: *What? How? When?* We didn't try to get them answered. We ran to the Zodiac, threw all our stuff in it, and drove over to the base of the hill. After all this, to miss the moment when Luna was actually captured would be bad.

Suzanne set up her tripod on the nearest piece of open ground she could find, then watched and filmed from sea level. I climbed and ran partway up the hill.

The first thing I saw was that the gate of the pen was still open, and Luna wasn't in it. The next thing I saw was that the jet boat was leading him right toward the open gate. I started the camera in a rush, but Luna turned away as he approached the pen.

So I gathered my breath back from the places I had left it in my mad dash up the hill. This was going to take some time.

We settled in and just kept the cameras running. Suzanne was far below, and Lisa was at her camp far above us on the top of the ridge. The three of us, out of touch with one another, watched the unfolding of the final hours of Luna's Nootka Sound adventure in the solitude of our own thoughts.

There was one more little irony here. Though in reality there was no longer any official videographer for the Mowachaht/Muchalaht or anyone, there were now three wholly independent cameras with a perfect view of the events, running continuously on the hillside, filming Luna's capture.

Down on the water near the pens, Clint Wright on the jet boat and Ed in *Rugged Point* gradually got Luna used to the wide opening of the pen. He began to go partway in.

There was finality in the air, both on our hillside and among the members of the First Nations. One canoe was already at the First Nations launching ramp, and the other was towed in, ignominiously scooting past Luna and the pen on a rope, behind *Wi-hut-suh-nup*.

Someone passed the news outside the locked compound. A Canadian media outlet reported on the radio and the Internet that Luna had been captured. Howie Garrett and Susan Berta, of Orca Network, who were anxiously watching the news on the Internet, picked up the report and transmitted it on the Orca Network's Web site.

The word went around. Donna Schneider started to cry. Eugene Amos felt the weight of it all over his body.

"My chest and my heart, everything was really heavy," he said, "and I was trying every which way I could to see if I could pick myself up. But there just didn't seem to be any way at all."

And even among the most ardent advocates of the reunion, there were those familiar mixed feelings—that division of wishes within one's own mind. One of the people who felt that way was Ed Thorburn, who apparently could never escape the power of his own empathy even when it tortured him. As Ed worked to bring Luna into the pen, he found himself thinking about the trauma of the truck ride that Luna was going to be forced to take.

"You know," he told us later, "when you are that involved, when you have that much contact in connection with the whale, I was afraid of what might happen. My biggest concern was having him trust me enough to follow me that long, and into the net pen, and then be stuck in a tank with foam on both sides. When you try and put yourself there, that has got to be a pretty scary situation. It is dark. You don't have any freedom of movement. You're not being heard, and you don't know what's going on.

"That's where I was thinking, If this animal has thought, what must he think of the people that he was trusting?"

Far away, in a small town in northwest Washington State called Anacortes, a man named Brad Hanson climbed into the backseat of a small seaplane. Brad was with the National Marine Fisheries Service in Seattle. He was the guy who was going to put that satellite tag on Luna's fin. He had arranged with a pilot friend to fly in his seaplane to Gold River.

Brad's tagging plan had been criticized by some, but he had spent a great deal of time and effort trying to make it right for Luna. Brad had spent hours testing flow around various shapes of tag enclosures in a wind tunnel, using porpoise models, and designing its position to miss blood vessels. Now he was going to make a cast of Luna's fin so he could make a perfect fit.

When the aircraft left Anacortes, the weather was perfect. They stopped for customs, took off again, and soon picked up the narrow stretch of blue below them that was Nootka Sound. Then the plane started to descend.

Eugene Amos was hanging out near the First Nations campground. "The general mood was dejection," he said later. "Lots of sadness. I guess the terminology was that the assholes got the whale." Then he heard the sound of an aircraft engine.

Brad Hanson was sitting in the back of the plane. As it descended, he could see the whitecaps on the inlet. From the air, he could see everything—all the docks, the pens, the boats guarding the edges of the boom sticks that blocked off the capture area, the boats leading Luna up to the gate of the pen. The air was bumpy.

The pilot brought the plane down, but he wasn't happy with his approach and aborted the landing. He went around and tried again. That didn't work out, either. So he came around a third time, this time at a different angle to the wind.

"I heard that great big whining engine," Eugene said, "and then the plane came in and crashed."

The plane touched the water, bounced up, slid sideways in the air, and slammed into trees and a field that was on Mowachaht/ Muchalaht land.

"Basically, we got blown sideways on landing," Brad Hanson said. "It wasn't a rough landing, I've had worse landings than that in a number of other aircraft in other areas. Essentially, the floats were up almost enough that I thought we were going to slide up onto the grass of the bank, but the left float clipped the bank, which caused us to tip up on the nose."

The small spruce and alder trees on the bank caught the left wing and the plane came to a rest at an angle, tilted up on the tips of the floats and the tip of the left wing. "We just came to a relatively easy stop," Brad said, "compared to what I was thinking at the time."

Gasoline poured out of the wings. People clambered out of the plane. They had crashed on the opposite side of the river from the Gold River docks, in a field owned by the First Nations but mostly used by bears.

On the other side of the river, Eugene and a group of Mowachaht/ Muchalaht pullers ran down to the water, piled into an open tin skiff that looked like a bathtub with an outboard motor, and zipped across the river. They were the first people to get to the wreck.

"And here we are, the guys who were battling to save the whale," Eugene said later. "And we were the first responders."

The group of pullers clambered up the bank, met the passengers, who were shaken but unhurt, and made sure they were okay.

"They looked a little sheepish," Eugene said. "Like, What are you guys doing here? It was kind of a morbidly funny situation. Of course we are going to charge them an exorbitant parking fee."

The Darth Vader boats came barreling over and got everyone back across the river, except for the First Nations pullers, who took the tin bathtub boat back. A few minutes later, Eugene was standing around the dock, talking to a reporter, and he said, "What is it with these people? Couldn't the message be any clearer? Don't play around with Luna. Just leave him be."

Then Luna went into the pen and stayed.

It started the way many of the other lead-in attempts had begun. The jet boat, with Clint Wright in it, tied side by side with Ed Thorburn's *Rugged Point,* moved slowly through the open gate of the net pen. Luna, right behind them, peeled away as the two boats crossed the pen boundary.

But almost immediately, he came back and went straight into the pen with the boats.

This was different. He went all the way into the back of the pen, where the boats were sitting, and just lay there on the surface. From where Suzanne, Lisa, and I watched, he seemed very peaceful, at least as relaxed as any of us had ever seen him. He lay near the surface, his dorsal not moving around much, breathing regularly.

Soon after that, Mike Maquinna gathered his people near a bonfire, just up the slope from the river. He seemed shaken and sad. He wore a T-shirt and shorts, his Yankees hat turned backward, the Maquinna medallion hanging around his neck.

"We have lots to be proud of," he said. Smoke blew across his face from the fire. He clasped his hands together in front of him.

"We have taken on something that is quite strong," he said. "Quite strong." He paused for a long moment, as if to consider the might of the Department and the dimensions of his defeat.

"You guys have a lot to be proud of," he continued. "You have been asked to stand beside a killer whale. You've done your nation proud. Don't let people take that away from you. In your lifetime, you pass it on to your children. You pass it on to your grandchildren, what you've gone through."

He stood there for a long time in silence, looking around at the faces, the same faces he had examined so searchingly just a week before, at the barbecue that preceded that first day, the day they had taken Luna away from the pen and splashed themselves triumphantly all over the newspapers. That was a long time ago. Smoke blew across in front of him again. His shoulders rose and fell.

"I think we owe ourselves a couple of songs to sing," he said. "Loud and proud. We take our paddles. We go down to that government wharf. We bang on that wharf and sing songs. Maybe Tsu'xiit will come again. Maybe he'll hear us again."

But his voice held no hope. People knew: It was stunning that this small band had held off the government of Canada for a week, but that was over.

CHAPTER FORTY-THREE

June 2004

A t the net pen, the gate was not yet closed.
        I found myself holding my breath to keep the camera steady for the lifting of the first layer of the underwater net that would close Luna in. But holding my breath didn't work, because time kept passing and they still didn't lift it.

First, several men, some in wet suits, came down ladders from the dock above and walked gingerly around the edges of the net pen. It looked as if they were being sensitive about a skittish animal, and that made me laugh, in a way, because laughing is hard to do while you're holding your breath. Since everyone knew that Luna actively sought human attention and seemed to revel in energetic activity, tiptoeing seemed silly.

The men stationed themselves on both sides of the opening to the pen. Some of them put on air tanks, masks, and flippers. Others stood braced, apparently ready to pull up the net.

They waited. At the edge of the pen farthest from the gate, Luna relaxed with Ed. But Ed was not relaxed. Why hadn't they pulled up the net already?

"I was willing to kill somebody," he told us later. "That's what I was doing. I was so furious. It was unbelievable. I thought, What the hell, why isn't the net coming up? Why don't we get this thing done? I mean, how many more opportunities were we going to get?"

He watched. It was not his decision. Luna played with a paddle and a pole over the side of the boat. Luna took a breath, then another. His tail moved lazily in the water.

It was 5:38 on the afternoon of June 22. Clint Wright, whose gesture would start the men raising the net, was down on one knee on the back of the jet boat, looking at Luna, who had been in the back of the pen now for about ten minutes. The opportunity was here.

Clint did not give the signal.

Luna turned and swam slowly out of the pen.

And from up on the hill, I heard the sound of distant singing.

What was this? How could this be? What was this place, Hollywood North? From behind the docks on the far side of the port area, where the river emptied into the sound, two canoes emerged, paddles flashing in the late-afternoon sunlight, hoarse voices singing so loudly that I could hear it way up on the hill.

Below, Ed went out of the net pen in his boat and tried to get Luna to follow him back into it. Luna followed several times, but he turned away at the pen's mouth for almost all of them. Twice he went in farther, but he no longer seemed at ease, as he had been that one time. Finally, he scooted out past the wharf. Where was he? Suddenly, it seemed that everyone had lost track of him.

There were now boats everywhere. The Darth Vader boats and the jet boat were moving around inside the big capture area that was behind the line of boom sticks. Outside the capture area were two canoes, *Wi-hut-su-nup,* and the big tin passenger boat from Maxi's Water Taxi. They were joined by the tiny little tin outboard-powered bathtub boat that had carried the pullers to the plane crash. It was being driven by a Mowachaht/Muchalaht guy named Rudy Dick, who had brought two friends with him. He drove it fast and wildly in the steep chop from the inflow wind. At any moment, I thought, it would capsize.

No one was going fast except the bathtub, and no one was going in a straight line, particularly the bathtub. Where was Luna?

I could hear motors, singing, wind, and an odd clanking noise. That came from the two passengers in the tin bathtub, who were banging on the bottom with the handle-ends of oars.

Finally, I saw Luna. He wasn't with the canoes or with Ed's boat. He was with the little tin bathtub. Rudy was yelling. He held the throttle in one hand and was waving the other hand around in the air, like a bareback cowboy. His passengers were hammering on the bottom as hard as if they were trying to set rivets. Luna leaped beside them and off they went, spray all around them, straight into the late-afternoon sun. The guys in the bathtub boat must not have been able to see anything in that glare except the flash of driven spray and the blasts of Luna's breath that surrounded them.

Ed went out to try to grab Luna and coax him back again, and it worked for about half a minute. The bathtub, clanking away like a nautical tin drum, curled around and picked Luna up again, as if to say, Hey, leave him alone; he's with the band.

Together, the tin boat and the whale charged off into the waves, with the guys pounding the bottom and Luna slapping his tail and the sun turning spray into gold, and they disappeared out into the dazzling wind of freedom.

Ed got close to them once more that evening, but Luna wasn't about to leave the rhythm section, so Ed turned and roared back and went inside the boom sticks. Ed is not the kind of man who sulks, but it sure looked as if his boat did.

The canoes eventually caught up with the bathtub and its soaked little crew, took over Luna, and led him all the way back to Mooyah Bay.

After Ed abandoned the chase, I sat down on the hillside and had no idea what to think. It had been a day full of energy, and now everything below me—all those buildings, the idling Darth Vader boats, the sterile net pen, the silent pulp mill, the pond full of logs— seemed to have lost all that energy with the departure of the little whale.

It gradually seeped into my mind that this crazy political fight was certainly unusual, but it was not the most special thing that had happened on this day. After all, there are crazy political fights among humans every day all over the world. But where else in the world could you see a wild whale take all day and swim something like fifty nautical miles just to spend his time with human beings?

We didn't think this was extraordinary, because we were used to it. But it was.

CHAPTER FORTY-FOUR

June 2004

The political fight escalated. On Thursday, large fishing boats came into Nootka Sound from a nearby First Nations fishing community, and on Friday, Jerry Jack took his own boat to Mooyah Bay and had a profane shouting match with one of the Darth Vader boats. And Luna didn't choose to leave Mooyah Bay.

This seemed to be the beginning of a long haul that was just going to get tougher over the next days. Then, on Friday, June 25, as I headed in to Gold River when the Darth Vader boats had given up for yet another day, Suzanne called me on our own little walkie-talkies, which had a range of about five miles.

"Hurry up," she said, sounding uncharacteristically worried. "They're threatening to arrest Lisa!"

What the hell was this? They didn't arrest Jerry Jack for directly confronting them, and now they were going to arrest *Lisa*?

I pulled up to the base of Lisa's hill. Suzanne was there, helping Lisa pack. Keith Wood was on his way from *Anon*. Apparently, Ed Thorburn had decided that Lisa was interfering with the capture because she could see everything from up there, and again he thought she was giving information to the enemy. He persuaded the owner of the mill, which owned the land, to suddenly declare that she was trespassing.

"We heard radio chatter," Ed told us. The chatter was between a voice that sounded like Lisa's and the First Nations' camp. "And so we felt she had a perfect spotting area. She was right above us, so anything we did was under that scrutiny."

The accusations were ludicrous. Lisa did not have a significant relationship with the First Nations, and she had always supported the reunion, though she didn't like the idea of the bolted satellite tag. I had been scanning frequencies on my VHF handheld most of the time every day and had never heard Lisa on it once. Was it possible that the Fisheries officers had confused her voice with the voice of the First Nations woman I had frequently heard talking on the radio from the launching-ramp office?

The only other thing we could think of was more of a conspiracy theory. Was this just an excuse to get Lisa off the mountain because, since they didn't seem to be aware of our presence on the hill, they thought she was the only independent person up there and they were planning to do something with Luna that they didn't want anyone to see?

That was far-fetched, but so was threatening her with arrest at all.

But whatever the reason, Lisa had been targeted, and we had to get her out of there in a hurry. Ed had set a deadline of 3:00 P.M. for her to be off the hill, and that was past. So Lisa, Suzanne, and Keith Wood clambered up and down that hill, carrying her tent and other gear, sweating and seething.

Why would Ed pick on the most vulnerable person around, a young woman working alone on a hill, making daily logs and recordings and endless observations, trying to do the only serious science with Luna that anyone had done since Rachael Griffin was here? Why would he flex his muscles this way, at someone so innocent and so ill-prepared to resist?

Finally, one of Lisa's friends from the *Uchuck III* crew, a big-hearted guy named Bill Mather, Fred's brother and one of the most helpful people I've ever known, came over to pick up Lisa and her stuff in an aluminum skiff that the crew called *Tinchuck*.

And then things changed again on Nootka Sound.

Suzanne and I met Bill partway up the steep hillside as we were carrying some of Lisa's stuff down. Bill climbed up to us and grinned. He looked at us over the top of his glasses in an amused way that we had learned was characteristic.

"It's over," he said.

Huh? What's over?

"They called it off."

Huh? What?

"DFO. They're done. They're going to pack up and go away."

We all piled into our various boats and rushed over to the public docks. On the upper dock, a small crowd had gathered around David Wiwchar, the reporter from the First Nations newspaper. He confirmed it. There had been a conference call with Ottawa that afternoon, and the Department had just announced that it was stopping all attempts to capture Luna, not as a short stand-down, but indefinitely.

"Outfoxed and outmaneuvered," one U.S. newspaper reported, "Canadian officials . . . pulled the plug on a floundering effort to capture the 4-year-old killer whale living alone on the west side of Vancouver Island."

We filmed the Mowachaht/Muchalaht people singing songs, and we filmed Mike Maquinna making speeches. "There are no winners or losers. There has been an education here."

"We did it," Jerry Jack said to a cheering crowd. There were winners and losers to him. This was raw victory. "We just did it with some water, junk food, and baloney sandwiches."

"The whale is symbolic of anyone who has battled for justice,"

Eugene Amos said, as always searching for the meaning. "Hooray for manpower! We outlasted the engines."

The story we had come here to cover was now over. It had ended in a very unexpected way, but it was over. We could write the article now, with a beginning, middle, and end, and people would find it interesting.

But we couldn't leave.

The canoes had been parked and the paddles were put away. The net pen was taken apart and shipped out. Ed Thorburn no longer went out to Mooyah Bay to pick up Luna and try to bring him to Gold River. The Department said something about further negotiations, and someone there mentioned possibly discussing another reunion attempt after the big potlatch scheduled for late 2005, but no plans were made. The bathtub boat did not make its clanging music again. Eugene Amos went back to making carvings of *kakawin*. No one was singing on the water.

The human fight was over. Someone had won and someone had lost.

But what was going to happen to Luna?

Part Three

~~~~~

DANCING IN THE SKY
WITH STARS

CHAPTER FORTY-FIVE

August 2004

It was early August. We drove out to Mooyah Bay in the Zodiac and sat on a beach of dark rocks, looking out across Mooyah Bay. The day was warm, and the water and sky were both a rain-washed blue. Everything was still except for a lapping on the stones. Luna was far out in the bay, by himself. Every once in a while, we could see him come up and breathe, but he was too far away to hear. The blue of the sky reminded me of the painting my father started but never finished that was going to be of the scene of my daughter's wedding.

My father had died in July. At the time, we were still in Gold River, tying up loose ends, except that we were finding out that real ends were hard to find, much less to tie up. We were interviewing Eugene Amos that day and received a message that my father had a slight fever.

Nothing to worry about, they said. But that told me it was time to get down there. This was the notice of change that I had feared and expected, the last stage in the long decline that had already taken most of him. So we left Gold River that afternoon to head for California.

The next call reached us an hour and a half down the road, as soon as we got into cell-phone range near the city of Campbell River. My father had gone to sleep in the afternoon and had not awakened.

The last, almost imperceptible remaining part of the man whom I had learned to love without reservation had evaporated away like the last water on his final painting, to become a part of the everlasting breath of the world. I would breathe him in now every day, and would look at the paintings he had left behind, and I would learn, with that love that will last as long as I do, to pay attention to the world of beauty with his eyes.

We did not return to Gold River for a month. But not much happened while we were gone. The Department had backed away and didn't talk about a reunion anymore, but it went back to trying to prevent Luna from having contact with people.

To the people of Nootka Sound who had loved Luna for a long time, this was another layer of cruelty.

"You just know that he must have had that feeling: 'What did I do wrong?'" said Paul Laviolette. "How would you get away from it? All of a sudden he has been ostracized. And you could feel that feeling: 'Why does everyone hate me?'"

Donna Schneider was just as forthright as ever: "I'm sure we confused the crap out of that poor guy."

The next time Luna was in the news, he had turned into a bad whale.

It happened out at Mooyah Bay. A sailboat called *Cat's Paw II* sailed in off the ocean into Nootka Sound, made its way up into Mooyah Bay, and then, the skipper said, was suddenly attacked.

"The whale came out of nowhere," he told a CBC reporter later. "We didn't know he was there. He just suddenly appeared in front of the boat, came right around the back, hit the back of the steering, and disabled the boat immediately."

The skipper, a man named Greg Middleton, described a disturbing attack in which he was afraid that his boat might sink.

"It was terrifying," he said. "I'm trying to be the good responsible skipper and take care of the safety of people first, then my boat, and then minimize the damage to the insurance company, and it was terrifying."

Luna had disabled sailboats' rudders before. He seemed to like to push on anything that could move, and sailboat rudders are not designed to be pushed sideways by a whale. But the aggressiveness that Greg Middleton described to reporters and later in an article for a magazine was foreign to most of the people on Nootka Sound who had experienced Luna's attentions, including us.

It turned out that Greg Middleton was a former reporter for a Vancouver tabloid newspaper. Among the stories he had written was a sensationalized article about urban coyotes, with the headline COYOTE INVASION SPARKS FEARS FOR KIDS' SAFETY.

After that, a columnist for the *Vancouver Sun* named Craig McInnes seemed to think that the public should now question the respect for orcas that research into their intelligence and culture had generated over the previous three decades.

"If Luna were a bear," he wrote in his first sentence, "he would have been shot and killed long ago." His essay went on to hope that Luna's "dangerous behaviour" would persuade people to swing their perceptions away from thinking of resident orcas as "docile, even fragile creatures that graze contentedly on salmon, while maintaining a lifelong commitment to their families."

He seemed to prefer a different image, one of orcas as "the most efficient killing machines on the planet, capable of hunting in bloodthirsty packs to bring down the largest creatures in the ocean." He also implied that guidelines to keep whale-watching boats away from killer whales might be important to protect "bite-sized tourists" as well as to give the whales room.

The Department did nothing to rebut the breathless fearmongering. In fact, it helped it along. After Middleton's furious article and television appearances, the Department put out a notice to mariners on the radio that was all warning and no explanation.

But that wasn't the worst of it. Greg Middleton wrote something in his yachting magazine article that fit our most cynical fears.

"I am told," he wrote, apparently describing discussions with people at the Department, "that it will take a 'serious incident' before they will consider the next options."

If that was what the Department was doing, it was disturbingly amoral. Waiting for an accident was using either Luna's pain or a human tragedy as a strictly political lever. Rather than actively looking for a benign solution that reflected Luna's own approach to humans, the Department appeared to want to step back until something shocking happened that would allow it to treat Luna like a dangerous bear.

"I think they're just waiting for Luna to force their hand," Cameron Forbes said. "I don't know how far it has to go. Are they just waiting for him to flip a boat, or to sink a boat, like a near miss? I think that would give him his walking papers. It would not be a net pen this time. They would lasso him, drag him, and he's gone."

CHAPTER FORTY-SIX

October 2004

That October, it sometimes seemed that the sky unloaded all the moisture it had gathered in the heat of summer all at once. Nootka Sound became a shrouded place where you wouldn't even think of mountains if you didn't know they were there. In this kind of rain, a downpour can seem eternal after only a couple of hours, and this one went on for days.

There was another gillnet fishery going on in the sound. It was scheduled for several days. Luna had been out there playing with the boats, and because they had rudders almost as fragile as sailboats, he had damaged at least three of them and made more enemies. This couldn't keep happening. We had already been told by a Department sharpshooter we knew that he had been chosen to do the job.

In the cool, wet morning, the inlet was absolutely still under the deluge. A huge storm was going on, but it was entirely vertical. The weather didn't blow. It just fell. It was as if the entire atmosphere was hammered into submission by the gravity of the rain.

Suzanne went down to the floating docks and got on *Wi-hut-suh-nup*. The First Nations had been given funds by the Department to do sporadic Luna stewardship, and on this day Jamie James, the Mowachaht/Muchalaht fisheries manager, was taking *Wi-hut-suh-nup* out to meet Luna. Ed Thorburn was one of the few Department officials who were not passive about Luna right now, and in this critical moment during the gillnet fishery, Jamie had an understanding with Ed that was like what Chantelle and Rachael had when Luna started playing with the seaplanes: Do whatever it takes to keep him away from those fishing boats.

Suzanne had gone along to watch what was happening. The rain matched her mood. There was a heavy storm in Luna's life. He was in serious trouble.

For the past two months, we had been working on how to stay up in Gold River to continue to follow the story of Luna. Our work for *Smithsonian* magazine was done; the story would be published that November. So I also took on a major assignment for *National Geographic* magazine. While Suzanne divided her time between working on our house and going to Gold River to find out how Luna was doing, I traveled in Denmark, Germany, and Great Britain, looking at new energy sources—windmills, solar panels, and a giant structure where scientists used high-speed cameras to watch split-second bursts of something close to fusion.

It was a refreshing thing to do after the political craziness of the past months, but I couldn't help thinking that we were closer to the edge of the unknown when we tried to comprehend the longings of a whale out on Nootka Sound than I was in a building full of nuclear scientists on the plains outside London.

For Suzanne, this day was not about exploration. It was about hoping that Jamie would figure out how to keep Luna out of trouble.

The little tin boat zipped across flat water plastered with rain to a logging camp across from the Gold River docks. The camp was in a bay called Jacklah. Just outside the log sort, Luna was hunting fish. His small black fin popped up regularly under a plume of breath after dives of a minute or a minute and a half.

Some of the time, he followed a tug that was working among the logs, occasionally he pushed a log, sometimes he spyhopped to look around, and often he would just lie on his side with one pec fin in the air, gently waving it like a flag or a greeting, as the tug went about its slow, grinding work.

But when the tug moved from one location to another, it picked up speed, and Suzanne saw an amazing thing.

The tug roared along, with a huge wave foaming at its bow, going ten or twelve knots, a very high speed for that kind of boat. And at the bow, immersed in all that moving foam, Luna was lying straight out in front of it, his dorsal upright just in front of the foam, with his tail braced against the tug's bow. He was completely in control, riding the boat's energy forward.

As the tug moved along, a huge fan of water arched into the air from Luna's head as he pushed his nose just far enough down into the swift water to peel a thin sheet of water off the surface and let the energy of his movement cast it into the air above him. It was an astonishing feat of balance and control, but he did it almost casually, and then broke away.

After that, he went out salmon hunting again. Then, apparently full of fish, he sneaked over to *Wi-hut-suh-nup. Poof!* Stealth Whale. He came up alongside the boat on the port side.

"He likes to get right up against the boat," Jamie told Suzanne, "and put his blowhole against the boat and blow as hard as he can."

Jamie is a slender, friendly man with a dark goatee and an almost continuous look of wry amusement on his face. Every meeting with Luna seemed to delight him.

At first when Luna came over that day, he started making raspberry noises with his blowhole. But then he came over with a piece of cedar bark sticking out of the side of his mouth and gave a long warbling whistle beside the boat.

Jamie couldn't resist that. He leaned over the side, tapped a few times on the boat, and put his hand out.

"All right," he said. "What've you got for me today?"

Luna came up very slowly, turned on his side, and looked up at

Jamie. Jamie just stood there looking at him. Luna went back down and came up with the piece of bark hanging out of his mouth again.

Jamie grabbed it. It came out of Luna's mouth. Luna came right back up with his mouth open, and Jamie put the stick back in. Luna went down in the water and came up with his mouth partway open and the stick just resting on his tongue, but as Jamie reached for the stick, Luna closed his mouth and moved the stick just a few inches out of Jamie's reach. Jamie laughed. Luna made a buzzing sound with his blowhole and a whistle with his internal sound chambers at the same time and let Jamie grab the stick. Then he pulled on it and gave a long, loud whistle. Jamie laughed. He whistled back. Then Luna whistled back at Jamie. It sounded almost exactly like what Jamie had done.

Suzanne watched in silence. This was not a casual thing. This was a relationship. This was two-way playfulness and trust. There was no shared language here, but there was communication.

"It's hard to describe the feeling that Luna brings to me," Suzanne wrote in her diary that night. "After all the indoctrination, it still feels a bit wrong to look him in the eye. I do, ultimately, want him to be back with his pod. But when I see him in the distance, it's like I am a teenager, staring at a boy across the dance floor, hoping he'll notice me and come over, but then when he actually does, I think, Uh-oh, now what do I do? I am hopelessly in love, but I can't dance with you because I am a horrible dancer, or some other reason that I can't tell him. That's how I feel with Luna, except it's more complex."

That day and for the last few days of the gillnet season, Jamie stayed around Luna and played with him when he came to the boat, and Suzanne took her cameras and her complex love out on the water each time Jamie went. Throughout that period, trying to be true to all the conversations she'd had with Lisa about not indulging our own needs to the detriment of Luna, she never touched him, and she tried not to look him in the eye.

Later in the week, the sun came out, and for some of the time Luna just rested on his side next to *Wi-hut-suh-nup,* looking up at Jamie, and Jamie leaned over and gently rubbed his side. It was impossible for Suzanne to believe that anything about this relationship was wrong.

On one of those days, Suzanne ran into Bill Mather at the dock. Since Bill was the skipper of a self-propelled barge, *A. G. Ford,* he saw a lot of Luna out at work sites or at night when Luna sometimes came to the dock when *A. G. Ford* was anchored there, so he and Suzanne talked about Luna for a moment.

"I see a definite change in his behavior in the past day or two," Bill said.

Oh no, Suzanne thought. She had heard too much lately about how bad Luna was getting. Now she was going to hear yet another story about how Luna was getting bigger and more dangerous.

"More aggressive?" she asked, trying to be casual about it.

"No," Bill said. "He's more mellow."

For the rest of the gillnet season, no more boats were damaged.

"Luna was a strong character," Jamie told us later. "He learned to survive on his own, you know? He did everything on his own, which is quite amazing. He does want some companionship and stuff like that, and I try to give it to him as much as I can, and let him know, You're safe here. See a friendly face, sort of thing. So I didn't do too much except be his friend. That was my greatest honor."

CHAPTER FORTY-SEVEN

October 2004

On a sunny day on the sound in *Wi-hut-suh-nup,* Suzanne put one of the cameras in a plastic container that was supposed to be leakproof down to thirty feet. She strapped it on the end of a pole that was shorter than thirty feet.

The big technical problem in her filming was seeing what the underwater camera was shooting. So I had rigged up a complicated little arrangement with a cable that led up through a seal in the leakproof bag to a second camera, which, connected to the wire, could be used as a monitor to see what was being filmed underwater.

It was unwieldy, but Suzanne is a coordinated person, usually. So with Luna near the boat, she plunged the contraption into the water, holding the pole in one hand and the monitor camera in the other.

The good news was that, yes, she could see what the underwater camera was seeing. The bad news was that all she could see on the monitor were teeth.

Luna had zipped over to the camera as if it were a magnet, opening his mouth wide and coming right up to the camera underwater. The camera made a small humming sound inside the plastic bag, far too quietly for humans to hear, but apparently Luna picked it up right away.

He didn't chomp. He came up, opened his mouth, and gently massaged the camera in its bag with his mouth and tongue. The bag didn't leak. The camera caught it all.

This wasn't exactly the image of orcas that you see on TV: the breaching, the grace. It was more like something in a dentist's office: the gaping multicolored insides of a killer whale's mouth, staked out around the edges by massive teeth. Nightmare for a salmon, big bucks for the orthodontist: Why, yes, I believe we can do something about that overbite.

During the next trips out in *Wi-hut-suh-nup,* Suzanne became more adept with the camera contraption. She got shots of Luna spyhopping next to Jamie from below, and of him nosing at the outboard's prop, plus plenty of images for the orthodontist.

Then on the last sunny afternoon, Suzanne was busy filming underwater, when something new happened.

The leakproof bag had lived up to its guarantee, and she was pleased with what she was getting. But then Luna turned in the water and twisted over on his back, which gave Suzanne an interesting upside-down shot of his mouth and teeth to go along with the right-side-up ones. Then, using his big tail like a scoop, he threw a huge bucketload of water right on top of Suzanne.

This was not a little mist from his breath or a splash from a pectoral fin. This was a tail-load of water—gallons. Suzanne experienced it much the way a coach experiences a cooler full of water and ice dumped over his head to celebrate victory.

In Suzanne's right hand was the second camera, the one used as a monitor, the one that had been so far from the water that it didn't need a leakproof plastic case.

She looked down at the camera's LCD screen, which served as the monitor. It was dripping. The whole camera was dripping. This did not have all the editing options John Ford's had, so the screen didn't say "Happy Birthday" before it expired. It just slowly folded up its pixels and went dark. The camera would now be useful, once it was dry, as a paperweight.

Luna was near the boat, making loud noises with his blowhole, but Suzanne didn't think it was related to what had happened.

CHAPTER FORTY-EIGHT

November 2004

On a day in November, a headline appeared in the *Victoria Times Colonist*: VICTIM SETS LAW ON LUNA. A man in Gold River had accused Luna of attempted murder.

The alleged victim was Keith Bell, a welder from Gold River. He had had encounters with Luna before in his sailboat and had seen his rudder damaged. But one day when he was driving a skiff with a friend across the inlet toward the Gold River docks, he got scared.

"We were just in front of Victor Island," he told us later, "and we were motoring along as fast as the boat would go, and I saw something in the water. And I think that the whale was lying in the water sleeping. It was just below the surface. And I pulled around it, and then the next thing I know, the front end of the boat is going up. And I turned the boat and went off of him. And then he would lift it up again, and I turned it, and three times he did that. And the guy in the front, he's a two-hundred-and-twenty-pound man and he's hanging on to the gunwales of the boat, scared half to death. It was just a miracle that somehow or other the boat managed to stay on an even keel, that it didn't tip over."

Keith had an odd relationship with Luna. He had been irritated early on in the stewardship program when stewards had told him not to interact with Luna. His family felt that they had seen Luna so often, they had a relationship with him.

"My daughter thinks that he had been so friendly with us in our different boats that he almost knew us," Keith said. "He was so, you know, congenial."

But Keith now seemed to think of the little congenial whale as a wild animal who was inconveniencing humans and should just be killed.

"So I went to the RCMP," he said. "Because if it was a cougar in our backyard, they would have come and shot the cougar."

The Royal Canadian Mounted Police always get their man, but perhaps not their whale. The person Keith eventually talked to said he was sorry but that he didn't think the RCMP had jurisdiction.

"He said that whale doesn't belong to us anyway," Keith told us. "It's an American whale."

The murmur that someone should bring death to Luna began to go around Nootka Sound. A lot of people who cared about Luna thought it was just talk, but some were worried and angry.

"Some people love the whale," Cameron Forbes said, "and the ones that love it don't speak loud enough, I guess. But the other ones: Just give me a gun and I will stick it down his blowhole and get rid of this thing. To hear the amount of people that are willing to go shoot it themselves because it bumped their kicker bracket says something. I'm not even sure what it says, but it is not good."

In the years since he and Catherine called the little whale Patch and went to see him just because he seemed lonely, the two of them had never wavered in their care for Luna.

"I have lost a few customers over discussions on this," Cameron said. "You just look at those people and you go, You know, it is a killer whale. Spend a day with it. If you can spend a day with this thing and don't feel some sort of attachment that is bigger than us, then you're pretty shallow. There is something missing in you."

As the year turned, we weren't sure what we were doing in Gold River. We felt just the way Cameron and Catherine did, but what was our role here? We were shooting footage, but for what? Nobody was interested in something for TV. We were writing a book, but the story itself wasn't clear. We didn't even know what was really happening here ourselves. After my father's death, the air of mortality drifted around me like a northwest winter fog, and I sought meaning everywhere, but I didn't find it.

Yet this determined, intent, and beloved character held us. And we could not bear to see this current of human fickleness moving across Luna's life, taking him to a place it did not seem necessary for him to go.

The choices for Luna's future still seemed to be no choices at all. The Department was not actively seeking creative solutions. So either Luna would be killed by someone who was tired of having him around or he would make a mistake and hurt a human. If that happened, he'd be shot by the Department or forcefully scooped up for an aquarium. When we talked to John Ford about what could be done, he was pessimistic.

"Clearly," he said, "there is going to be a challenge to keep him safe, and keep people safe, and have a happy ending, if he stays in Nootka Sound."

Yet any doors that might open to new ideas about what could be done for Luna if he couldn't or wouldn't get back with his family seemed resoundingly closed and padlocked by the Department. The only options seemed to be captivity or death.

So what were Suzanne and I doing here? If we were just sitting around waiting for a tragedy that would break our hearts, what was the point? Or was there something more than that in the compulsion that held us here, watching? Eugene Amos kept saying that Luna was a teacher. We didn't believe the supernatural part of that. But even if Luna wasn't a spirit sent to Earth to change human hearts, even if he was just a young whale seeking companionship, there still seemed to be something going on here that mattered.

CHAPTER FORTY-NINE

February 2005

The phone rang at about 3:30 in the morning. In my slow awakening, I missed the call.

Oh no! What had happened? Was it my mother? Luna?

Our other cell phone rang. This was a determined caller. We were fully awake now. We got it.

It was Lisa Larsson. Her voice was more excited than I had ever heard it.

"The G's are here!" she said. "The G's are here!"

What was this? It was completely unexpected. Lisa was working as a winter caretaker at one of the fishing lodges in Nootka Sound, and she had a couple of hydrophones in the water to listen to Luna.

Lisa had worked with the Northern Resident orcas for twelve years, recording and analyzing their calls. She was accustomed to waking for whales. But she had never expected that when she awoke to the calls of Northern Resident whales, it would be here. But here they were, whales that spent their summers around the northeast edges of Vancouver Island but normally vanished all winter to places unknown. Now it turned out that one of those places was Nootka Sound.

She recognized the characteristic calls immediately. They were whales from a group that contained several individual pods, but was known collectively as G Clan.

"I had the speaker turned toward the bedroom and I heard this ping," she told us. "And I was like, No! What was that? It must be something. And then I heard another couple, and I was like, Oh my God, it must be whales!"

She was wide awake right away. She got out of her sleeping bag and went to the speaker. The calls started out on a hydrophone at a distant location, then started to come in on one that was near her. Identifying the calls was not difficult.

"Oh, for sure," she said. "I feel like I know them, I've heard them for so many years. I was like, Oh my God, they're here! It was like old friends coming to visit. Oh, I was just so surprised."

The calls came in louder and louder, and she could tell there were quite a few whales and that they were spread out, because while she heard some on the local hydrophone, others were still only coming in on the more distant one.

"I was just really happy to hear them and that it was the G Clan; they have such beautiful calls."

But of course her excitement wasn't just about G Clan. What about Luna? What would he do? These were not the transient whales, the meat eaters that Luna hid from when they came into Nootka Sound. These whales were very similar to the Southern Residents, his own family. Though they were never seen mingling with the Southern Residents, their habits and diet were similar. In this extraordinary situation was there a chance that he'd go with them? We talked with the hushed excitement of hope, as if that slender hope would be helped if we didn't speak about it loudly.

As Lisa sat by the speaker, the G Clan's calls faded away. So she put her sleeping bag on the floor near the radio receiver and lay there in the warmth with her headphones on so she wouldn't miss anything. And then she heard them again, first faint, then stronger.

Now they were being picked up by the hydrophone she had put at Anderson Point, right by Mooyah Bay.

"First they are distant," she said, "and then they are fairly close.

But they are not really close on the hydrophone. So I think they were on the far side of Anderson Point by Bligh Island. Like they were hugging the shore."

Then, through the same hydrophone, she heard Luna.

At first, she thought it was a call from another Northern Resident clan.

"So I hear that one a couple of times until I realize, Oh my God, it sounds like Luna. By then the G Clan's calls are getting faint again and so Luna does his little sound. And then it's quiet and I hear him moving and then he comes close to the hydrophone really quickly."

In the urgent darkness of that amazing night, Luna was near Anderson Point, calling. And other resident orcas were easily within underwater-communication distance, which is believed to be at least ten miles. It may have been the first time in three years that Luna had heard calls of whales that were even close to being like him.

He made more of his characteristic calls, what Lisa called an "*Eee-ah*" call. Then he stopped and seemed to wait. After that, she heard more G Clan calls, but fainter.

"They were definitely hearing each other," she said. "And also he reacted. He made contact. If he just wanted to observe them, he wouldn't have made his calls. And also, to make his call and then be quiet is what they do. They make calls and then listen for a response."

She sat there in the darkness of that early morning, wrapped in her sleeping bag. She was far from any other human being, in a big empty lodge where furniture was covered by sheets and shutters were closed, on the edge of one of the most remote parts of Vancouver Island, in the middle of a winter night, but what she heard was the drama of possible connections. As a chatty crowd of orcas passed by, the little lone orca she had learned to love so well reached out to that passing crowd with his single lost voice cast through the sea.

"So then he keeps doing his sound," she said. "And then it's quiet for a few minutes. Then he repeats it again. And then all is silence."

Suzanne and I rushed around, packing things. As the first light came, we got in the airplane and flew north. At the same time, Jamie James and Roger Dunlop also went out in their Zodiac, and Kip Hedley, the lighthouse keeper at Yuquot, got his binoculars. We all had one goal: to look for G Clan and Luna and see how far apart they were. Or, in that hope that we all had but didn't quite believe was possible, find out if they were together.

But when we got there, the sea stared blankly at us, inscrutable as always. The weather was calm, but the restless swells still cast moving shadows on the water, and distant surf on reefs made us look carefully to be sure it wasn't whales.

It seemed such a long time since we had been out here looking for L Pod, hoping that it would come and fetch its lost child. So much had happened since. Back then, Luna had almost everyone's goodwill and affection. He had done nothing since then except try as hard as he could to regain a little of the human embrace he had been given for those few weeks the previous June.

We had recently met a Gold River couple originally from Poland. Anne, the wife, once lived on forty acres in the British Columbian interior, and one winter she had fed a young deer. She had called the deer "Zipper."

"I know I wasn't supposed to do that," she said. "But I didn't want him to die. Every time I heard coyotes in the night, I couldn't sleep." The deer lived through the winter.

When their daughter, a university student, came to Gold River for Christmas, the three of them went down to the dock on Christmas Eve. They were the only people there. Luna was drifting between boats in still water, the amber lights around the dock shining on his back and lighting the occasional misty burst of his breathing. They wished him a Merry Christmas.

There they were, a family of Polish émigrés, building their new lives in Canada, standing on a lonely dock on Christmas Eve on Nootka Sound, wishing Merry Christmas to a whale. For some reason, when we heard this, it made us happy. It meant something. We weren't sure what it meant, but it was good.

CHAPTER FIFTY

March 2005

The forecast was for an east wind and sunshine. We got down to the dock early. Luna wasn't there, and he had not been seen for days.

It was now March. My *National Geographic* work was finished. We had a check coming that would help keep us in peanut butter and outboard-motor fuel for a few more months.

We went west with the wind up the familiar passageways. We landed in the lee of a little island. The tide was very low, with mussels and oysters and starfish above the waterline, and I climbed up into a baby forest to brace the binoculars on the rough lichen-thickened bark of a tree.

In the distance to the east, there was a boat that looked like a skiff. But my perspective was off, and when I realized it was ten times as far away as I had thought, I recognized the two crane booms of *Uchuck III*. We pulled over to the rocks when it was coming by, and I called the ship on the VHF.

"Come over," Fred Mather said on the radio. We jumped back in the Zodiac and went up next to the big black hull, and Fred slowed down for us. Another of our friends on the crew, Glenn, came to the rail. He was carrying a white paper bundle for us. It had two multiberry muffins in it.

"I was just going to send one," Glenn said, "but Glenda said two."

Glenda was Fred's wife. She was in the galley today because Donna Schneider had the day off.

It was just a little thing, but it felt good. It was a little token that we were becoming part of the community of Nootka Sound, that we had friends out here who would slow their ship to toss us muffins.

I looked up that wall of black paint and at the people along the rail—Glenn and a couple of passengers. The view I had today was Luna's view, the angle from which he had watched people for many years.

When we thought about that little lonely creature out there in his big sea, making the acquaintance of that black rumbling wall, it made me wonder, What kind of familiarity brought him to us humans? After he got to know people, did the eye contact and the waves from the people give him any of that same feeling of belonging and friendship that we had just received with the package of muffins? What was that thing that we shared, deeper than we understood, that goes a very long way back to that ancient past out of which we and whales both grew? What was it that is somehow as fundamental to both of us as the way our blood flows from the heart to the brain and back again?

Glenn tossed us the muffins. We caught the bag and took a tour along the starboard side of the old ship as it picked up speed again. As it built a wake at its bow, we peeled away.

We got over to Anderson Point, and there was a splash back there where we'd come from. Lazily, Luna came across the front of the point, giving us slow glimpses of a black back in the silver water.

Then a little dozer boat came out across the bay from somewhere up Hanna Channel, transferring from one log sort to the one in Mooyah Bay. It growled along like a bulldog across the open water, a powerful little blunt-faced diesel thing. Luna seemed to perk up as it approached.

He was puttering along on his back, and he started flapping his tail on the surface. Then he went over to the dozer boat and accompanied it all the way to the log sort at Mooyah Bay. He went inside the boom sticks and hung out with the boat as it shoved on a large bundle of logs. At one point, the dozer boat shut down, and the guy in it went to the edge of the logs, leaned over, and talked to Luna for a minute or so, as if giving him a muffin. Then the boat driver got back into the dozer boat and drove off again, the young whale working beside him in the maze of fallen forest.

Much later, when we got back to the Gold River docks, Rick and Sheila Millard were there with their boat. We talked about how hard Luna worked to make contact with humans, in spite of the fact that he had no need for anything physical from us at all, not shelter, not food, not transportation, nothing we would think of as concrete. Yet he seemed so dependent on us for something, just for that elusive something that living souls have carved out of the big mystery as necessary: one another. There are some animals that are cats, Rick said, but there are some animals that are humans or whales or dogs, and we need to be together. It's something about the way the blood runs from the heart to the brain and back again.

CHAPTER FIFTY-ONE

May 2005

The big gym at the Mowachaht/Muchalaht village of Tsaxana was full of echoes and flat light. We paid attention to that because we were going to film in there, and in terms of sound and light it was going to be ugly.

That didn't necessarily apply to the message. This was a workshop on what to do about Luna, sponsored by the Mowachaht/ Muchalaht First Nations. There were about as many experts here as there were people in the audience. In fact, there weren't really any spectators at all. Everyone was involved; no one was just a watcher.

Ken Balcomb was there—the guy who had made those proposals to lead Luna home. Kari Koski, who had been so involved with the stewardship, was also there. There was Keith Wood, who had spent so much time in his sailboat looking for L Pod in order to try to give Luna a soft trip home. Paul Spong had come from OrcaLab's island research station far to the northeast. Jamie James was there. So was Roger Dunlop, the First Nations' official biologist, who had been counting otters with Jamie when they'd seen the wolf coming out of the water.

The two outside experts were Toni Frohoff, the biologist who had studied solitary whales and dolphins elsewhere in the world, and Catherine Kinsman, who had the most experience of any of us with those kinds of situations. She ran the Whale Stewardship Project in

Nova Scotia, which was formed to help protect solitary beluga whales who showed up regularly on the east coast between Massachusetts and Newfoundland and seemed to want social contact with people the same way that Luna did.

Eugene Amos was also there, but with tubes in his nose from an oxygen bottle. In the months since he had done all that pulling in the canoes, his heart had started giving him grief. There were others in the audience from the group of pullers: Sam Johnson, who had always worn a woven Maquinna hat in the boat; Wayne Lavoie, the young guy with the booming voice whose hands had shaken when the three Darth Vader boats had tried to intimidate the single canoe; and Rudy Dick, who had driven the tin bathtub boat that rang like a drum. Mike Maquinna came into the room for part of the time. Ray Williams and his wife, Terry, the last residents of Yuquot, came to town by boat and sat through everything.

And in the back of the audience sat Ed Thorburn. Though he described his presence as personal, not official, he was in uniform.

Not many people talked to Ed. It was May 2005, almost a year since the lead-up to the capture attempt had begun, but even now a lot of people, including us, didn't have much to do with Ed. There was still bad feeling across the lines created by the First Nations' resistance, and the chaotic craziness about threatening to arrest Lisa Larsson was still in a lot of minds.

The workshop was long, but the messages that came out of it were simple.

"I really don't know what to do now," Ken Balcomb said, "and I don't know what to recommend." Most of the others agreed, and the only First Nations person to speak during most of the conference, Jamie James, said there wasn't much they could do except enforcement. The two outside experts, who were quickly embraced as colleagues by most of the people in the group, expressed a very clear mandate: Continue to try to keep people and Luna apart.

"It's very hard because we care so deeply about these animals,"

Catherine Kinsman said, standing in front of a slide in a Power-Point presentation that showed a woman riding bareback on a wild beluga. "We'd love to be their playmate, if we could. But we can't. We can't fulfill their needs."

In a brainstorming session after the formal presentations, Kari Koski brought up an idea we'd been thinking about, too: whether the only chance for Luna might be to actually give him intentional controlled interaction, like what Jamie had done, to keep him out of trouble.

"Would it be appropriate to have the time and the place and the boat," she asked, "where you knew you're going to have interaction and you limited what those interactions were to whatever people thought was good for him?"

The reaction from Toni and Catherine was largely negative. Toni thought there might be a place for that kind of approach, what she called "enrichment," particularly using objects that were not obviously human-related.

"My opinion is that there is no justification for intentional human contact from a boat or from land without trying something else first," Toni said. Catherine Kinsman was similarly uncomfortable with the idea.

"The more appetite he gets for that," she said, "he may start doing things, he may be creating a problem. I'm just really cautious about that."

The meeting ended with an informal resolution that the First Nations would pursue funds from the Department to conduct another stewardship operation, focused once again on the effort to keep people and Luna apart, but that the band would also consider leading Luna to the mouth of Nootka Sound to expand his territory.

And there was a lot of discussion of the possibility of designing a nonhuman "playground" for Luna to distract him from boats and people. The playground might include things like an underwater keyboard that Luna could press to get something to happen, like the broadcast of underwater sounds, and tactile stuff like brushes to rub against.

But the most immediate thing was the stewardship, and for us that was discouraging, because we had seen how it had not worked except when the stewards and Jamie had interacted with Luna themselves.

Earlier in the week, Jamie had taken Ken, Toni, Catherine, and Suzanne out on *Wi-hut-suh-nup* to see Luna. The day started out sunny, but soon the weather changed to gray sky and rain. Once they got out to Mooyah Bay, it was another one of those odd moments. The very people who were opposed to interactions went out on the water, stopped, and let Luna come up to their boat. Though no one touched Luna, there he was, trying to make eye contact with everybody. We didn't think the interaction was wrong, and neither did Ken Balcomb. Catherine and Toni did in theory, but they were there. They didn't touch him, and they worked hard not to catch his eye. But how could they possibly turn away?

They now were among the many people who—like Suzanne and me, all the stewards, Donna Schneider and Jamie and pretty much everyone else here who loved Luna—found themselves torn by what they wanted to give Luna and what all the theories and fears told them should not be given.

That night, I was thinking in pictures again, too tired to translate them to words. Since I had begun traveling with a whale, there was something else going on in my head. In the face of Luna's apparent acute consciousness of his own life and the lives of others, I found myself thinking of human language itself as just a clumsy shadow of what is real compared to the intricate mercy and love and sacrifice that the hearts we have been given by life and time can achieve. Here was a creature who seemed to have a complete awareness of life, who used nothing that resembled our language, but who nevertheless could build social relationships that worked. We humans have associated our kind of language with consciousness for a long time. What if consciousness and language, as we understand them, are not linked after all?

In the images of that evening, I could see us humans paddling along in imaginary life jackets at some ocean's perimeter, some kind of drop-off, where the last view of secure land disappears beneath the water we tread, and there is nothing down there but endless depth. We find illusions of solid ground in what we imagine is our superior life of language and reflection, but if we look in the eye of the whale, there is vertigo.

CHAPTER FIFTY-TWO

May 2005

Kari Koski told us a story at dinner the evening after the work-shop. It was about when she and Kristy Zeidner were in Gold River in 2002, at the end of the first year of stewardship. They were staying in that tiny trailer down at the dock, and in the middle of the night, Kari woke up and heard a noise outside.

She put her hand on the edge of the window and lifted herself partway up from her bed, which was actually the dining room table, by the window. At the same time, a small bear put a paw on the window and looked in.

She looked out and the bear looked in, and both recoiled. She fell back to the bed, and the bear fell down to the ground. She then looked out again, and the bear looked in again. They continued looking at each other, inches apart.

In the morning, because Kari and Kristy were worried about the bear coming back and getting into the trailer, they called the RCMP, and an officer came down and set a humane trap, a big barrel on a trailer, with a door that slammed when the bear touched the bait.

The bear got in the trap right away, and Kari and Kristy called the RCMP down to pick it up. According to protocol, the RCMP would relocate it and let it go. But the officers didn't come for quite a while, and during that day a lot of people came around, looked at the bear, and poked at it, doing all the bad things people sometimes do to trapped wild animals.

The RCMP finally came and took the bear away for relocation. But the RCMP officer told Kari afterward that the bear was not relocated. He said that the RCMP officers usually just took the traps away somewhere private and shot the bears. Relocation just moves a problem, he said, so there was no point in it.

The question was whether it was actually more about convenience. Maybe it was more that the RCMP officers didn't want to be bothered driving the trap fifteen miles up a logging road into the woods just to give a bear another chance.

When Kari told the story, we all put our heads down.

People are not good for the planet, Kari said that evening, though I know she doesn't fully believe we are hopeless. She is a cheery person, but she saw the difficult things and was sensitive to the sad choices that we make that eat holes in the beauty of the world. The great thing about Kari, I thought as we said good-bye and she went back to the United States, is that she knows these things we do are choices, not fate.

The day after the workshop, Lisa Larsson was out at Yuquot, helping Keith Wood install a satellite dish. They were working together on something Keith called LunaLive. It connected one of Lisa's hydrophones to the Internet and let the world listen to Luna in real time. This involved using the transmitter that Lisa already had at Anderson Point, where the hydrophone was. Within a week, he had it working, and when Luna was in Mooyah Bay, you could hear him from anywhere in the world.

Now we divided our time between finding people to interview about Luna's history and going out on the sound to watch him. That spring, he spent most of his time at Mooyah Bay, so we spent many days on Anderson Point, sitting there with Max and Maple and our tripods, taking note of what Luna was doing. But there were also frequent days in which we followed him from a distance as he traveled with *Uchuck III* or *A. G. Ford* as the ship or the self-propelled barge made their rounds from logging camp to fish farm with supplies and hardware.

On a sunny day in June, we found Luna dashing around, being Bruno, with a little yellow dozer boat at the Mooyah Bay log sort.

We tied up at the dock at the logging camp and got permission from the camp foreman to hang out there for a while. I left Suzanne on the dock to film and took the Zodiac over to the edge of the boom sticks. I climbed out and stood on one, with my camera on a pole to brace it, and filmed away as Luna played with the dozer boat.

Then Luna disappeared. The dozer boat was still growling around, doing its fierce little bulldog pushing and shoving, but Luna wasn't popping up beside it. I stood there looking around—at the bunkhouse barge, over near the ramp where the skidders dumped loads into the water. No Luna.

Poof! I turned around. There Luna was, right behind me, his nose gently moving our Zodiac. He wasn't Bruno anymore. He was Stealth Whale.

"Um, hi, Luna," I said, thinking, Damn, this isn't good.

Luna started pushing our boat around at the end of the rope I'd tied to the boom stick, moving it back and forth, back and forth. I climbed into the boat, and he pushed me around some more. But we weren't there to give Luna things to play with. We were there to watch him but to avoid him. So I took the boat back to the dock, where Suzanne was, and we pulled the boat right up onto the planks.

There. We were out of his way, as legal as we could get. Go back to your boom boat, Luna. Go be Bruno. Go away. We're not your friends.

But he didn't. He rolled over on his side and looked at me.

262 • The Lost Whale

Well, it wasn't as if I snapped or anything. It was just the most natural thing in the world. Suddenly, all that stuff didn't matter anymore. Leaving the little guy to his loneliness just no longer seemed to be the kind of thing that I would do.

I put my camera facedown on the dock. I kneeled and then lay down on my stomach with my head over the edge of the dock. I looked back at him.

I looked across a short space of water at a face that did not have any flexible skin that could transmit emotion. But nevertheless, his eye did pass on something, indecipherable but strong.

It was like looking over a cliff into time. Whales have been in the sea for fifty million years and have been apart from us on the tree of evolution for longer. Yet we share something.

In that grand ticking void of unimaginable time, I thought, we have traveled, you and I, Luna, and in our blood flows the record of our journey. Our minds cannot read that record, but it informs every hour of our lives.

We have carried it in every breath. Across sea or sand, we have carried it in every choice, every moment of survival, century upon century, millennium after millennium. Sea levels rose, sea levels fell, the ice came and went, and still we have traveled in life, carrying with us only what we must. And now, here at last, you and I know only that it matters; we don't know the story of why.

But this thing we share came to us through every single drama of our unbelievably many lives only because it is necessary. If it had just been optional as we wandered across those deserts or those storms, we would have thrown it aside. In the tumble of time and the ferocity of living, the casual falls away. Nothing we did not require could pass through the stone filter of time: If you don't need it, it's gone. Yet it came with us, you and me and all like us, because we had to have it. It made us who we are because it got us here.

Every day our hearts read the message in the blood and act

upon it, and the message overwhelms us: We do not live alone. We care about one another.

Rain again fell on a flat calm Nootka Sound like a hurricane of gravity. No wind blew, and the rain made a hiss on the water in a million splashes. When you looked low along the water, the edge between the surface and the rain was a silver haze. The mountains faded up into an indefinable dark sky that seemed heavier than the stone.

I was alone. Suzanne hadn't come with me. I stood in our Zodiac with rain-splotched binoculars, looking for Luna at a tug about a quarter of a mile away, where I thought I'd seen him fifteen minutes before. But he wasn't there. I thought I saw a roll of water and a fin behind it, but I was wrong.

He was behind me. I didn't know this. But when he came up and goosed the boat, I knew it with a jolt. Hey, Stealth Whale!

I looked back. There he was: a dark shape, green-brown patches moving below the surface, his white patches seen through thick water, which was colored now by the outflow of Gold River's rain-made flood.

Luna put the leading edge of his dorsal up against the side of the boat, like a longshoreman leaning a shoulder into a load, and gave the boat about five big shoves.

I didn't want this. When he did this, his head was right in front of the outboard leg. If I gunned it, I'd run over him, so I couldn't get away. I looked away from him for a couple of minutes. More pushing.

I was right in front of Gold River. This was not the place to have a Luna encounter. If I was caught, there would be consequences, and it would be easy to be caught here. So I talked to him.

"Hey, Luna," I said. I could feel the emotion in my voice, the tangled confusion of wanting to give welcome but fighting both my need and his. "This isn't fun. It's not fun at all."

He stopped what he was doing. He came up alongside, suddenly peaceful. I was surprised by his abrupt attention.

"Hey, Luna," I said, "I think it would be good if you went off and did something else."

He seemed very calm beside the boat. Then he moved a little and tilted partly sideways, not enough to bring the whole side of his face above the water, but enough to bring up an eye. He made a very short raspberry sound with his blowhole.

And he started to call. It was the same call that I'd heard on Lisa's recordings, the *Eee-ah* call, except that I could hear it directly, from the surface, and it seemed smoother, and quite soft. It was his short call, the one people heard most often on the hydrophones. He called, then called again and again and again, and looked up at me.

What was this? Why had he stopped so soon when I asked him to? It wasn't language he was hearing. Was it my emotion? Could he detect my worry about being caught with him? What were his calls about? Was he asking me for something, as we'd always thought? Or was he offering something?

The rain fell hard, and he moved away from the boat. I started up the motor and left him. I drove the boat hard into the rainstorm of gravity and made the rain sting my face.

Luna has never asked us for anything but friendship, I thought. But we think we know better. Once, trying to keep people away from him was a great idea, an experiment in tough love, to see if the starvation of solitude would push him toward home. But it didn't work, and now it has been four years. Four years! Yet we persist in trying to administer loneliness as if it were a leech.

No history informs us that this arrogance is wisdom, I thought, but we embrace it. No depth of experience tells us that this cruelty is necessary, but we commit it. No science tells us that this pain is truth, but we inflict it.

A great life has come to us, I thought, without guile and without fear, asking for something. Like an inept parent, we have offered him hardware, politics, transportation, medicine, advice, and money. But we haven't offered the one gift he's asked for: companionship. Luna has asked only for the very best of who we are: our kindness, our understanding, our love, and that ability we have to care across the wall that separates individuals—our empathy. But we turn away.

Yet we know the feeling. We, too, cannot live alone. We carried that need with us across time, too. We know that to turn away is to pronounce death.

Surely, I thought, we will never be forgiven—by nature, by life, by ourselves—if we let you suffer just because you are trying to be our friend.

When I got home, my face was raw from the rain. Suzanne and I talked. We had both come to the same place. We were no longer conflicted. We had made a choice.

CHAPTER FIFTY-THREE

July 2005

I n our frustration with what seemed to be a fatal status quo for Luna, we could no longer bear to watch the hurricane we were covering just go by. We stepped into it. If our lives got swept up in its turbulence, that would be a price worth paying. Our empathy for Luna was not wrong. It should not be set aside.

Suzanne and I started writing a proposal for what we thought should happen. We proposed intentional interaction.

The rationale to keep people away from Luna had two different components. The first was based on Toni Frohoff's research and Catherine Kinsman's experience: The more interaction solitary, sociable whales and dolphins had with people, the more likely they were to be injured or killed. The second was the argument that interaction with people would make it more difficult for Luna to have a reunion with his pod.

The second argument was null. Luna wasn't going to get worse. He was fully acclimated to interacting with humans. And there were plenty of arguments against this theory anyway. Springer had managed to reconnect even though her mother had died. If a vegetarian found a starving wolf pup and managed to keep it alive on tofu, spinach, and potatoes, that wouldn't mean that the wolf would never eat meat again.

What about the first argument against interaction, though? That was tough. That was real science that spoke about real danger.

But it was clear that nothing except taking all the boats off Nootka Sound could stop the interaction. Luna was determined, and no matter what the stewards had done, interactions could not be stopped. So if you took that science of doom at its toughest, tragedy was inevitable. But was that pessimism necessary?

Maybe interaction itself was not necessarily the problem. Maybe it was the type of interaction that was the problem. All the interaction that Toni and Catherine had experienced and studied was the same kind of thing that Luna was having in Nootka Sound. It was completely chaotic; it just depended on which boat happened to be going past. Old freighter or fishing boat, kayak or sailboat, they were all part of the mix. And none of the people who were interacting with him had any training in what was safe and useful and what was destructive and dangerous.

What if you could change the nature of the contact? What if you could make it planned, consistent, safe? What if you could have one or two boats that Luna considered his temporary pod?

Was that possible? Certainly. It had already been done. On those few occasions in which the stewards had been given the right to interact intentionally, and when Jamie had been told to keep Luna away from the gillnet boats, Luna had not been difficult to keep out of trouble by using just a single boat, as long as that boat didn't make a habit of ditching him. It was like real friendship as we understand it: It was consistent.

So maybe coming up with a way of interaction that was safer and more helpful for Luna was not impossible.

We wrote the proposal. We went through all the arguments and advocated two things: first, that someone be given a permit to give Luna carefully designed, consistent, intentional interaction to satisfy his needs and keep him away from danger; and second, that while that interaction was given, that same organization should repeatedly lead Luna out to the mouth of Nootka Sound to make it more possible for him to have a reunion with his pod if it came by. If no one else would do this, we said, we would organize and administer this operation, but we hoped that it would be a cooperative effort with the First Nations, scientists, and the Department.

We sent the proposal to the Department and the press, and we waited for something to happen.

It was a crazy step in a crazy situation. It turned us into partisans, advocating a radical position.

It got press coverage. It was covered by the main Vancouver Island newspaper, the *Victoria Times Colonist,* and by Canada's national newspapers, the *Globe and Mail.* The proposal got immediate support from Ken Balcomb and Susan and Howie at Orca Network. But the Department absorbed it into its offices as if it were an oil spill. We knew a response would take a while. So we waited.

I had my computer set up in our little office upstairs in the apartment in Gold River. I often signed onto Keith Wood's Web site, LunaLive, which broadcast the feed from the hydrophone at Anderson Point to the world. It was a good way to try to keep track of Luna. When I heard his calls, I could sleep well. When I didn't, I stayed up to listen just a little longer.

It was remarkable to be able to listen to the sounds of the ocean from that landlocked room filled with darkness and worry, and to see comments from people who were also listening in Scotland and London and Finland.

But though it seemed wonderful that so many people in so many places wanted to care for Luna and pay attention to him, even among many of those, there was no strong effort to solve the problem of apparent loneliness that Luna himself identified every day as the most important thing in his life. Yet it was the very same thing we humans consider most important in our own lives: relationships.

And now, as he asserted those needs more desperately, more humans turned away from him. What hope was there for this whale, so present in our lives but still so lost?

One night when there were no calls on LunaLive for hours, I wondered why people were so determined not to give him what looked like simple kindness, even when there was no scientific or rational reason to withhold it anymore. Why did so many people see offering it to be almost immoral? Were those things that he seemed to need—affection, kindness, companionship—too soft for us to see as important? Were they too mushy for our taste? Did it seem like a weakness in him to need these things, or in us to offer them? Is that why someone could describe an orca's efforts to find a social life—the most natural thing for an orca to do—as aberrant? Lance Barret-Lennard had said the need for social contact in orcas was probably as strong as the need for food. Why did so many of us humans think that caring enough about that need to try to solve it was somehow a lack of toughness and character?

I listened and listened and listened for Luna's calls. He must have been somewhere else. It was now almost 2:00 A.M. There were just the sounds of waves gurgling, the small clicking of shrimp, the croak of fish, and the distant, steady rumble of an engine, probably a generator at a fish farm. Not silence, but emptiness.

CHAPTER FIFTY-FOUR

August 2005

I sat in our Zodiac next to Jamie and Roger in a new inflatable boat that Roger had purchased for the band's fisheries operations. We rested on the water beside a kayak whose calm paddler did not seem as worried as we were. As we sat there on the water, Luna came up and bumped against my boat. There was a loud hissing noise. In this old boat, it was a familiar kind of noise—familiar but not good.

"Uh-oh," I said to Jamie. "I think I have a leak."

"No," Jamie said. "It's Luna."

Really? Since when did Luna make that noise? I was sure it was the boat. Then it stopped and started again. Jamie was right. I could see the little bubbles around Luna's blowhole as he made the exact sound of leaking air.

The little goofball had scared us again, but not just about the leak.

Kayaks worried everyone. Luna had paid attention to several over the years and had treated them gently, but now that he was at least sixteen feet long and weighed about three thousand pounds, his size and power and the kayaks' vulnerability made them seem the biggest risk. The deep waters of Nootka Sound are bitterly cold year-round and can drain the life from a human in minutes. So for all of us, the kayak scenario was the one we thought could lead to an incident that would bring on the Department's guns.

Like Roger, we had a new boat. Well, it was a different boat, much older than the small red Zodiac. That one had been damaged at the dock while we were away and would take a long time to fix, so we'd bought an ancient black used Zodiac. Bill Mather, the most helpful man in the world, had helped us modify it so it would actually hold together, though it sprang a leak so often that I thought of it as incontinent.

We called it *Blackfish*. That was the boat I had been out in that day, watching from a distance as Jamie and Roger led Luna back toward Mooyah Bay from an encounter with a sportfishing boat in Cook Channel, a few nautical miles west of Mooyah Bay.

Everything was going smoothly; I could see Luna coming up regularly beside the First Nations' eighteen-foot Zodiac, cruising home. But then all of us, including Luna, saw the solitary kayak crossing a passage ahead.

I had talked briefly with the kayaker when I had seen him earlier. I had told him that Luna was around. But I had hoped that Luna would not get close enough to get interested. That hope was not realized.

Because of all our conversations about this kind of thing, I could probably read the minds of Roger and Jamie:

Uh-oh, thought Jamie.

Uh-oh, thought Roger.

Uh-oh, I thought.

Luna apparently thought something different. He bailed on Jamie and headed east, his dorsal slowly submerging at speed like a sub lowering its periscope for action.

We all just watched. It was another one of those moments on Nootka Sound. Hold your breath and wait. This was now in Luna's hands, so to speak. If it was a violent meeting, we were there to help the paddler, but that would be the Department's call to action. If Luna was gentle, Jamie could probably intervene and there would be no news, no event, no splash.

Luna's dorsal popped up behind the kayak.

The kayaker's name was Alan Dunham. He was a computer programmer from the interior of British Columbia and did most of his kayaking on large lakes. He saw Luna coming.

"There is a certain sense of apprehension," he said later.

Luna came up under the kayak and lifted it, but only slightly.

"He didn't do it forcefully enough to tip me over," Alan said later. "He was cautious about it." Alan put the starboard paddle flat on the water as a brace. There was no splash.

About that time, Jamie arrived and came alongside the kayak. Alan reached out and took hold of one of the rope loops on the Zodiac. I called Jamie on the radio and asked if he'd like to have me over there, too. "Yes," he said.

So we all gathered around Alan on the calm water of a dazzling, hot day on Nootka Sound. Luna spyhopped gently a couple of times, as if counting the participants at the meeting and trying to figure out what was on the agenda. Then he came up horizontally and rested quietly between Jamie's boat and Alan's kayak.

Things were so quiet that they felt bizarrely normal. And maybe they were. Just another whale day on Nootka Sound. Did we wonder why Luna was so cautious, so gentle around Alan's kayak? Not at the time.

Alan was calm, too. He was completely at home in his kayak, with his body wrapped in a blue rain suit and flotation gear, streamlined down into the boat with a kayak spray skirt that made him look part boat himself, like a nautical centaur. He looked around thoughtfully, sort of speculatively. Hmm. Well, look at this, a killer whale. How interesting. "He gives a bit of a push sometimes," I said. Alan smiled. He already knew that. "Yeah," he said.

We all chatted in a matter-of-fact way, as if this was the kind of thing we all did every day. Check your oil, sir? Would you like your windshield washed? How about we remove your whale, sir?

"Hey, you," Jamie said to Luna. He gave Luna a little rub on the head. Alan reached out and gingerly touched Luna's head himself.

Jamie slowly moved back along the length of his boat. Luna followed him.

"Be a good whale," Jamie said. "Go get some chinook." Jamie lay full length on the boat's tubes, facing aft, and Luna came up at the stern of the boat, looking right at him. "Be a good whale," Jamie said again. Luna came up and leaned his head on the tube by Jamie's head and lifted one pectoral fin out of the water.

The tension in the air ebbed away. Eventually, Jamie started back toward Mooyah Bay, and Luna went with him. Alan headed to shore. I followed him and asked him what he thought of what had happened. If the Department had been watching, it might have been called a near miss. What would he call it?

"An experience of a lifetime," he said. "A positive one."

CHAPTER FIFTY-FIVE

August 2005

Another day, and we couldn't find him. Sunshine in the air, shadow on the mind. Nobody seemed to know where he was, and no one had seen him the day before.

It was another summer gillnet-fishing opening, and there had been some contact between him and the gillnetters, but we didn't hear of anything bad, except that one boat had been pushed around more than the fisherman wanted. But nothing had happened since then.

We headed out on the water and tried the familiar places along the route, but there was no sign of Luna. Because of the recent voices of aggressive fishermen both in our own interviews and on television a couple of nights before, where one fisherman wondered aloud about how Luna would like the taste of dynamite, we were worried. Mooyah Bay was calm but empty. We were starting to make vows that if he turned up okay, we would motor along behind him twenty-four hours a day, like a bodyguard in an SUV, just to try to keep him safe.

But then we went back to the Gold River dock, where Luna had hardly been seen for six months. *Uchuck III* had just arrived, and there were people standing around on the dock, some looking over the edge. And at last we heard the sound we had been missing: the quick, deep breath of Luna.

It was a relief. We'd been waiting far too long to hear again that salute to life from the sea. Ah. He's okay. He's alive. He's up to the same old stuff.

Things were chaotic. Kids' voices called out, "Luna! Luna!" People at the lower dock splashed their hands in the water to try to lure Luna over. The last of the afternoon's chop rattled boats together and rocked the dock floats. And the breath of Luna punctuated it all with regular bursts of that presence that seemed both strange and hauntingly familiar.

But though this looked benign on the surface and in many ways seemed full of good-hearted friendliness, that wasn't what we wanted for Luna. Although there was joy at hearing Luna's healthy breath after what we had thought was a frightening absence, this reminder of the chaos of interaction that he got here was not reassuring. When we argued that Luna needed a real connection with humans, some people thought this inconsistent, chaotic way of life was what we meant. We didn't.

Then, long after sunset, something happened. From out of nowhere came the boxy aluminum shape of *Wi-hut-suh-nup*. On it was Jamie James. He saw the crowd on the dock and motored over.

A half-moon was up. In its glow and the late-summer twilight, *Wi-hut-suh-nup* worked its way around the edge of the docks. Jamie shut down the motor and let the boat drift. He tapped out a little rhythm on the side of the boat as it drifted farther from the docks.

Jamie waited for Luna to approach, to recognize him and the boat, and become accustomed to its familiarity. In the mix of twilight and moonlight, I saw the breath and heard it faintly. Luna had gone back to his friend.

The twilight deepened and the aluminum shape of the boat disappeared into darkness. As the boat drifted away, I could hear the calm voice of Jamie just talking quietly to the whale, and the occasional breath of Luna.

I last saw *Wi-hut-suh-nup* off in the distance, its three lights now condensed into just one glow, moving slowly west. It made me happy. Luna had headed for Jamie from the dock's chaos as if he at last knew where to go.

The ache of the day's worry dissolved in the moonlight. This was the model of what could be done for him. Not flashy, not noisy, but, in its consistency, something more like real friendship as we know it—and perhaps as orcas know it—than what he had had from anyone but Jamie for all these years. It could be done.

We relaxed. For the next hours, Luna would be safe and in a familiar place. He was, for a little while at least, not entirely alone.

CHAPTER FIFTY-SIX

August 2005

Roger and Jamie were building a playground, and Keith Wood was building a phone.

The playground was modeled on something that Toni Frohoff had talked about at the workshop, but it wasn't the same thing. It was designed to provide Luna with something interesting to play with without human contact.

Suzanne and I went up to the camp where the First Nations stewards spent nights near Mooyah Bay and watched them building it. It was based on a short raft of logs with a wooden platform. On the platform were strapped three red and three white large round boat fenders, a battery, and a bilge pump with a hose mounted on a stick. The battery ran the bilge pump, which ran water through the hose and squirted a thin stream of it over the edge of the platform and into the sea. The little hose wasn't quite as energetic as the full-out fire hose we had seen Luna playing with a few weeks before at a work barge near a fish farm, but it was running water, which he loved. There was a floor brush on the side for him to rub against, and, in a final touch, a string from the platform was attached to a life-size plastic decoy duck.

When they got ready to test it on Luna, they asked us to hide with our cameras and film how he used it.

They couldn't get permission to anchor it in deep water because of navigation issues, so they put it a few feet out from the shore in a little cove not far from Mooyah Bay. And they turned on the hose.

They didn't actually think that Luna would race over there to interact with it, so they went to get him.

Suzanne was up the hillside from the playground, filming through a gap in the trees. I was on an island about a hundred meters away with a big telephoto lens on a tripod-mounted camera. We waited a long time.

Finally, *Wi-hut-suh-nup* appeared from behind a point. Luna was with it. With Roger and Jamie on board, it gradually approached. Jamie was leaning over the side of the boat with a light blue swimming pool speaker attached by a cable to a CD player. He was playing wolf calls to Luna.

Luna loved the sound so much, he tilted his head above the water and rested the active speaker on the side of his jaw, the area through which orcas gather sound. He seemed captivated by it. When it slipped off, he lifted his head up until Jamie gave the speaker back to him.

For Suzanne, there was no avoiding a certain way of describing this. If Luna couldn't have L Pod, she thought, at least he had an iPod.

Though the playground seemed goofy, it mattered. If this or something like it could distract Luna from going after gillnet boats or others that didn't want him around, it would be a huge solution, without being so radical as to offer interaction from humans. So we kept filming.

Luna went over to the playground and put his nose under the water flow. He took a look at the duck. Jamie got out and stood on the platform. But when *Wi-hut-suh-nup* left, so did Luna. Jamie stood there, looking forlorn, until Roger came back to pick him up.

"He stuck with the thing for a bit," Jamie told us later. "But I don't think he really liked playing with things that wouldn't interact back with him."

The phone that Keith Wood was making was a different kind of idea. It wasn't animal management. It was an offering of the latest tools of our tool-making species to an animal who didn't use tools but maybe could.

Keith Wood's idea about LunaLive had been a success around the world, and there were quite a few passionate listeners.

The idea about the phone expanded on that idea. Would it be possible, Keith wondered, for the hydrophone at Mooyah Bay to send live calls from Luna into the waters near the San Juan Islands, where Luna's family would be for the next several months? If Luna's relatives responded to the calls through this remote connection and created what could almost be called a conversation, perhaps the repeating station could be put in a boat and the family could be led north to pick Luna up at the mouth of the sound.

We helped Keith out as he got started with the project. And we interviewed him about his plans. When I talked to him on-camera in his boat, when he was anchored near Anderson Point, I kept trying to get him to talk about it in terms of the Spielberg film *ET: The Extra-Terrestrial*. Basically, I was trying to feed him a pop-culture line.

He was reluctant. I think, given his preference for referring to Luna by his number instead of his nickname, that it wasn't scientific enough for him. But I finally got him to say it, though he looked characteristically sheepish as he got to the key words.

"What we're going to do is have both L-67 [Splash, Luna's mother] and L-98 hear each other's voices at the same time," he said. "In effect what we're establishing is a phone call. I mean," he said with that faint embarrassed smile, "this is ET, phone home."

And during that summer, too, summoned not by a phone call but just by chance, one of the two Mowachaht/Muchalaht canoes that were used in the fight over the capture came back to Mooyah Bay. Most of the people in it had not been part of the fight, but Wayne Lavoie was there, the young guy with the big voice, the shaking hands, and the ready jokes. So was Jerry Jack, following in a small outboard-powered boat, along with his fiancée, Fran Prest.

Jerry had brought a hand drum, and he led the singing. He sang some of the songs that people were already starting to practice for the big potlatch for Ambrose Maquinna, now scheduled for the coming November. This was the potlatch that would mark the end of the four-year-long period of mourning for Ambrose. Some people said this was also the time when the spirit of Ambrose might leave Luna's body, or Luna might leave Nootka Sound.

Luna found the canoe across from Anderson Point. He followed it as it moved slowly around another small point opposite Tuta Marina, under the hill where Lisa Larsson had camped. Lisa was back in Sweden now, but she listened regularly to LunaLive.

Did Luna remember the canoe? The sound of the paddles cutting through his water? The booming voice of Wayne Lavoie? What did he remember? Did he know that he had followed this same canoe away from the capture pen of Ed Thorburn and Clint Wright?

Whatever his memories were, he seemed happy with the canoe. He spyhopped and did pec-fin slaps; he moved slowly alongside the canoe and rubbed against the black wooden hull as the hands of men and women reached out from above to caress his dorsal fin or his white underside. In the stern of the canoe, a young guy scooped water up with a bailing pitcher and poured it over Luna's nose, and Luna kept coming back for another splash.

Jerry Jack followed the canoe in the little skiff, singing. It was the first time Fran had seen Luna. She looked solemn and in awe. She saw Luna completely as Tsu'xiit, not as an animal to manage but as a transcendent life to learn from and to revere, who felt empathy and offered kindness to ease the experience of human suffering.

"He wasn't just a whale," Fran told us later. "He was brought here for some reason. I could not get over the sense of feeling that I get from him. It changes your whole body; it is almost like an instant feeling of healing, just an awesome feeling. When you think about it, that is why Luna, to me, seemed to be around, and that is to wash away hurt, wash away the pain in our lives."

CHAPTER FIFTY-SEVEN

October 2005

I awoke in one of those days of mixed sun and cloud in October, feeling as if Luna was alone and we were unable to make life better for him, or even to protect him. It had rained all day the day before and we hadn't seen him, which always left us on edge. Now the weather was better, but not my spirits.

The First Nations stewardship was over. It had been a stopgap measure, full of the same good and bad moments that all the other stewardships had gone through. Like the rest, it had been inconsistent and had no real outcome.

The stewardship had ended a couple of days before it was scheduled to finish, when *Wi-hut-suh-nup* broke down. Now the stalwart little tin boat was sitting on a trailer up on the band's land near the blank-eyed empty houses where the old village had stood. It looked as if this little boat, which had so much history with Luna and Jamie, was just going to sit there until the aluminum was corroded down to drifts of dust by the years.

Suzanne and I got up and went out early. The water was still, and in the distance to the south, a thin mirage picked up strange silhouettes of logs and a boat superstructure. When we went across the inlet, it resolved into a bunch of logs being pulled by a tug.

As we approached, we saw the small black fin in the smooth water near the tug's bow. The tug was moving very slowly, carrying along its logs. Luna was there.

We tied off to the slow tug and climbed aboard. One of the crew told us stories—about how Luna had picked up the end of the boom chain and handed it to him when he needed it; about Luna pushing log bundles along in the right direction to help. Up on the bow, Suzanne peered over at Luna, who rolled over on his back, put his tail up by the bow, and let the boat push him slowly along. Then he came up, took a breath, and turned sideways to look up at Suzanne.

Later, we stood in the noisy little cockpit with the two men. We talked about people threatening to kill Luna. Then the skipper said something that cleared my head.

"We're out there all the time," he said seriously. "And we're looking out all the time."

Suzanne and I talked about that afterward. We had sometimes joked with Jamie that Luna was a blue-collar guy, most at home among the hardworking men and women of the sound. When he had free time, Suzanne had said, he probably went to the gym and lifted weights. But that wasn't just a joke. Most of the people who worked on Nootka Sound were long-term friends of this little whale.

Who were they? Cameron and Catherine, going back and forth from Gold River to run their resort. Rick and Sheila in their old gill-net boat. Radar, the beachcomber, in his old boat that looked like a truck had run over it. A guy named Bob Christiansen, who told us affectionate stories about working on the logs and being surprised by Luna. "I'll tell you," he said, "you haven't been goosed until you've been goosed by a whale."

They were people like Donna Schneider, the owners and crew of *Uchuck III,* and Bill Mather on *A. G. Ford*, as helpful as always, who had a broom he would use to give Luna a scrub. They were like the people who worked up at the Spirit Lake Timber logging camp in

Mooyah Bay, one of whom once told us that if one of the sportfishers killed Luna, "the next one would be him."

So we were not alone. It was just that our allies were quiet. They didn't have anything to do with television and newspaper reporters. They didn't have anything to do with the Department of Fisheries and Oceans. But they formed a kind of Luna Underground, keeping their eyes and ears open, giving companionship where they could. They hadn't been shooting at Luna; they'd been watching out for him.

We were becoming more like those people than like the outsiders we once had been. So we changed things in our lives again. We were in deep with Luna, so we got in deeper.

The famous potlatch for Ambrose Maquinna was coming up in less than a month. Oddly, the closer it got, the less the event seemed attached to Luna directly. There were no canoe trips to Mooyah Bay to see Luna or to communicate with him. There seemed to be no discussions between the band and the Department about Luna's status after the potlatch was over. We didn't expect anything to change. So we rented a boat trailer and a pickup truck, drove home, and picked up yet another boat to use on Nootka Sound. This was our island commuter boat, the one that got us back and forth from the island where our home stood, still unfinished. We were pulling out all the stops for Luna by taking that boat north.

The boat was nothing special, except to us. It was a twenty-foot-long former sportfishing charter boat that had seen better years—a lot of better years. It was two feet longer than the black Zodiac, but it was better because it had a tiny cabin up in the bow just big enough to sleep in.

It wasn't a very dry boat in the rain, and as winter approached, a lot of rain was on its way. I put together a shelter out of a blue tarp. This made the boat look like a refugee tent, but made it a lot drier.

We bought our own hydrophone, and I started going out on the water for several days at a time. If we couldn't get a permit to help Luna get the kind of friendship we thought he should be given, at least we could keep watch and try to prevent someone from shooting him. The men and women of the Luna Underground were out there, but the workers were not always around. There didn't seem to be anyone else who had the time or the boat to just be there for Luna as the stewards and Jamie had been there in the past. So we decided to try.

CHAPTER FIFTY-EIGHT

November 2005

Typically, I had a sweet daydream about the day of the Maquinna potlatch. In my tendency to write movie endings in my head, I daydreamed that on that day a canoe would be launched there at Tuta Marina, manned by Eugene Amos, Sam Johnson, Wayne Lavoie, Ed Thorburn, Mike Maquinna, and a bunch of other pullers, men and women. The canoe would pick Luna up at Anderson Point and turn the corner into Zuciarte Channel, then would head out to sea, and there—a crowd of plumes, a thunder of breathing . . .

That's how my daydreams always ended. But how wonderful. And, I thought, arguing with my appalled realistic side, just remember what happened that day when Luna was in the pen and the canoes came out again after even Mike Maquinna had given up. I didn't daydream that, and it was Hollywood all the way. Why can't we have Hollywood again, on the day Ambrose Maquinna is sung into eternity?

Well, if it was going to be Hollywood, the sky would clear. It didn't. The sky was glum and rainy.

We decided that Suzanne would attend the beginning of the potlatch, scheduled for 10:00 A.M., and I would go out and see what Luna was up to on that special day.

The sound was an easier place to travel in our bigger boat. It wasn't much more comfortable, because at speed the rain was blown into the cockpit through the various pieces of plastic and duct tape that were supposed to protect me. But I got to Mooyah Bay in forty-five minutes. I stopped, and *poof!* Stealth Whale.

He arrived about 2:45, rubbed on the boat, then rolled over to look at me.

When a human looks in the eyes of a dog, the dog often turns his eyes away. When Luna looked at me, I was the one who felt the dog's shyness. To Lance Barrett-Lennard, the Vancouver Aquarium marine mammal scientist, Luna's gaze seemed contemplative, but to me it was more forthright than that. And the sense of complexity beyond what we understand was pronounced.

It was not only clear up close that we could each recognize a need in the other. It was also clear, when I looked at him and remembered all the many ways he had tried to communicate, that his thought process might be even more layered than ours, more intricate, more complex.

We think that language liberates us, makes us learned and wise, but it often seems ineffective, as well. Thousands of books have been written about the meeting of lovers' eyes, yet that moment remains inexplicably complex. Looking at Luna, it seemed to be our failure that we cannot operate except with these cumbersome symbols.

I looked at him, thinking vaguely that I had better figure out how to ditch him before somebody caught me doing this. Then a sense washed over me that this orca was just as aware of living as I was: that he could perceive all the details that I perceive, the feeling of atmosphere and sea, the texture of emotions, the knowledge of our own position on the Earth, and who we are and who we are not, and what makes us feel safe. This was overwhelming. It was not comfortable, but it included awe.

I left Luna to himself and went to anchor in a bay not far from Anderson Point. The anchor did not hold, and as darkness fell, sudden and hard, I was looking for another spot, using the GPS, without Luna.

Then very slowly, so slowly that I didn't understand it at first and got chills from it, a wall of muted lights the size of a mountain slowly materialized to the southwest.

For a few minutes, this was shocking, huge, hard to comprehend. Then I began to understand it. It was a ship, so far out of scale in the normal collection of boats on Nootka Sound that it did not seem real.

It was Canadian Coast Guard Ship *Bartlett. Bartlett* is an ice-strengthened navigational aid tender, which sounds like a small boat. It isn't. This ship is about 190 feet long and has superstructure that stands about 60 feet above the water. It would dwarf *Uchuck III.* The ship was named for a great Arctic explorer who was born in Newfoundland and was known for his monumental seven-hundred-mile walk across the Arctic ice to get help for his stranded crew.

The ship moved majestically into Mooyah Bay through the mist and sleety rain, its lower windows glowing, its engines a low murmur that filled the canyon. It seemed to occupy the entire space of the sound. Its hull was painted red, like that of all Canadian Coast Guard ships, but in the wet darkness the hull was just moving dark space, lighted only by the reflection of the ship's own lights off the moving water below.

I was bobbing around like a cork in the water below it as it pulled into Mooyah Bay. There was a river mouth there and some sandy bottom, so it was a decent anchorage. I heard a massive rattle and roar of chain. The ship was in for the night.

I called the ship on the VHF radio. I had renamed our new boat *Blackfish,* like the old Zodiac. I figured that *Blackfish* was easier for people to remember than what we called it at home: *Margaree.*

"Vessel anchored in Mooyah Bay, this is the *Blackfish.*"

I think crew members on *Bartlett*'s bridge were a little surprised to hear me. But eventually a woman's voice answered. She told me the ship's name, and I asked about Luna. She knew about Luna, and, yes, he was presently beside them.

Not a bad place for him, I thought. Warm-water outflows, lights,

288 · *The Lost Whale*

rumbling engines, people looking down from the forward decks at him, most likely talking to him. Luna would be with them all night.

I said thanks to *Bartlett*. I decided not to anchor. Luna had his company for this evening.

I headed back up the inlet to the Gold River docks. Because of the darkness, I had to open the front windscreen in order to see well enough to detect logs in the boat's spotlight, and the rain stung my face all the way. When I got to the potlatch, I was bitterly cold.

In the gym at Tsaxana, the potlatch had been going on for eight hours already, with its speeches and songs. The place was jammed. The Mowachaht/Muchalaht dancers had magnificent shirts bearing elaborately stitched images of orcas, and sometimes when they sang, they carried paddles.

I had timed my arrival perfectly. Everyone was sitting down to paper plates laden with hot food. I got a plate and sat down with Suzanne. But soon Sam Johnson came over, his eyes serious. He sat down and put an arm around my shoulders. He talked to me very quietly.

"I want you to stay here tonight," he said, practically in a whisper. "Don't go out." I turned to look at him, questioning.

"Don't go out," he said. "Tonight he's speaking with the ancestors."

But out in Mooyah Bay, Luna was with a Department ship. The Canadian Coast Guard is a branch of the Department of Fisheries and Oceans.

That seemed ironic to me, and then I thought that Sam himself might have enjoyed the irony, too, and might have floated the notion that the ancestor Luna was out there speaking with was not a ship, but a great explorer.

Then there was another thought. The ship was based near Victoria, near where L Pod spends the summer and fall. The Southern Residents had not yet left for the winter. What if in the morning Luna went home with *Bartlett*?

CHAPTER FIFTY-NINE

November 2005

Luna did not go home with *Bartlett*. That was just another romantic daydream. Luna needed to cope with real life right now.

I was back out in Mooyah Bay as yet another night fell. It was later in the month. I was anchored along a shoreline where the forest came right down to the sea about a hundred meters north of Anderson Point. From there, I heard Luna on the hydrophone almost every night.

Luna's presence in my life had become settled and natural. It was like when you move to an amazingly beautiful place or a great city. In the beginning, you amuse the old-timers with your awe, but when you are no longer as amazed, those surroundings become unremarked but vital to your life. No longer are you set back on your heels by the scene; instead, the scene is what keeps you on your feet.

Now, when Luna was around, my Nootka Sound world was complete. I wasn't lonely. There he was, out in the middle of the bay during the daytime, or off at some fish farm, or playing with a dozer boat, or, in the dark, calling through the water in his eternal hope of being heard. I would have the speakers on all night, and I would never sleep through his calls. I would just awaken, start the recorder without getting out of the sleeping bag, and smile.

Real life was troubling. A few days earlier, I had been down on the dock, talking to a fisherman, and he'd said flat out, "Luna's going to be killed this winter."

I told him that if someone killed Luna, he'd be arrested. The guy looked at me as if wondering how much of an idiot I was.

"There's a lot of bad weather out there," he said. "Nobody will ever find out."

In the morning, Luna wasn't calling and I couldn't see him, so I pulled up the anchor and went over to Tuta Marina. There had been snow two days before, and nobody was using the marina. I took my camera and binoculars and walked up the hill past a little trailer and into the woods.

The words of the fisherman haunted me. Too many people were talking like that. That's why I was out here, but I couldn't be here every day.

In the snow, there were tracks. They were the tracks of a wolf—just one.

There was something good about seeing that print. Luna had peeled my layers back, too. My wish to be aware of the interweaving of human and other lives was acute, and if this wolf wanted to watch me cross his landscape, that was fine.

I walked up the old logging road into the hills above Mooyah Bay, heading toward Lisa's old observation site. Slender young alders about two or three feet tall were growing in the middle of the road. It felt as if they had all grown up since we had been there last, back when Luna's imminent reunion with his pod seemed so certain.

That was before we knew about the Department's low expectations that the reunion would work and the extent of its plans for captivity. It was before we had seen the first canoes. It was before the shadow of the Darth Vader boats, before the gate to the pen was not closed, before Ed's threat to arrest Lisa. It was before the apparent willingness of the Department to give Luna the time to make a deadly mistake.

The Department could not say it had no options. The only thing that stood between Luna and active, careful engagement with efforts to lead him to the mouth of Nootka Sound by us or by Ken Balcomb was the ideology that Luna should not have human interaction. Not even to entertain those options was clear evidence that the Department had consigned Luna to the unhappy ending it predicted. If something happened to him, the Department would immediately announce that this was the inevitable consequence of a wild animal's contact with people, but that would not be true.

There was more than one option on the table. Earlier in the year, a well-known orca scientist from New Zealand had come to the Pacific coast, and Ed Thorburn had invited her out to meet Luna. Though we didn't know this at the time, she had written up a recommendation to the Department concerning what to do with Luna. It was similar to ours: It suggested that intentional, controlled interaction could keep him occupied and safe.

Then, in early December, a workshop was held in San Diego as part of a major conference about marine mammals. Among the speakers were Toni Frohoff, Catherine Kinsman, Ken Balcomb, and Suzanne. Suzanne gave a PowerPoint presentation on Luna and our proposal. Among the people present was Marilyn Joyce. At that meeting, Toni and Catherine agreed with Suzanne that something involving some form of enrichment of Luna's life to help keep him safe was necessary, and Toni started developing a proposal of her own.

But the Department did nothing. And it did not respond to our proposal. The reasons for this reluctance to take action still seemed based on the philosophy that Luna should not have any human interaction unless he was in an aquarium.

A few weeks before, I had talked to John Ford about the day Luna had come up beside our old Zodiac and had whistled directly at me. I had asked him if he thought it was humane to keep trying to deny Luna the contact he seemed to need so much and was getting only chaotically. John had chastised me for saying that and for staying with Luna to listen to him. "People can't do that," he said. "You have to hold yourself back, because he needs to be a real whale."

"A real whale." There was moral condemnation in both his words and his tone, not just of me but also of Luna. Somehow, it seemed, a whale who stooped to seeking humans to fill a void was less of a whale than he should be, and people who stooped to trying to help him were lacking proper self-discipline. Empathy was weakness.

But wasn't it a form of arrogance to think that humans could make Luna anything less than what he already was just by interacting with him? I used to buy John's argument. No longer.

I worked my way up the hillside on the old road. At last, the view opened out. I had guessed right about the route. I was in the familiar place. Below me the angular shapes of the corners of Mooyah Bay emerged from the trees, and I could see the two arms of Zuciarte Channel and Hanna Channel leading off to the south and west. The distant horizon was of low ridgelines of points of land and islands, but just beyond them was an indistinct glow in the air: the muted, cloudy shine of the Pacific.

This was the old clear-cut where Lisa had put up her tarp, where she had sat listening to Luna and watching him from afar for days and weeks. Unexpectedly, her blue tarp was still there.

That was a surprise. Lisa is a tidy, careful person who always worries about the environment. Now here was this torn blue artifact of her months here. It was partly under snow and partly visible, and it looked forlorn. Lisa never would have left it here unless she had expected to come back.

I looked out across the water. I saw no distant plume of breath. The day felt leaden. We had not expected things to happen as they had. Over and over, our expectations had been wrong. I stood there for a long time, trying to envision something, something that was not bleak. I looked around. In a snowfall, there is always hope, in the melt that nourishes life, in the new leaves that I could see close to the ground, lifting their heads through it, and in the clean new slate that snow brings to the world. This clear-cut hillside had been hammered by human machines, but life was coming back.

Time and life. I need to know of nothing else to be in awe.

CHAPTER SIXTY

November 2005

A few days later, I thought we had lost him. Another storm swept across Vancouver Island. Wind up to hurricane force thrashed the water. Fog and rain shrouded the coast. I slept one windy night in the shelter of Mooyah Bay, but I went back to town after that, then came back out a couple of days later. There had been no calls on LunaLive since the storm began, and when I got back out to Mooyah Bay, no one had seen Luna at any of the fish farms or the logging camps.

I spent the night at Mooyah Bay with the hydrophone in the water and the speakers turned up high. But there were no calls.

I widened my search zone. I moved out on the west side of Bligh Island, south of Cameron and Catherine Forbes's place, well west of Mooyah Bay. I had forgotten my binoculars, so I used the camera's telephoto lens to magnify my view. Each time I thought I saw a distant spout, I raised the camera and stared through it, recording, waiting for the next. But it was always waves breaking on distant rocks.

So I put the camera up automatically but without expectation when I thought I saw another spout, out near a place called Strange Island. I focused on the distance and pushed the button. I'd have to film for a minute or so to be sure it wasn't him, so I just kept rolling.

Without warning, joy flooded into my life.

Right in the middle of the lens, Luna leaped clear of the water.

There he was, the whole length of him, about 150 meters away, twisting in the air as he jumped, almost as if he were wiggling his hips.

And what were my thoughts at this wonderful moment? Keep the camera steady!

Wow! He was back! He was alive.

To hell with the Department of Fisheries and Oceans and the barge it came in on, I thought. I slowed the boat. Luna came up in the distance for another breath; then he was with me. I looked over at him as he slid up along the side of the boat. I thought, I'm not going anywhere, Luna.

He came up beside the boat, looked at me, and rolled over. I reached out and rubbed his belly with my fingertips. It was the first time I had intentionally touched him. In the cold water, his skin was warm.

I looked around and checked the GPS. Well, maybe we would go somewhere after all. Together. We were about four nautical miles from the mouth of Nootka Sound. He was out here anyway, over half the distance from Mooyah Bay to the mouth, so why not take a cruise to the open sea?

Luna had been to the mouth of the sound before. Ed had led him out while he was training him for the capture. The canoes had taken him to Yuquot, where Ed had led him back, in the Tug of Whale. Once Jamie and Roger had led him out in the First Nations' inflatable. He had also been there with *Uchuck III*.

He had never stayed there long. Maybe the big sea made him uncomfortable. But the whole idea behind leading him there was to do it often enough that he would get comfortable out where he would be more likely to hear his family members' calls if they passed. Today, I thought, I might as well just give it a shot, in case we would have a chance to do it some more.

The current was outbound. I just let it move us. I sat in the boat and Luna played around it. The GPS indicated that we were going two knots right out toward the sea. For a while, I sang to him. Then I whistled to him. I gave him the little whistle that my parents called our "family whistle." It was a version of the chimes of Big Ben. When I whistled it, it was the first time I had heard this sound since my father died. When it came from me, I heard it from him, clear.

When I was eleven years old, I started attending a boarding school in Brazil, and I was desperately lonely. My parents had said they would come to see me, but it wasn't clear exactly when. I went up to the bunkhouse one night to get ready for bed, but then from outside the bunkhouse I heard that whistle, and I knew my dad was there. Complete happiness lived in that whistle.

After I made that whistle for Luna and remembered the welcome of that night, I wished as strongly as I could wish anything that I could give Luna that kind of call from his family.

Maybe teaching him to feel comfortable out at the mouth would at least open that door.

Luna and I drifted south, and on this day of light breezes, the big ocean seeped into Nootka Sound like a rumor. The big restless energy that came from somewhere far away slipped beneath us and grew, but the current still took us south, outbound. At last, we were even with the lighthouse at Yuquot. We were at the mouth of Nootka Sound.

At first, Luna didn't change what he was doing. But after we passed Yuquot, with the swell now a long, soft undulation, he slipped away. And pretty soon I saw a little dark fin in the distance to the north. He was heading back to Mooyah Bay.

I headed back, too. But there was something different on this boat now. I remained convinced that the gift people can give most wild animals is to keep away from them, but this was completely different. We had already rejected the ideology that Luna and people should be kept apart no matter what, but now fighting it directly seemed the only way to keep him safe.

In fact, there was evidence that maybe connections of any kind, including those with people, were necessary if we ever hoped he would be able to reunite with his family after years away.

While I was out in Mooyah Bay, I did some reading. I read Matthew Scully's magnificent *Dominion,* a watershed book about animals written by a religious conservative, not an animal-rights radical. And I read books by Temple Grandin, the autistic student of animals who has helped make farms more humane.

I read in these books and others about the hormone oxytocin. Oxytocin, Grandin wrote, is essential to social memory. It helps you recognize your friends and family. And its presence in social mammals' brains is increased by social contact. When a human pets a dog, oxytocin in the brain is increased in both.

So it seemed likely that what Luna needed was not solitude to drive him back to his family, but attention and a socially structured life, both to give him comfort and to maintain his social instincts. If we were teaching him to deny his most fundamental needs to be with a small group of familiar individuals, then maybe we were ruining him for a reunion, not saving him for it.

He was still engaged with humans. He still trusted us. There was still time to save his life.

I drove the boat against the stream of tide that still flowed out from Nootka Sound, following a distant small black fin that was going back to the place where he felt safe. But I wasn't going to be safe. If I could, I would become a part of that Luna Underground that had been here for Luna all these years. Without calling attention to it, I would try to smuggle friendship into Nootka Sound.

CHAPTER SIXTY-ONE

December 2005

I n the early morning, with the temperature below freezing, the rivers poured mist down onto the sound. I awoke to an eerie, still world, with drifts of mist floating in curls across layers of softly shining water and with the sound of a distant whale call in my ears.

What I smuggled into Nootka Sound was just the bare bones of something like friendship. It wasn't what Suzanne and I thought it should be. We proposed a clear intentional system, designed by people like Ken Balcomb, to provide safety through consistency. But I couldn't do that.

It was, as things always seemed to be with Luna, a dilemma. If I wanted to give Luna what we thought he needed, I would have to be consistent. But if I wanted to be able to stay out there even just to watch out for him without being charged with a crime, I had to be sneaky about it, which meant I could do nothing consistently.

The Darth Vader boat had radar, which I did not have, so it could creep up on me. I had to keep looking over my shoulder and be ready to ditch Luna at any moment.

The main difference between what I did and all the original stewardship programs was that I tried not to ditch Luna. I did what Jamie had done in 2004 and what Chantelle and Rachael had done in 2003. I never deliberately engaged him when he wasn't seeking it; I always let him make the interaction decision.

So I never got near him when he was out in the bay by himself. I'd stop over near the shore and watch, usually several hundred meters away, in a place where he'd have to make a deliberate effort to find me. If he was hungry for attention, he'd come over, but if he was fishing or goofing around with a log, I wouldn't distract him. The only other way that I got involved was when he was already interacting with people in a situation that looked like a problem. If a fish farm or a logging camp was having difficulty with him, or if what he was doing looked dangerous, I'd go over and entice him away.

Then, once he was with me, I wouldn't ditch him. I'd just leave the boat drifting and interact with him as he seemed to want it. Usually, the boat would gradually drift out of the boundaries of the zone he had set for himself and he'd just go off into the middle of the zone and fish or spend time paddling around on his back, waving his pectoral fins in the air.

It was odd just to be hanging out, watching him come up and look at me, talking to him, having him looking at me again. I would listen to the odd little noises he made, letting his breath out with a hiss or a blast; then I'd watch him come up and again slap his pec fin or his tail, or press a fender against the side of the boat with his nose for some reason, as if trying to figure out what it was made of.

My awareness of his consciousness was changing the way I felt about my own species as well as his. I did not feel as special as a human as I had before, but I also did not feel as isolated. It was a curious combination: The more I got to know him, the more complex he became in my eyes, and the less likely it seemed that we humans would ever be able to understand his life, with its incredible focus on sound. But at the same time, that consciousness and complexity seemed familiar to me in more fundamental ways than I had expected.

Social contact is such second nature to us that we don't pay attention to many of the details that provide the glue: the banter at the shopping mall, the watercooler conversations, the moments of eye contact that transmit messages—I'm with you on that; What an idiot he is; Catch up later; Yeah, I know; I like you—all the many tiny gestures of friendship that get you through the day. With Luna, all that was fresh because he was looking for details that I didn't know. What were the slaps of water, the blown bubbles, the squeaks, the little building blocks of social comfort that he needed?

Almost all of it seemed to be about touch, sound, and moving water. He spent a huge amount of time around the boat, touching things with his nose and the side of his head, and sometimes, underwater, touching something with his tongue, such as ropes attached to fenders or pieces of cedar bark. When I filmed what he was doing underwater, much of the touching of the boat was done very precisely but firmly with the tips of his pectoral fins or with the edges of his tail.

What made all this clearly social was that he seemed dramatically less interested in doing these things if nobody was on the boat. For instance, he would hang out with Bill Mather on *A. G. Ford* for hours while Bill and his crew delivered equipment, nets, and huge bags of fish food to the fish farms, but when Bill tied the boat up at the Gold River docks and went home, Luna would leave within minutes. However, when Bill stayed on the boat to sleep, Luna would often stay with that boat through the night.

Not that he always let people sleep in peace.

Sometimes when Bill spent the night on board, Luna would get his nose under the edge of the barge's massive anchor, which hung on a chain close to the water on the side of the barge. He would lift and swing the anchor away from the barge, then let it go.

Boom! The anchor would slam against the metal hull, ringing the whole boat like a gong. When Bill would come out on deck, Luna would quit ringing the barge and would look up at him. Bill would give him a rub with the Luna broom he had handy, and the night would be peaceful again. Bill would sometimes hear the sound of breath outside his open window as he drifted off to sleep.

And there was something else. Luna responded to our needs, too.

One day, Luna started playing with my kicker motor—a smaller outboard mounted on a bracket beside the main engine, to be used if the main engine failed. He started lifting it on its bracket and letting it fall abruptly back down. This was one of the things people got angry with him for, because sometimes he would do that so often that the bracket would break. Bye-bye outboard.

So after he played with it for a while, I decided I'd better get it off of the bracket and on board. I climbed back on the boat's transom, which was a difficult place from which to lift off an eighty-pound motor. Also, I guessed that if I went back there and started moving the motor myself, he would think of it as even more of a game and would push the thing around even more enthusiastically, which would be dangerous. So I said to him, trying to project the worry I felt about this procedure, "Hey, Luna, this isn't working out very well. Could you leave that alone for a while?"

I didn't expect what happened next. He immediately left it alone. He backed away. He watched me take off the motor and lift it into the boat. Then he came back up and rubbed the side of the boat with the tip of his pec fin.

Thinking that he had understood my language would be foolish. But something had happened.

Whales have an abundance of the same kinds of cells in their brains that humans use when they feel empathy. And that was the only thing I could guess was going on. Maybe by hearing something in my voice, Luna had been able to pick up a bit of my emotional state, my worry, and had guessed what he needed to do to make me worry less. Maybe he had empathy.

Empathy. That seemed like a very human thing to expect in an animal. But not really. Scientific studies have shown that something like empathy is at work in several species. And when I thought about the social nature of orcas, it turned out to be obvious. If an orca has social needs, he also has to have something that at least resembles empathy.

302 · The Lost Whale

If you need something social—connection, friendship, a pat on the back, cooperation in building a house or raising a child or hunting salmon—the only way you can make a genuine connection with another being is for that other being to volunteer it. A true social connection cannot be created by force. It can only be made by mutual choice.

And to be motivated to volunteer to complete the connection, you have to care about the other being's needs. For someone to exist in a social world, he or she must have both parts of the ability to connect—both the need and the emotional understanding of another's need. That's empathy.

So to live in a social society, you must both suffer loneliness and offer empathy. They are connected. Both are required to make the connections that drive beings to live and thrive together.

It made sense. It also answered another puzzle: How did Luna know to be gentle when he pushed Alan Dunham's kayak—and all the other canoes and kayaks he had encountered? He had played with the kayaks and canoes far more gently than he had pushed my Zodiac, and he pushed me more gently than he pushed sailboats. If he had pushed Alan as hard as he pushed me or a sailboat, Alan would have been flung out of his kayak and the little boat would probably have been damaged, and the paddler endangered. But Luna pushed it gently.

Empathy.

CHAPTER SIXTY-TWO

December 2005

In windy darkness, I was anchored up against the forest near Anderson Point again, looking across at the rain-smeared lights of the fish farm on the other side of Hanna Channel and a green light flashing on the point of Gore Island. There was no other form in the darkness. Rain and cloud and mist hid everything, making the rest of the world just simple darkness. You could fall in any direction.

Yet out of this formless darkness, there came Luna's call, distinct and clear on the loudspeaker from the hydrophone. It was his simple short call, the one heard most often on Lisa's recordings. In a way, his call seemed, well, civilized. It was like an expression of culture, making shape in shapelessness: the shape of living intention, the shape of belonging.

On this evening, I had been talking on the VHF radio to Kip Hedley, the lighthouse keeper at Yuquot, about our own different travels in life, his to Nepal and mine in Antarctica. We were a couple of guys who could cope with solitude and liked being out in places where weather collided with life in vivid ways, but we liked talking to each other on the radio, too. It was one of those gestures of friendship, that hardest of relationships to describe and even to understand, which grows like mist but holds like iron.

We had signed off, but I still had the radio on, automatically scanning frequencies. One of them clicked on.

"It is emotionally disturbing when one of these things happens," the voice on the radio said in a French-Canadian accent.

"Yeah," said another voice. "That's the sort of thing that makes you think you'd just pull the pin and retire."

It was a couple of tug skippers out there somewhere nearby, doing the same thing that Kip and I had been doing, just touching base.

I knew what they were talking about. It had been in the news. A bargeload of logs had been blown over in a storm recently. The barges were big; a lot of money went into the sea. Fortunately, the cargo floated, but it took a while to retrieve.

"Can't retire," said the French-Canadian. "No money, no candy."

Once again, the lights of a big vessel materialized in the sky to the west of me, doing an impressive imitation of the vast intergalactic mothership appearing over Earth that has been a feature of science fiction movies forever. It was one of the two tugs that had been on the radio, coming into Mooyah Bay to take away the bundles of logs that Luna had been pushing around lately. These tugs came into the sound day or night. Up on their huge cranes were mounted dazzling lights that turned the whole log pond into day.

As the ship and its huge barge positioned themselves next to the log pond with their lights on, I saw Luna there with the tug, a tiny fin in turbulent water, Bruno putting on his hard hat and his goggles and his corks, going to work in the logs.

The scene was dazzling and chaotic. I sat well outside the halo of light, watching the two huge cranes, each with a massive grapple, reach down into the water and pick up bundles of logs, wrapped together by cables, heaving them high into the air, the seawater draining off of them in heavy rain back into the bay. The cranes would swing and the bundles would curve across the lighted sky, the last water draining off behind them in a trail of glitter, to crash-land in piles on the barge. Below, in the chaos of boom boats and smaller tugs moving the log bundles up to where the cranes could grab them,

Luna's fin appeared here and there, the tiny fin of a working guy, right in there with his friends. In our lives, and in the lives of orcas, even work is social.

I watched this through the night, talking to Luna a couple of times when he emerged from the roaring work site to check in with me, then watching his fin appear again in the turbulence. At 6:45 A.M., the big tug moved the laden barge away from the pond and got under way, and Luna followed him. I talked to the skipper on the radio. "Yes," he said, "he usually keeps us company when we load."

I anchored again next to the forest by Anderson Point and got some sleep. But Luna didn't go far from Mooyah Bay that morning while following the load of logs. At 10:30, he was back, and he woke me with a call.

The wind picked up all day. It was December 23, Christmastime. Spray and rain moved across the water; there was a low white haze blowing along the surface down toward Gold River. The blue tarp overhead flapped and rattled. Time to go home for Christmas. Suzanne and I had family coming. I couldn't help thinking that Luna did not.

I was anchored on a rock bottom. I'd had a hard time setting the anchor and now I had a very hard time getting it out of there. Finally, I pried it loose and moved into the deeper water. Luna was not around and it was too rough for the hydrophone. So I tidied up for the lumpy trip back to Gold River and drifted through the area where Luna had been before. No squeak on the hull. Then I drove slowly past the fish farm at Atrevida Point, and suddenly the boat lurched and squeaked. Ah. You're back.

I drifted with him all the way across the bay. After all that action the night before, he was as mellow as a sleepy toddler walking hand in hand with me. He just stayed with me most of the time, swimming on the port side, his head between the hull and a little white fender,

306 · *The Lost Whale*

the fender resting on the top of his head on the port side of his blowhole. His breath smelled like clean, raw, fresh fish, like fish smells in a market.

I talked to him a lot. It was Christmas. Why not? Mist and iron.

Everybody needs gestures of friendship, so I gave him as much as I could, tokens of the belonging that I wished he could have complete. I sang Ambrose's paddle song to him and whistled my old family whistle to him, hearing my father. I rubbed his belly. I poured water over his nose. Then I cut a chunk of the gaudiest bit of woven rope I could find, something with blue and red woven into it, and tied it to a fender. I gave it to him when I had to leave.

Something of a Christmas present, Luna, I thought, about all I can manage. He didn't seem to want to take off with it at first; he just pushed it against the hull with his nose, feeling its softness. In the past whenever he'd gotten hold of a fender on a loose rope, he'd taken off with the fender immediately and played a form of Keep Away with it for a couple of hours. I thought he might want to take off with it this time, too, so I draped the rope across his mouth, but he didn't open up to grab it. He just stayed next to the boat. I was feeling sad about having to leave him. Was he picking up on my emotions again?

He looked so small—not when he ran his body under the boat and rubbed, but when he came up and looked at me. He was a small whale, still just a small whale; he was only a kid.

So I gave him a kid's toy, and when I absolutely had to leave so I could get back before dark, I dropped the fender with its little Christmas string on it and motored slowly away. He stayed there with the fender. When I looked back, he was pushing it around, then finally decided he'd take it down and grabbed it by the rope, arched his back, and disappeared.

I went back to Gold River in wind and rain, and Suzanne and I headed home for Christmas. Everyone on the water was busy getting their work done so they could be home, too. The big barges with the logs were heading for the mills, trying to get off-loaded in time. The fish farms were on skeleton crews. The loggers were gone from the camps along the sound. *A. G. Ford*, running a hectic, sleepless three-day race from fish farm to fish farm, and wharf to wharf, back and forth to a place called Port Eliza, had delivered everything on time. The big barge and *Uchuck III* were now tied up and silent. Luna was alone.

CHAPTER SIXTY-THREE

January 2006

Keith Wood also left Nootka Sound before Christmas. His efforts to make a phone for Luna had been valiant. The technological challenges had been acute, but he had almost done it. But all the details that had to fall in place didn't, and L Pod vanished into its mysterious winter. Keith went back to Texas, but he would be back in the spring with L Pod and would try again.

I kept going out to keep watch. Once, I got a call on the radio from a fish farm where repair divers were uncomfortable with Luna around, so I led him about three miles back to Mooyah Bay, and nobody turned me in. But most of the time, I just recorded his calls and echolocation. LunaLive was still working, and I kept taking batteries up the hill to the transmitter so that people in other parts of the world could listen, too.

I continued to keep track of where Luna went, often following him around at a distance. Once, I had been looking for him all morning and finally saw him playing with a fishing boat. I popped over to the shore, jumped out, and ran up a little hill so I could set up a tripod. As I started filming, I heard a sound in the tree above me. I looked up and saw wide, worried eyes. It was a little bear I hadn't seen that I had scared up the tree with my uphill sprint. I went back to the boat and watched the bear come cautiously back to earth.

On another beautiful day, I wound up finding Luna far up another inlet at a logging camp called Nesook. The day was calm and luminous and he was playing with a boom boat, with the morning sun behind him. Every breath he blew was silver.

While I sat in the boat in Mooyah Bay, I starting writing this book. I had a laptop with me, and a car battery to keep it going. Working on it took me back to the beginning, to those unexpected days for Rick and Sheila Millard, Cameron and Catherine Forbes, Donna Schneider, Jamie James, and Ed Thorburn. It was now four years since Luna had started interacting with people that winter and spring.

"I think it was best then," Cameron Forbes had said of the time when they had called the little whale Patch and you could let your heart respond to him without guilt.

By now, we had become such good friends with Donna Schneider that she let us do an on-camera interview. She was terrific in front of the lens. She told us a story about a passenger whose stylish Tilley hat had blown off. The boat had stopped for Luna, and Luna went out to get the hat. And when he came up under it, he placed it perfectly on his head between his nose and his blowhole, in exactly the place where you would put a little hat. Everyone on the ship laughed.

"Glenn got a pike pole and retrieved the hat," Donna said. "I said to the man, 'Do you want us to wash it? Wash the salt off?' And he goes, 'I am never washing this hat.' "

And good old Eugene. Man, he can talk. I am not sure how many conversations we had with him up in his little house in Tsaxana while he carved his small models of Tsu'xiit with those eyes he had learned to recognize from the canoe battles.

Eugene's good humor never failed. His heart didn't, either. Soon he wasn't using the oxygen anymore. When we interviewed him for about the fifth time, he didn't talk about the potlatch being the end of Luna's time in Nootka Sound; he said that Luna might leave just because he was losing patience with us.

"I can foresee the time," he said, "when he figures, Well, I've done my best. You folks aren't learning anything. It's time for me to go. I think there is going to be more than a couple of times we say, My

God, I think we blew it. We had it and we threw it away. That is so darn true of a lot of things, when we've had the opportunities and we've blown them. Here is an excellent opportunity; he is giving us every chance, every break, saying, Here, come on, check it out. It is still a beautiful world."

I think the earliest days with Luna were the best for Ed Thorburn, too. We used to think Ed was going to be the hero of our little story. Now it almost felt like his experience was the tragedy of it. He had put everything he had—his time, his heart, his reputation—into trying to get Luna home. But his efforts put distance between him and both the main community of Gold River and the First Nations' reserve of Tsaxana because of the hard edges in the capture attempt. About a year after the capture failed, he was transferred to Campbell River. He seldom had a chance to see Luna after that. His enforcement partner, Greg, remained.

We mended fences with Ed. I eventually gave him a tape of the time he canoed with the First Nations on that sweet night before the capture, when we all thought they had gone out in the canoes to honor the little whale and say good-bye. Later, we went to do an interview at his home in Campbell River, up that hour and a half of winding road from Gold River that he no longer drove so often.

"I think about Luna all the time," he said. "Just about every day. I call Greg to find out how he's doing, and stuff like that. There are so many things that happened over that time, from the time I first met Luna until now, that will be with me forever. I mean, just the experience of knowing that whale was worth everything that happened."

He sat in his living room in Campbell River, the memories taking over. His face was no longer severe. It was still windblown; I don't think he would ever choose to be an indoor worker. But when he spoke of Luna, he did not look tough. He looked like a man who loved a whale.

"I think that for everybody who has been connected with Luna," he said, "it is something special. If Luna goes away—if he goes back with his pod—nobody can take those four years away from me."

CHAPTER SIXTY-FOUR

January 2006

Out by Anderson Point, it was the kind of weather that Graeme Ellis complained about when he kept coming up here during storms in the fall and winter of 2001 and 2002, when he identified Luna. Along the coast, there was a brutal steady wind, forty knots and higher.

"It's really blowing," Kip Hedley said when I talked to him on the radio out at the light station at Yuquot. "And it's going to be a good one tonight." Farther up the sound, where Luna and I were, was better, but there were bursts of wild wind, swept down by eddies on the mountains, and continuous heavy rain.

Work went on, and so did fish hunting. There were a lot of echo-location clicks from Luna throughout the morning. I suspected that he was chowing down. Then the calls and clicks stopped.

Luna had taken off to meet a friend. Looking off in the distance to the west up Hanna Channel, I saw a faint shape in the rain against the gray of the land, more of a shadow than anything distinct. It looked like a tug pulling a barge. I could hear the sound of its prop on the hydrophone.

It was a relatively small two-man boat called *Yucata Scout,* a familiar boat in these waters. It was towing a barge carrying heavy equipment in to the logging camp at Mooyah Bay. "Yup," the guy said on the radio. "Luna's with us."

The boat came up to Mooyah Bay and docked the barge. As the big machines on it started driving off, I came up alongside *Yucata Scout,* and the crew invited me into the small pilothouse while Luna moved around both our boats, giving little nudges.

I didn't know the guys, but they were part of the Luna Underground. It was good to talk to them. They talked about petting him, rubbing his nose, rubbing his belly with a brush, rubbing his teeth. "If he'd a wanted to bite somebody, he'd a already done it."

I talked about people threatening to shoot him. "The guy who shoots him, they should take him out and shoot him, too." Ah. Our kind of guys.

In the rattling wind outside the little pilothouse, you could still hear Luna's occasional blast. We talked about Luna a lot, but the statement I liked best came out when we talked about the question of aquariums. "Hey," one of them said, "if the aquariums take him, we'll go get him back."

After they left, I anchored back out on the rock bottom near Anderson Point, taking a bit of a risk that the wind might drag me. Luna was still hanging out near the log sort, so he wasn't far away. I went back to reading Matthew Scully's book and found a quote I wanted to use: "It should tell us something important all by itself that animals have this way of constantly confronting us with ultimate questions—about truth and falsehood, guilt and innocence, God and sanctity and the soul—forcing us to define ourselves and our relationship to the world."

The boat danced on waves only a few yards from the lee shore, where a corner turned to the south. But I was knee-deep in ultimate questions.

I sat in the boat in the early darkness with my computer, typing, while the refugee-tent tarp flapped overhead and rattled with light rain. Out here on the water, things seemed very simple. In reaching to understand Luna's orca culture and the way he tried to express his needs with sound and slaps on the water that I couldn't understand, I felt my own cultural ties growing less important. Out here, things were simplified down to what we needed, Luna and I, down to what has come to us through time, and to what will go on.

When I looked at Luna up close or in the distance, I felt connected in time to all those other lives that had preceded us. It was as if a little window had opened in the wall of the room called Today. It gave me a glimpse down a pair of tracks, rolling into the distance of the past like welded railroad tracks shining in a sun break through the rain. Each track was made of a million lives linked far back, all of us connected by the hot weld of blood to blood, back to the time where the tracks met and our lives no longer diverged. Back to the time of those early mammals—small, weak, wise; bonding, binding, sharing, and surviving amid the thunderous footsteps of cold-blooded giants because they needed one another; building the force for connection that we call empathy.

I heard Luna's call on the hydrophone, and I thought, I've learned some stuff from you. If you are as I have seen you, as complex and as aware as I am myself, then that truth, that sanctity, and that innocence are more significant than I had imagined. You have taken me to a place where human language is just one way to get at the consciousness of living, and if our language is not the only passport to awareness, we have some redefinition to do.

Hey, Luna, I have leaned over the edge of a boat and looked through your otherness at you. As different as you and I are and will always be, we are familiar. We know loneliness and we know empathy and we see those things in each other's eyes, and they build our bond. These fundamental forces of emotion came with us across the greatness of time because they are necessary, not optional. This thing we call friendship is bigger than we know.

I felt immortal. We both were. Not our individual lives. Our choices.

Hey, Luna. Thank you.

———

The wind has gone quiet, probably for just a moment, and the rain has stopped. There is stillness in Mooyah Bay. The other boat's little anchor light is shining over there, where friends of Luna sleep. I stick my head out from under the tarp. There is still moisture in the air, a light, cold mist that puts prickles on my skin.

I am here, and I am privileged to be here, in Luna's place. From somewhere out there, not far away, I hear a breath.

This is where I choose to stay, in this moment.

EPILOGUE

March 10, 2006

Transcript of Transmissions Between *General Jackson*, a 237-Ton Tug Based in New Westminster, British Columbia, and Tofino Coast Guard Radio

GENERAL JACKSON: Ah, Tofino, ah. Coast Guard, ah, *General Jackson,* two-two Alpha.

TOFINO RADIO: Calling Tofino Coast Guard Radio?

GENERAL JACKSON: Yeah, the *General Jackson.* How do you read?

TOFINO RADIO: *General Jackson,* Tofino, copy you fine.

GENERAL JACKSON: Okay, I'm barely . . . We're in Nootka Sound here, Mooyah Bay, and, ah, just thought I'd report that, ah, you can cancel that—that Notice to Shipping about Luna, he just went through our prop. He just went through our prop.

TOFINO RADIO: Can you tell me what happened?

GENERAL JACKSON: Well, I'm runnin' slow here with my log barge waitin' for the swell to go out. . . . He's been kinda playin' around the boat here this mornin' and, ah, well, he, I guess he got in too close to the prop and . . . and it hit him, I guess.

TOFINO RADIO:	Okay, any, ah, any idea on, ah, how he's doing?
GENERAL JACKSON:	Well, I . . . He didn't survive. That wasn't, ah. That wasn't. I'd say he didn't survive. . . .
TOFINO RADIO:	Yeah, sad end but inevitable, I'm sure, ah. It would have been a sad end anyways. Okay, I appreciate that information.
GENERAL JACKSON:	Okay, yeah, right-oh. Yeah, not, ah, not the best of news, eh? But I thought I'd better report it.
TOFINO RADIO:	Yuh, roger, thanks.

On June 6, 2006, three months after Luna died, Donna Schneider and Suzanne, with the help of the people who owned *Uchuck III,* organized a memorial journey for Luna up Muchalat Inlet to Mooyah Bay. We were surprised at how many people came.

Most of the people who are in this book showed up, some from far away, and there were people on the ship whom we had never seen. Among the familiar faces were those of Chantelle Tucker and Rachael Griffin, Ryan Lejbak, Paul Spong, Gail Laurie, Keith Wood, and many others. Lisa Larsson couldn't come because she was in Sweden. When I boarded the ship, the first people I saw were Ed Thorburn and Mike Maquinna, chatting amiably on the upper deck. Jamie James didn't come, but I knew why; it would not be comfortable for him to show his grief in public.

The day was calm and gray. Occasionally, very soft washes of sunlight came through the clouds, nothing strong and bright. My father would have loved this light. I did some storytelling on the public-address system from the bridge, but mainly I stayed up there in that small space with Glenn, who was the skipper that day, and Alberto Girotto, from the head office.

I was pretty much in the same situation as Jamie, but I also felt some blame because when it happened, I had been away taking Su-

zanne to the airport for a trip she had to make. And though it is foolish to set oneself against the past, I was still thinking I might have
prevented it. I had a hard time talking about that to our friends.

So I talked to them on the PA where they couldn't see me, about
places Luna had been. The places and stories came to my tongue easily and without effort. I had grown familiar with this landscape and
the whale who lived in it. It was a piece of my instinct, these gray
waters, these dark blue-green hills and the patches of white snow
showing among clouds in the mountains higher up. This rain, this
mist, these logs on the water, these dozer boats, all so familiar. Luna's
adopted home.

Everything was very quiet around the sound. There were just two
or three fishing boats in the distance, moving slowly.

We stopped in Mooyah Bay, and Glenn shut down the ship, the
generator and everything, and drifted as I used to drift through the
middle of the sound, with Luna making squeaking noises on the side
of the boat by rubbing his pectoral fin tips along the hull.

After this, the next years for us would be all about Luna. As *Uchuck
III* moved across those still waters that day, we had no idea that we
would eventually make a full-length movie with the footage we had
shot and with footage from so many others who had loved him. We
had no idea that eventually people in many countries would learn to
love Luna through the film. We had no idea that Luna's efforts to
make contact would resonate with people in China and Africa and
the Middle East and even in the whaling nation of Japan.

But also as the years passed, we would still see empathy set aside
in a society in which corporate ruthlessness is praised and the politics of destruction are rewarded. In a presidential campaign to choose
a leader who should, of all things, have compassion for his people,
we would see a candidate's call for empathy mocked and twisted to
define him as weak. And as the years passed, I would come to believe that some people attack empathy not because it is weak but

because they fear its power. If you thrive on cruelty, empathy can defeat you.

As I think Luna knew, not in words but in action, empathy is the opposite of weakness. Without it, life is as fragile as grass, blown down by a breeze. But when it links us, we are as strong as chain, as welded steel. That's how orcas live. And as Eugene Amos might say, orcas know justice and truth.

As we drifted along in *Uchuck III,* Mike Maquinna spoke and threw a flower on the water. Then I told the group about another ceremony that had been held on *Uchuck III* for another death. On that trip, people had thrown ashes and flowers, and right after that Luna had done Stealth Whale, bursting up through the flowers and ashes like life reborn in hope. The people who had thrown the ashes that day had smiled. They thought it was perfect.

I don't recall what I said after that. It didn't matter. I was just glad to be on the water with these people, who also knew what it was like to share friendship with a little whale.

The farthest we went before turning for home was the log sort at Nesook, where the water was flat calm and black. I remembered being there when his breath was living silver in the morning sun.

Transcript of Interview with Jamie James, Fisheries Manager, Mowachaht/Muchalaht First Nations

This is one of the many ways for me to remember Luna. It is the easiest way.

The clouds were out. No moon. It was totally dark. And you know that phosphorescence in the water that glow when they're disturbed?

So we had Luna coming with us, and, oh, man, it was the

most amazing thing you've ever seen. He was just coming next to us, while we were bringing him over.

You didn't see Luna. You saw the outline of Luna. The way he glowed. It was like Luna was dancing in the sky with the stars.

So, every time at night when I think of Luna, I look up in the stars.

ACKNOWLEDGMENTS

Our gratitude, first of all, is for patience personified. This book has taken longer than anyone predicted, partly because of the twists and turns of the story as it evolved after the book was initially planned, and partly because of the twists and turns in our own lives both as authors and, unexpectedly, as filmmakers.

So to our editor, Daniela Rapp, and to our agent, Kris Dahl, our undying appreciation for your patience, forbearance, and understanding and, equally, for your affectionate insistence on the achievement of ultimate deadlines. This is a special combination, not always balanced as gracefully as it is by these two talented and effective people.

And we also wish to express our deep appreciation for the inspiration and work given to us and this project by Kathryn Mulders, who first represented the book in Canada. The tides of life have taken Kathryn out of the world of literary combat for the time being, but we hope that this book adequately matches her early vision of what it could become, and we will always appreciate her ongoing enthusiasm for it.

And from the start of the bookmaking process to its conclusion, our deep gratitude to Carol Edwards, who did the copyediting with similar patience and terrific attention to detail, and to the others in the vital chain of painstaking and unsung work that still underpins the publishing of words in whatever form they may take in these complex electronic times: Geraldine Van Dusen, production editor; Sarah Jae-Jones, editorial assistant; James Sinclair, book designer; and Ervin Serrano, jacket designer.

All of this began with an innocent question from Sally Maran, at *Smithsonian* magazine. It was along these lines: "Anything going on in your part of the world that might be interesting to us?" When we told her about this little whale who was approaching people for social contact, she and Don Moser, the editor, gave us the assignment. Many thanks to both of them, and also to Alison McLean, who also worked on the editing of the story that was published in the magazine in November 2004, and who had excellent questions about Luna and the people around him that had an impact on our work long after the article was finished.

The relationship with *Smithsonian* continued during the tenure of the next editor in chief, Carey Winfrey, who did what I didn't think was possible: He carried on Don Moser's tradition of excellence in his own way and style, making *Smithsonian* one of the very few magazines that bucked the trends of the Internet age to fully maintain its subscription base through the continuing strength of its content. Carey eventually published a follow-up to Luna's story in August 2011; many thanks to him, as well.

We also want to thank Douglas Chadwick, author of many *National Geographic* articles and of books on a wide variety of subjects, whose elegant, amiable, and informal style hides a very serious and competent scientist at work behind the scenes. Doug has been a role model for many years. His book about whales, *The Grandest of Lives,* is required reading for anyone who cares about animals, but is also, like all of his work, highly accessible and entertaining. We had many conversations with Doug about both writing and orcas, and often about Luna himself, dating back to before we ever met the little whale. Through Doug's observations, we learned the complexity of Luna's story before most of the complications actually became visible, and he continued to provide invaluable insight into events as they developed.

In the world of orca studies, one voice stands out in terms of this book, both as a source of information and as a friend: Ken Balcomb, senior scientist at the Center for Whale Research on San Juan Island, Washington, whose work with the Southern Resident orcas, Luna's family, has gone on for close to forty years now, and whose interest and enthusiasm has never flagged.

No one scientist can claim to be the scientific godfather to these whales, and when you talk to Ken about pioneering work, he immediately refers to Michael Bigg, who worked in Canadian waters on orcas before Ken arrived on the scene in the mid-1970s; but Ken is certainly one of the whales' best friends. The painstaking assembly of information that he and his indefatigable crew, including Dave Ellifrit and Astrid van Ginneken and dozens of others, have gathered is a treasure. If these endangered whales manage to survive and recover to healthy numbers, Ken's work will have been a major part of the search for solutions. And we also much appreciate the help and friendship of Howard Garrett and Susan Berta, whose Orca Network is an invaluable aid to both orcas and to the human friends of orcas all along the Northwest coast.

Also in the world of science, we much appreciate the help of Dr. Lori Marino, a leading neuroscientist in the field of cetacean studies, whose advice, work, and friendship helped us to appreciate the magnificent complexity of orcas' brains and minds. Lori is a senior lecturer at Emory University and is the founder and executive director of the Kimmela Center for Animal Advocacy. Lori's work on behalf of the animals she studies, and her defense of their rights to life, health, and freedom, is insightful and determined. She is a terrific role model for the pursuit of responsible science.

We also want to express our appreciation for two people who appeared in our lives late in the story but who have grown to be close friends and advisers: Dr. Toni Frohoff and Catherine Kinsman. We first met them when they came to speak at the workshop on Luna sponsored by the Mowachaht/Muchalaht First Nations. Toni is a scientist who has focused for years on cetaceans and particularly on dolphins. She has done a great deal of work studying the few but persistent animals known as "solitary sociables," who have done exactly what Luna did in seeking contact with humans when they found themselves isolated from others of their species. Her rigorous scientific effort to seek and incorporate new evidence into the body of her work, and her outreach in friendship to us and many others, makes her a beacon in this field.

And Catherine, who has taken her love of cetaceans to very practical and intense levels as she has sought to protect other solitaries from the same chaotic situations that Luna encountered, has become a good friend. We are deeply grateful for her long history of helping these other lives, and for her work to celebrate them as well as to save them, in her work as a singer and performer. We were very lucky to be able to include her song in honor of Luna, "Your Friend," on the DVD of our film.

We are grateful to all the many other people we interviewed and spent time with who appear in the book, but we cannot present that list here; it's very long and would inevitably be incomplete. But there are many others who also helped beyond the process of journalism.

Special among these is Donna Schneider, who has become a close friend and always a sounding board, for her thoughtfulness, her awareness, and her ability to look at whales and other forms of life in a way that seeks reality, gritty as it may be, but does not shun love.

Shirley and Larry Andrews, who were neighbors of ours as we lived in Gold River, were invariably hospitable, enthusiastic, and curious about the world. Though they are not a major presence in the book, they certainly helped to form it. One morning we will never forget, Shirley brought us a rose to throw on the water, showing us without saying anything that she shared what we were feeling.

The entire crew of *Uchuck III,* including Fred and Glenda Mather,

Sean Mather, and the late, truly lamented Bill Mather, along with Alberto and Glenda Girotto, gave us a huge amount of help—and many berry muffins—and never asked for favors in return. Their old ship is always polished, and we cannot imagine a better way, even these years later, to spend a day or two than on its calm and friendly decks. In a burst of spray at the bow or a cresting wave in the wake, Luna still swims beside *Uchuck III.*

And we will always be grateful, with a smile, for Eugene Amos, who wields a delicate and artistic blade when he carves yellow cedar, and who has been a constant friend for all these years after the story ended and our work appeared to be all wrapped up. Eugene has the ability to laugh at both good fortune and misfortune, and he has taught us many things.

There are two others who deserved to have a far greater presence, in both the book and the film we made, who helped us a great deal while we were on the waters of Nootka Sound, and who worked very hard for Luna. They are Keith Wood, who set up the remarkable Web site, www.LunaLive.net, and tried so hard to get a signal through to Luna's family from the depths of Nootka Sound; and Lisa Larsson, who spent all those months leading up to the capture attempt listening to Luna's calls and keeping a log of what the little whale was doing. Both of them, and particularly Lisa, gave us hours— days—of time, yet because of the vicissitudes of both filmmaking and writing, they appear only in cameos in the final product. Yet their work and their ardent determination to help Luna shaped the way we understood the story.

We were also fortunate to have access to the many archival photos of Luna from some of the people who knew him best: Sandy and Roy Bohn; Fred and Darlene Lazuk; and Paul and Judy Laviolette. Despite concerns about possible repercussions from the Department of Fisheries and Oceans, these individuals shared their photos and stories of Luna with us and helped us understand Luna's early presence in Nootka Sound.

We also benefited from the insight of other journalists who were covering Luna's story; in particular, David Wiwchar, who, with his wife, Andrea, spent a lot of time in Gold River both during the capture events and thereafter. We are grateful for the fine reporting on Luna's story by Judy Lavoie, from the *Victoria Times Colonist,* whose even hand and understanding of not only Luna's story but the larger story of the Southern Resident community of orcas have been critical in bringing awareness to orca issues.

We will always appreciate the ongoing encouragement and support from Andrew Johnson, at CBC's *The Lens.* Andrew embraced Luna's story, and his willingness to commission a one-hour documentary film about Luna, which later turned into a full-length nonfiction feature, allowed us to stay in Nootka Sound for longer than would have been otherwise possible and directly contributed to the making of this book.

We'd also like to thank Marc Pakenham, who helped to organize the Luna Stewardship programs. Marc gave us a great deal of time in several interviews, yet he is also underrepresented in this story. Kari Koski, one of the other stewardship leaders, who does appear more significantly in the book, has remained engaged in the Luna story, still thinking about the meaning of Luna's complicated and emotional link with humans and what it means to our relationship with all whales and other forms of life. Kari has always been concerned that people may get the wrong impression from Luna's story and might force themselves on whales who do not have a need or any use for a human presence in their lives. We share that view and much appreciate her efforts to make that perspective known without in any way turning it into conflict. In all our contacts with Kari, and in our many discussions about the questions that remain unresolved in the history of Luna, she has been a good friend and a wise adviser.

And we want to thank all the women who, like Kari, worked on Nootka Sound as Luna's stewards. Theirs was a thankless task; they all struggled to figure out what was best for Luna. Although the task they had been assigned was impossible to accomplish, all persevered to try to make it work. Then, so much later, when we interviewed several of them, they honored Luna and their efforts with a level of openness and continued affection for him that revealed the power of the experience and the sincerity of their effort to try to make life better for a little whale who seemed as lonely as a lost child.

Cameron and Catherine Forbes, owners and operators of Critter Cove, were also particularly important both in helping us get our work done and in caring for Luna. As described in the book, they were indefatigably Luna's friends, and they both have the ability to observe human nature and the natural world with a refreshing blend of skepticism and engagement, which, we believe, made Luna's life in Nootka Sound better than it might otherwise have been for many reasons.

We also remember with fondness our visits to Critter Cove, the Forbes's marina. At Critter Cove, we spent a lot of time talking not only with Cameron and Catherine but with many of their guests, and we always felt welcome there. We also enjoyed many fine slices of pie baked by Cameron's mother, Julie Forbes.

We came to Nootka Sound as journalists, not expecting to stay long; what we found as the weeks in Gold River lengthened to months, then years, was a warm and welcoming community that became a second home to us. Because of the hospitality of the members of the Mowachaht/Muchalaht First Nations—who invited us to many meals and events, including the much-loved Yuquot Summerfest and the ultimate potlatch for Ambrose Maquinna—and the kindness of long-time Gold River residents like Rick and Sheila Millard, whom we would often encounter at the Gold River dock, where we would chat about Luna, we never felt like strangers in town.

The community was very sympathetic to Luna's plight; those who thought he should be killed were in a tiny minority. The large and small gestures of friendship that people so willingly gave us brightened our days and led to our awareness that Luna had many friends, even among those who hardly ever saw him. The genuine friendliness of people in unexpected places like the Kleeptee log sort, the fish farms, and the Mooyah Bay logging camp, and that of the people we met casually at the grocery store or the gas station or out along Nootka Sound, gave us a sense of becoming part of a true community. We will always remember our time in Gold River with great fondness for both the striking landscape and the people who filled it with grace.

There were losses over these past years that we also wish to honor in the same way we remember Luna—as lives fully lived in connection with others. Each of these losses, as they came, reminded us again about what a writer once said in a Christmas column when he knew his last days were upon him: that "the only gift that matters is a spark of brave forthcomingness, an unshuttering of spirit, from another living person, so soon, like us, to disappear."

We are lucky to have known Jerry Jack, a man of joyful enthusiasm for living and for political engagement and human drama. We will always miss Bill Mather, the skipper of *A. G. Ford,* who repeatedly helped with physical things, such as making our old Zodiac float right, and with insights that helped us understand Luna's situation. And we can never forget the kindness of Kip Hedley, lighthouse keeper at Yuquot for many years, who welcomed us to his remote home often and helped us and many others with efforts to find a way for Luna to have a natural reunion with his family. Kip was there again and again during the weeks Mike spent alone on Nootka Sound, with radio conversations that, in brief but always reassuring moments of contact across the miles, chased loneliness away and reminded us why friendship is such a vital and necessary force in all our lives.

And we can't forget David Parfit, Mike's son, who has been a source of constant engagement in the whole story, who worked very hard on the film, and who has provided a very steady and thoughtful voice of reason, which we hope is well reflected in these pages; and Mike's daughter, Erica, who, while farther away from us geographically, has been a voice of inspiration, well attuned to the way words sound on paper, as this book has developed.

Finally, we want to thank two friends of Luna who are described at length in this book, but whose empathy for Luna deserves one more comment.

First, we tip our hats directly to Ed Thorburn, the Department of Fisheries and Oceans fisheries officer who spent so much time with Luna in the early days and who, without question, was a loyal and consistent friend to the young whale. Ed always spoke frankly with us, and his care for Luna was always unambiguous. Though we sometimes disagreed and had conflicts with him both on and off the water, Ed made the effort to reach across those divides to a place where we could meet in recognition of our shared affection and awe for Luna. We will always respect Ed for who he is and what he tried so hard to accomplish, against long odds that included some of the policies of his employer. He gave everything he had.

And so did Jamie James, the Mowachaht/ Muchalaht First Nations fisheries manager, whose perspective was different from Ed's but whose devotion was also complete. Always kind, always cheerful, always honest, he gave us respect and time and, sometimes at his own personal risk, access to a view of Luna that we would otherwise have missed. More than that, if we can be so bold as to offer thanks to some degree on behalf of the whale friend for whom we, too, felt love, Jamie was with certainty Luna's best, most consistent friend on Nootka Sound, far more than we were able to be.

When we saw Luna with Jamie, there was an ease in Luna's moves and eyes that seemed unique to their specific relationship. Something about the calm and careful way that Jamie related to Luna, the playfulness they shared, and the moments of mutual eye contact that flickered across the water made it clear that when he was with Jamie, Luna felt safe. In a way that was no doubt short of what orcas could have given him but was probably the best that humans could provide, in those times with Jamie, Luna seemed to be content.

So, to Luna, thank you for what you gave to all of us to help us understand the nature of living, the depth of the spring of time from which it rises, and the importance of the loneliness and empathy that we share and weld into friendship; and thank you, Jamie, and all these others, for what you gave Luna.

Michael Parfit
Suzanne Chisholm